D1562770

The Game of the Impossible

W. R. IRWIN

The Game of the Impossible .

A RHETORIC OF FANTASY

UNIVERSITY OF ILLINOIS PRESS

Urbana Chicago London

LIBRARY OF CONGRESS CATALOGING IN PUBLICATION DATA

Irwin, William Robert, 1915–
    The game of the impossible.

    Bibliography: p.
    Includes index.
    1. Fantastic fiction, English—History and
criticism. 2. Fantastic fiction, American—
History and criticism. I. Title.
PR830.F317   823'.8'0915   76-13459
ISBN 0-252-00587-2

To my wife, my companion
in many ventures

Contents

Preface

There are critics who at times seem persuaded that art should be shielded from scrutiny. Accordingly, E. M. Forster once permitted himself to complain about the anatomizing of fantasy:

> If critics had not their living to get they would seldom handle any literary fantasy. It makes them look so foolish. Their state of mind is the exact antithesis of the author whom they propose to interpret. With quiet eyes and cool fingers they pass from point to point, they define fantasy as "the unserious treatment of the unusual"—an impeccable definition, the only objection to it being that it defines. A gulf between the critical and creative states exists in all cases, but in the case of a fantastical creation it is so wide as to be grotesque.[1]

This passage occurs in an essay on Ronald Firbank, a major writer of fantasy half a century ago. Forster's complaint is, of course, a familiar deprecation of analysis, in which he displays less than his usual acumen. I hope that his praise for this inept definition is a joke. Be this as it may, he has a point, and with his warning in mind, I have undertaken a critical study of fantasy as it has appeared in English and American literature since 1880. To be accurate, I should call the subgenre with which I am concerned "long prose fiction fantasy," but this phrase is intolerable, and hereafter I shall use the one word "fantasy" for that kind of extended narrative which establishes and develops an artifact, that is, plays the game of the impossible.

Why is 1880 taken as an arbitrary starting point? Simply because about that time fantasies began to appear in England and America with increasing frequency, some the work of authors who were or became eminent. After 1860 there were isolated signs of the coming flow in the Alice books, the works of Edward Lear, Kingsley's *Water Babies*, and the *Phantastes* of George

---

1. *Abinger Harvest* (1936; reprint ed., London: Arnold, 1946), p. 113.

Macdonald.[2] But the two books of Lewis Carroll are sports. They provide more than objective narration, and the verisimilitude they establish is speculative in ways not typical of fantasy. In short, the Alice books are more diversified than orthodox fantasy. Lear wrote no prose narrative. *Phantastes* can be adequately described by retrospect from the works of C. S. Lewis. And *Water Babies*, aside from being a mélange of story and moralizing, stimulates too little interest to justify my beginning with the earlier date. The continuing prominence of fantasy began about 1880.

Since 1957 this spate has all but run dry. Concurrently, authors as diverse as John Barth, Anthony Burgess, Iris Murdoch, and William Burroughs have shown a growing engagement with the fantastic and with modes of thought and sensibility appropriate to it. But for reasons that I shall suggest in the last chapter, they did not choose to confine their energies within the formal and theoretical requirements of fantasy, which is radically incompatible with most purposes of "postrealistic fiction." This impetus toward the fantastic, persistent with gathering momentum throught the 1960s and into the 1970s, has left fantasy behind. Indeed, paradoxical though it seems, the rise of the fantastic has been a major contributor to the decline—temporary, one hopes —of fantasy.

A further statement is needed of what this study will and will not provide, so that the reader will form only such expectations as can be satisfied. I make no attempt to trace the history of fantasy. Such an effort might be interesting, were it possible. But in no significant sense does fantasy have a history. Chronology may be followed, and evident lines of influence on concepts and means, for example from Novalis to George Macdonald to Charles Williams. But inherent in fantasy is a fixity of method that, for all the variety possible within it, precludes development over the course of repeated performances.

I say nothing, apart from a few incidental comments, about fantasy drama or the fantastic in drama or versions of either in film. Likewise little about the fantastic short story, though this

2. See Louis Macneice, *Varieties of Parable* (Cambridge: University Press, 1965), p. 82ff.

offers rich material. The dramatic and short story manifestations, despite evident similarities with my chosen object, embody differing technical and tactical features, such as would repay separate considerations.

Indeed, restricting for what I believe a liberating purpose, I do not even attempt to discuss all the fantasies in English that appeared between 1880 and 1957. Rather, I have chosen to develop a rhetoric of fantasy and to examine selected works that have both intrinsic importance and remarkable illustrative value. For I intend that this study be central rather than encyclopedic, and suggestive rather than prescriptive. Thus it may aid the curious reader, but it will leave him or her with the privilege of knowing fantasy directly and judging it with a mind informed rather than surfeited.

I face now the pleasant obligation of expressing gratitude for assistance I received as this study was in progress. It is my good fortune to be a member of a department and a university in which that tradition known as the community of scholarship is so highly honored that it is taken for granted. Accordingly, my colleagues at the University of Iowa have been most generous, willing to answer questions, discuss speculative propositions, suggest reading I had not discovered for myself, and offer critical comments on portions of the manuscript. I am grateful to them for their time, which is a scholar's most precious and most vulnerable possession, but even more for their candor. The mark of their integrity and friendship is that they have not knowingly allowed me to get away with anything. Thus I take pleasure in thanking Nancy Andreasen, Paul Baender, Michael Cooke, John Gerber, Jenefer Giannasi, John Grant, John Huntley, Robert Kelley, Carl Klaus, Frederick McDowell, Margaret Mangan, Baldwin Maxwell, K. K. Merker, William Murray, Eric Rabkin, Robert Scholes, and Oliver Steele for aids so numerous and various that they cannot now be specified.

To Duane C. Spriestersbach, Dean of the Graduate College, and the University Research Council I am grateful for an Old Gold Summer Fellowship and an appointment as a research professor during the first semester of the academic year 1968–69.

From the Graduate College also came the funds to provide me at various times with research assistants—Robert Sutherland, David Fratus, Thomas Van Demark, Thomas Lamont, and Marcia Noe—who promoted my work by solving problems of investigation I imposed on them and by offering valuable suggestions I had not anticipated.

W. R. Irwin

The Game of the Impossible

All of us have reason to know that we are finite creatures, limited in attributes and potentialities. This is an uncongenial truth, as frustrating to most as it was to Adam and Eve in that paradise we imagine the state of innocence to have been. What, then, do we do? Live and think in obedience to a notion of our immutable nature? Much of the time. But even within the habit of conformity a restiveness is lurking; many of us are ever hoping to break out and be as gods. When liberation occurs, the result may prove one of those fulfilled quests of human understanding that provide the bright spots of history, or it may prove a sheer chase after vanity, or, more likely, something between. From insatiable curiosity about the unknown and the mysterious have arisen not only the triumphs of Newton but also the dubious enterprises of astrology, alchemy, magic, cabalism, divination, spiritism, and a host of other means that, no matter how diverse otherwise, are bound together by their seemingly unattainable purpose. Some of these are now relics of foregone folly; others are in some guise more than lively at this moment. It is easy for reason's zealots to be scornful of all such aberrations. But the unreflecting scorners among us may profitably listen to R. G. Collingwood: "A society which thinks . . . that it has outlived the need of magic, is either mistaken in that opinion, or else it is a dying society, perishing for lack of interest in its own maintenance." [1] Ultimately, attitudes toward curiosity are beside the point. The inquiring spirit is there, a dynamic beyond the reach of praise or censure. It is ineradicably human, a symptom of our being the glory, jest, and riddle of the world.

All this punditry on a familiar theme is intended only to indicate the general range of desire within which the fantastic casts a lure to the imagination. Our appetites for strangeness are powerful, but they do not necessarily end in Faust-like efforts to abro-

1. *The Principles of Art* (Oxford: Clarendon Press, 1938), p. 69.

gate finitude or to penetrate ultimate mysteries. They may as well produce a kind of mental play that speculatively violates the binding intellectual conventions of a world that is too much with us. Who among us has not wished, for sheer relief and variety, that apples might sometimes fall upward through the earth's atmosphere, that we might talk with Socrates or Ben Franklin, that we might meet a platitude walking down the street? Thus it is no cause for wonder that literature is pervaded by the systematic representation of what we generally think antinatural or impossible and of what contravenes intellectual conventions in such a manner as to become temporarily within credence. Ancient examples come to mind—the pseudo-Homeric *Batrachomyomachia*, the fables of Aesop, almost the entire canon of Aristophanes, the *Vera Historia*, the *Menippus* and *Icaromenippus* of Lucian. And behind these in time lie the early versions, shadowy and fragmentary, of what we now know as fairy tales. Through periods of congenial and hostile intellectual climate, literary excursions into the fantastic have persisted, often undertaken by the partisans of reason itself—More, Rabelais, Bacon, Pope, Swift, Voltaire, Sterne. Some works of these men, and of others, are indeed fantasies within the meaning I hope to establish.

And what are these fictions that I call fantasy? As a preliminary definition, to be expanded and examined later, I suggest the following: a fantasy is a story based on and controlled by an overt violation of what is generally accepted as possibility; it is the narrative result of transforming the condition contrary to fact into "fact" itself. All of us have played this game in private reveries, in conversation, perhaps in writing. It is at the least a welcome release from dailiness.

Late in the nineteenth century various authors turned to writing fantasy. What impulse drove them can better be guessed at than ascertained. Most likely they were seeking alternatives to the hegemony of the novel of social realism; this has been a powerful and sustained impetus behind many well-known departures and experiments in modern fiction. Whatever their motivations, those who contributed to fantasy between 1880 and the mid-1950s make a roster of distinguished names: Max Beerbohm, Edward Bellamy, G. K. Chesterton, John Collier, Walter de la Mare, Norman Douglas, Ronald Firbank, E. M.

Forster, David Garnett, William Golding, Kenneth Grahame, Robert Graves, James Hilton, W. H. Hudson, Richard Hughes, Aldous Huxley, Ronald Knox, C. S. Lewis, Arthur Machen, George Orwell, T. F. Powys, Victoria Sackville-West, James Stephens, J. R. R. Tolkien, Mark Twain, Rex Warner, Sylvia Townsend Warner, H. G. Wells, Rebecca West, T. H. White, Charles Williams, Virginia Woolf, Elinor Wylie. These authors and others brought fantasy to its highest execution and left us a body of fiction that deserves to be known and understood, even though its kind has all but disappeared from the literature of the past eighteen years.

For all its recurrence in recent literary history, fantasy as a subgenre of prose fiction is not clearly understood. Few critics have granted it sustained attention, and among them, as well as among common readers, there is little agreement on its characteristics. Everyone is confident that he can recognize fantasy, and each year such helpful publications as the *Fiction Catalog* enumerate titles so classified. But the principles behind identification are usually obscure and unfixed. Some definitions are exclusive and say in effect that fantasy is only such narrative as embodies extrapolations from science or pseudoscience, or deals with pragmatic societies of the past or the future, or with the supernatural, especially magic.[2] Others make the opposite error and include in fantasy any narrative projection of orders of fictive reality beyond the familiar. Some make "fantastic" a synonym for "untrue"; for some it means only "exotic," "implausible," or "deviant," or "escapist."

Much of this confusion can be accounted for and an access to clarification can be opened by a brief excursion into one aspect of psychology, a discipline in which "fantasy" is a prominent subject for study and speculation. As a term in psychology, extended into psychiatry and psychotherapy and thence into the academy of the cocktail party, "fantasy" can have three meanings: a psychic capability,[3] the process by which this capability

2. See Patrick Merla, " 'What Is Real?' Asked the Rabbit One Day," *Saturday Review of the Arts*, 45 (November, 1972), 43–50.

3. In older usage "fantasy" and "fancy" were often made synonymous. As faculty psychology has been superseded by a unitive concept, this identification has disappeared. But as a term outside psychology, "fancy" may yet be discussed.

exercises itself, and the product of such exercise. Hopeful perhaps of promoting clarity, Jung proposed some distinctions. For him, one frequent manifestation of psychic energy is "phantasy," in which term he fused the capability and the process. The product is a "phantasm"; this he defines as a complex that "corresponds to no external state of affairs." [4] Jung has much to say about "phantasy," but the essence is expressed in the following statement:

> This peculiar activity of the psyche, which can be explained neither as a reflexive reaction to sense-stimuli nor as an executive organ of eternal ideas is, like every vital process, a perpetually creative act. Each day new reality is created by the psyche. The only expression I can use for this activity is *phantasy*. Phantasy is not inextricably inter-related with other psychic functions. At one time it appears primordial, at another as the latest and most daring product of gathered knowledge. Phantasy, therefore, appears to me as the clearest expression of the specific activity. Before everything it is the creative activity whence issue the solutions to all answerable questions; it is the mother of all possibilities, in which too the inner and outer worlds, like all psychological antitheses, are joined in living union. Phantasy it was and ever is which fashions the bridge between the irreconcilable claims of object and subject, of extraversion and introversion.[5]

Jung further proposes a discrimination between passive and active phantasy. The characteristic form of passive phantasy is the dream. The active is markedly different, in that consciousness participates in shaping material from the unconscious. Active phantasy is "the principal attribute of the artistic mentality." [6]

Presumably the active phantasy disposes the person to any kind of artistic creation that is congenial to him, and not specifically to literature. Nor does Jung give any hint that the formation of narrative is a result of the activity. The compensatory self-aggrandizing daydreams that Freud discusses from time to

4. *Psychological Types*, trans. H. Godwin Baynes (London: Paul, Trench, Trubner; New York: Harcourt, Brace, 1926), p. 573.

5. Ibid., p. 69.

6. Ibid., pp. 574, 580.

6

time are narratives, and the means by which they may be transformed into literary romance I consider in a later chapter. A direction toward story is also central in a standard psychological test, the Thematic Apperception Test (TAT), a program of twenty pictures, one a complete blank. From each picture the subject is asked to make a story that has a beginning, middle, and end. The testers assume, however, that the picture controls only the topic or context of the fantasy which emerges and that this represents in turn a "series of generalizations drawn from experience, never the experiences themselves." [7] Indirectly the narrative responses express what has for some reason, usually the requirements of society or a societal group, been repressed. Analysis and interpretation then may be conducted by comparison of the subject's fantasies and the norms of his society.

Insofar as phantasy in the psychological usage originates in free play of the psyche, it resembles the intellection that can lead to literary fantasy. But surely the products of the Thematic Apperception Test and of daydreams as Freud understood them express a limited freedom of invention. The makers are subservient to pressures that thwart and may be circumvented in this substitute fashion. There is little evidence in literary fantasy itself, or in the wit play which incites and sustains it, that release from the author's idiosyncratic repressions is a significant motive. Jung's description omits any mention of an egocentric factor, but from the general conformity of his formulation of phantasy as quoted and his ideas about the artistic potential of emanations from the collective unconscious, it may be safely assumed that he did not consider ego involvement important.

No doubt active phantasy could yield the material for a fantasy. In his autobiography and elsewhere, C. S. Lewis provides evidence that with him just this occurred. But the narrative development of a fantasy is deliberative, and I see no reason to doubt that its intellectual inception may be—indeed, most often is—deliberative as well.

With this background of lay explanation, some generalizations can be projected. The process described by Jung is one source of

7. William E. Henry, *The Analysis of Fantasy* (New York: Wiley, 1956), p. 36 and passim.

what I have called "the fantastic," and his phrase for such constructs, that they "correspond to no external state of affairs," goes far toward defining "the fantastic." But not far enough. Jung's phrase does not indicate a purposiveness that separates the fantastic from the accepted and thus introduces a predominant rhetorical factor. The test of difference is more than noncorrespondence; a matter is within the range of the fantastic if it is judged, whether on the basis of knowledge or of convention, to be not only outside "reality" but also in knowing contravention of "reality." Thus within the concept of the fantastic is a competition for credence in which an assertive "antireal" plays against an established "real."

Much of the confusion in literary criticism originates in an assumption that the fantastic and fantasy are identical. Of course, they share a large area of congruity. But the fantastic, that is, the factitious existence of the antireal, is actually material. It is not of itself a literary form, and its presence, even preponderance, in a narrative does not necessarily make a fantasy. Elements of the fantastic may be introduced, singly or in combination, into almost any form of imaginative literature from heroic epic to farce. It can have a place anywhere in the range from the remotest chivalric romance to immediately contemporaneous satire, from the sheerly entertaining to the purely didactic. It seems to be independent of those differences in sophistication, of writers or readers or both, which are often associated with cultural levels or social class. Thus the fantastic is just as evident in the folk tale and the popular ballad as in postrealistic fiction. It can be a functioning part of a novel whose main purport is realistic, as a moment's reflection on *The Heart of Midlothian* or *Bleak House* will confirm. In short, to define a genre by its material or content alone is a mistake, and this mistake repeatedly occurs in discussions of fantasy.[8]

8. It will have occurred to the reader that "fantasy" is used in discussions of music, the fine arts, and film. In music it can designate instrumental improvisation, free-form sonatas, operatic potpourris, pieces in contrapuntal style for the virginal, even various kinds of composition intended to convey a dreamy mood—a wide range of possibilities, in which there seems to be no conceptual center. A number of art historians and theoreticians, chiefly French, have considered the fantastic; they rarely concentrate on *fantaisie*, presumably following the logic of

Whatever the material, extravagant or seemingly common-place, a narrative is a fantasy if it presents the persuasive establishment and development of an impossibility, an arbitrary construct of the mind with all under the control of logic and rhetoric. This is the central formal requisite. Without it even the most bizarre material may be mobilized to produce something other than a fantasy. An author's purpose may be, for example, to incite the reader's participation in wonder, in which disbelief contributes to a drifting pleasure detached from any kind of intellection. This is the charm of Maeterlinck's *Pelléas et Mélisande*, or in the prose fiction of Eleanor Farjeon's *The Fair of St. James* and Peter Beagle's *The Last Unicorn*, in which the reader is actually encouraged to consider the events beyond credence. Such, too, was the repeated effort of James Branch Cabell, a name conspicuously missing from my previous list of major fantasists. These works and many like them promote reverie, not intellectual play, and any attempt to make them factitiously credible would be destructive. Paradoxically enough, the fantastic can be used to make an antifantasy.

To repeat, narrative sophistry, conducted not to make the worse appear the better reason but to make nonfact appear as fact, is essential to fantasy. In this effort, writer and reader knowingly enter upon a conspiracy of intellectual subversiveness, that is, upon a game. Moreover, this game, led by the writer prompting participation by the reader, must be continuous and coherent. Misunderstanding of fantasy can result from the oc-

Pierre Castex, who, concerned with mystery, rejected *fantaisie* as a term on the ground that "dans l'usage français il évoque d'aimables caprices, des visions gracieuses ou riantes." These studies in the fine arts actually deal with the fantastic as previously described, that is, as material which reveals and perhaps gives access to what is unknown or otherwise beyond rational cognition. Roger Caillois, for example, finds in *l'art fantastique* a means of apprehending and rendering, as best can be, visions of essence, glimpses of "ces réalites intérieures qui n'ont ni forme ni stabilité." *Au coeur du fantastique* (Paris: Gallimard, 1965), p. 171. Though much more might be said about his excellent study, it is evident that he is dealing with matters far different from the manipulation, intellectual play, and controlled narration of literary fantasy. As a term in cinematography, fantasy is unfixed. It can describe any presentation or style in which dreaminess, whimsy, distortion, or horror is prominent. In short, it designates any nonrealism. Altogether, the usages from these disciplines contribute little to the understanding of literary fantasy.

9

currence within a long fiction of passages, episodes, descriptions, or interludes that are self-contained manifestations of the fantastic. Because these are often impressive and decisive—as is Stephen Dedalus's hallucination of hell or the Nighttown sequence in *Ulysses*—it is easy for readers to assume that the whole work is so colored. Perhaps it is, but tincture does not make a fantasy. A better example is the legend of the Grand Inquisitor in *The Brothers Karamazov*, which both Ivan and Alyosha several times call a fantasy. As a unit it is, but the total work is not. Fantasy results only from the persistence of a main and substantial tendency throughout the whole. No matter what is the central arbitrary nonreality that generates the fantasy-illusion, all elements of the narrative are determined by it. Characters, action, and setting appear more credible than the accepted norm they displace. The author of a realistic novel can permit himself more laxity in overt verisimilitude, in the contribution of devices to purpose, in the relationship of parts to the whole. The fantasist has much less freedom; his margin for error is almost nonexistent. It was not simply to amuse his readers that Swift labored to establish in Books I and II of *Gulliver's Travels* a flawless consistency of detail, all related to size proportions. This was indispensable to his rhetoric.

Here, then, are the basic intellectual and literary principles of fantasy, briefly stated. But this is only the beginning, no more than a sketch of the anatomy and distinctive features that may be rightfully expected in a full—and I hope persuasive—theory of fantasy. This is the next task, and it occupies the next four chapters.

two

Fantasy and Play

Actually I would mistrust an "impeccable definition" of fantasy as much as E. M. Forster does, though for a different reason. He suggests that definition is an instrument to dismember a work of art. But I have been forced to abandon several ingenious definitions because of results in application either too exclusive and arbitrary or too permissive and undiscriminating. In this respect my experience has repeated that of many students of literary genres. Better, then, for the present purpose, to undertake an extended description of the normative aspects and practices of fantasy. In the end this will likely prove more enlightening than a definition.

As approaches to this discussion I shall follow three lines of inquiry. None reaches to the heart of the matter, but all facilitate progress along the way. First, it will be helpful to consider certain speculations about the nature of play and to connect these with suggestions about the dynamics of wit and fancy proposed by Freud. Next, I shall examine such theories of fantasy as have been advanced by recent critics, some of whom have the authority of also being writers of fantasy. These theories are diverse, incomplete, often specialized, but from them can be extracted, after the rejection of what is either impertinent or dubious, some suggestions bearing on the central description of principles that will follow. Finally, I shall review the general characteristics of kinds of prose fiction that in some way resemble fantasy—fairy tale, gothic romance, ghost story, pornographic story, science fiction—in order to distinguish them from fantasy proper.

Of the many persons, from various disciplines and with various interests, who have concerned themselves with the nature and cultural significance of play, I shall concentrate on a few, selected because their conclusions are essentially coherent or complementary and because their work can be used to illuminate fantasy. These authors are Johan Huizinga, Elizabeth Sewell, and Roger Caillois—a seemingly diverse lot, with whom others will be occasionally associated for incidental illustration.

The career of Johan Huizinga shows a progression from *Altertumswissenschaft* (Sanskrit and Indic culture), through medieval European history, to modern affairs. His was no series of changed directions, but a growth and an ever-extending integration of knowledge. He became an eminent historian of culture and philosopher of history, a reproach to all narrow specialists. At his installation as rector of the University of Leiden in 1933, he chose for the subject of his inaugural address "the play element of culture." Soon thereafter he published *Homo Ludens*, a full study, ranging through a wide variety of cultural evidence, of play.[1]

Ordinarily it would be my obligation to formulate a synopsis of Huizinga's principles. In this instance, however, I take the liberty of quoting instead Professor Karl Weintraub's succinct formulation of them:

> Play is non-earnest. Human life can subsist without it. It is unnecessary for survival. From the point of view of our material needs and the immediate utility of our actions, play is a useless squandering of vital energy. Play lies outside our highest moral commands and is neither sin nor virtue. It lies outside the distinction of true or false. Its nature is neither biological nor logical nor ethical. Yet it occupies a large part of man's life. It may be useless; yet play has its own meaning—*zwecklos aber doch sinvoll*. It fulfills a social function and possesses its own forms, rules, and demands. It is a freely accepted activity which submits the player to its own rigid order. Play has its own ethics and its own seriousness which may even entail the question of life or death. It is always contest and strife. Play demands intense concentration of body and mind and has as its reward only satisfaction, possibly a prize, or glory. It is negated by dis-

1. In a foreword Huizinga remarks: "For many years the conviction has grown upon me that civilization arises and unfolds in and as play. Traces of such an opinion are to be found in my writings ever since 1903." *Homo Ludens: A Study of the Play-Element in Culture* (1939; reprint ed., Boston: Beacon Press, 1967), p. vii.

honesty and unfairness, by disregard for its order. It is meaningful only when its outcome is uncertain, when chance has a
chance. It must take place among equals, and yet it is pro-
foundly "aristocratic" in "discovering" the best. It expresses itself in styled forms and is always linked with our aesthetic sentiments. It is strictly outlined and has a firm structure. It is
repetitive in form, yet infinitely variable and unpredictable
within its own order. It has rhythm and clear harmony.[2]

Beyond this summary, just a few generalizations are needed to
complete the basic concept. Huizinga insists that play is pre-
cultural, a fundamental and independent aspect of the human
spirit that cannot be explained by physiology or psychology,
though its manifestations can contribute to bodily, emotional,
and psychic health. Thus Huizinga feels no embarrassment about
making his title-phrase, *homo ludens*, coordinate with *homo
sapiens* and *homo faber*. So deep is the play component that it
cannot be understood as the schematic opposite of an equally
powerful disposition to earnestness. In a chapter on linguistic
evidence, Huizinga concludes:

> We can say, perhaps, that in language the play-concept seems to
> be much more fundamental than its opposite. The need for a
> comprehensive term expressing "not-play" must have been
> rather feeble, and the various expressions for "seriousness" are
> but a secondary attempt on the part of language to invent the
> conceptual opposite of "play." . . . The significance of "car-
> nest" is defined by and exhausted in the negation of "play"
> —earnest is simply "not playing" and nothing more. The signi-
> ficance of "play," on the other hand, is by no means defined or
> exhausted by calling it "non-earnest," or "not serious." Play is a
> thing by itself.[3]

2. *Visions of Culture* (Chicago: University of Chicago Press, 1966), pp. 222–
23. I have omitted Professor Weintraub's documentation. He notes that the
phrase in German is quoted from the chapter entitled "Die Liturgie als Spiel," in
Vom Geist der Liturgie (1922), by Romano Guardini. In the immediate context
Father Guardini is arguing that the liturgy, in contrast with canon law, has a
self-contained and valid meaning, outside any criterion of purpose.

3. *Homo Ludens*, pp. 44–45. In the course of the chapter, Huizinga cites evidence from several ancient and modern languages that the images in words for
play specify movement and lightness, that these are basic throughout a great
variety of applications and extensions, and that these original images are the
hidden metaphors in abstract terms.

Huizinga stresses also that play is essentially free, in the sense that a person may participate and stop participating at will; there is no inconsistency between this and the absoluteness of rules within any play activity. From this it follows that there is a clear distinction between "play," often a pretending, and "real," which is not forgotten, no matter how intense, absorbing, even holy, the play activity may be. This kind of freedom or separateness causes the limitations of time, space, and binding convention that Professor Weintraub specifies, and causes also in the resulting manifestation an inescapable element of display, performance, tour de force.

The originating dynamic of play Huizinga believes to be decisive in almost all cultural phenomena from the most awesome, sacred rituals or riddles in search of cosmic wisdom, to the most frivolous invective matches or the extravagances of the periwig. He gives his most careful attention to religious observance, the generation of myths, legal forms and practices, warfare through all its degrees of deadliness, philosophy and the quest for knowledge, fine arts, and poetry. Steadily the competitive, the "agonistic," relationship persists in some way, again either deadly or facetious or somewhere between. Play and contest are no less than "civilizing functions."

For this study poetry is the most important manifestation of play. Huizinga asserts that whereas in other forms the original nexus often becomes obscured, it remains prominent in poetry. He stays with the vatic idea of poetry. The poet is even more than the "unacknowledged legislator of mankind"; he is the divinely possessed seer, a natural aristocrat who nonetheless serves his community, whose work "is at one and the same time ritual, entertainment, artistry, riddle-making, doctrine, persuasion, sorcery, soothsaying, prophecy, competition" (p. 120). The creation of beauty, though it may occur as an effect, is not the direct object; if the object can be reduced to a phrase, it would be the exercise of power. Even the formal and rhythmical arrangements of poetry and the deployment of images do not have organic beauty as an end, though they may have a beauty of their own. All the devices of poetry are emanations from play with language. Indeed, in his chapter on poetry Huizinga never discusses the "aesthetic purport" as such beyond noting that in "the social game" of poetry it is either absent or but incidentally present. His judgment of poetry as sheer art-object and the provocation of sensuous response may be guessed from his scorn, which he scarcely conceals, for what happened repeatedly in art and music after the eighteenth century, when decoration and romantic self-indulgence displaced function. As a wish for "the satisfaction of personal aestheticisms" grew, play and its agonistic energy dwindled or disappeared.[4] This was one of many corruptions, results of the decline and fall inherent in the romantic ideal, that oppressed Johan Huizinga, and threatened civilization, in the 1930s.

Huizinga's study is treated with great respect, despite some serious reservations, by Roger Caillois, savant, literary director for UNESCO, and editor of the journal *Diogenes*. Of his many works I am here concerned with *Man, Play, and Games*.[5] Callois's principal effort is to construct a sociology of games, with implications for understanding the societal modes that contain them, according to a comprehensive classification. Agreeable as it would be to discuss his speculations for themselves, I must restrict myself to those of his observations that can be applied ultimately to prose fiction fantasy. He notes certain games, illustrative of the fundamental condition of freedom in play, that have no stated or understood rules; generally these games are developed by improvisation. Their conduct involves a central "as if" factor, a sustained and governing pretense that displaces the known truth of ordinary experience and observation. This "fiction" operates in the same binding way as the conventions that Huizinga keeps in the foreground of his attention, though it lacks the prior formulation.[6]

I believe that it is not falsely extending Caillois's principle to suggest further that this controlling fiction, or make-believe,

---

4. Ibid., pp. 201–3. Elsewhere Huizinga is not so consistent in stating the exact association of play and beauty, and he admits that his "judgment wavers." In general, however, there is no place in Huizinga's consideration for poetry as sheer aesthetic activity, either for writer or reader.

5. First published as *Les jeux et les hommes* (Paris: Gallimard, 1958).

6. *Man, Play, and Games*, trans. Meyer Barash (New York: Free Press of Glencoe, 1961), p. 9.

must not only be different for each improvisation generated from it, but also must have its inception in a counter to something already established by daily life or routine thought. I surmise that improvisation is especially conformable to one of Caillois's four major "attitudes" of play, mimicry or simulation.[7] In his leading remarks on mimicry, Caillois says, "All play presupposes the temporary acceptance, if not of an illusion . . . then at least of a closed, conventional, and, in certain respects, imaginary universe" (p. 19). It must be added, I believe, that mimicry, like parody, cannot be conceived without an inciting object and cannot be developed without sustained and controlled invention.

Perhaps I have made Caillois seem a disciple of Huizinga, concerned with extending the master's principles. This is not the case, though the two are agreed on many fundamentals. The cultural manifestations that occupy Huizinga may have about them something of the spirit of games, especially in the all-important competitive aspect. Beyond this, they are games in a figurative sense only. Caillois concentrates on the games that people play or have played, especially gambling, in which he sees a challenge to Huizinga's proposition that play is without material interest. Huizinga excludes psychology as a means of studying play, because at best it can provide a partial answer to the problem and at worst it denies the independence and primal quality of play. Without denying this reason, Caillois examines in depth the psychology of players, as demanded by their games, and thus illuminates another component of play itself. Their works are complementary; together they provide a concept of play that may be applied to the understanding of fantasy.[8]

7. The other three are *agon* (competition), *alea* (chance), and *ilinx* (vertigo). Each of the four may be embodied in games ranging through a progression or along an axis from *paideia* ("an almost indivisible principle common to diversion, turbulence, free improvisation, carefree gaiety . . . uncontrolled fantasy") to *ludus* (i.e., discipline, routine, method) (p. 13).

8. In an appendix to *Man and the Sacred* is a further critique of *Homo Ludens*. Here too Caillois expresses high regard for Huizinga's study, but he examines also "the defect in this admirable work": "It studies the external structures better than the intimate attitudes that give each activity its most precise meaning. And, the forms and rules of play are the object of more attentive examination than the needs satisfied by the game itself" (p. 154). From this he continues to attack Huizinga's identification of play and the sacred.

The works of Huizinga and Caillois describe fully the nature of play and its cultural range. Huizinga discusses the primacy of the play element in *poiesis* and concludes that in poetry the original impetus is less diffused by later accretions than in other cultural manifestations of play. Even so, he attends more to the poet as *vates* and to poetry as a "social game" involving competition that prompts the mobilization of resonances in language, imagery, and figuration, and to poetry as an embodiment of a mythical way of dealing with cosmogonic questions than he does to the products of a principally literary art. He draws his most persuasive material from "primitive" poetry and its continuations into later periods. Though Huizinga cites many literary examples, most of them in an ad hoc manner, he makes no attempt at systematic study of literature. Some of his examples are from narrative poetry (he has a particular affection for *The Rape of the Lock*), but he has nothing to say about prose fiction, and nothing that bears directly on wit and fancy as instruments of play, though the general consistency of both with play seems self-evident.

Accordingly, it is necessary to seek some literary manifestations of play that may be more directly related to wit and fantasy. These exist in the kind of writing usually called nonsense. Most critics who take nonsense seriously complain about the term. Likely it has been used as the result of an assumption that all is non-sense that does not conform to conventional understanding and established logic. But "nonsense" as applied to such works as those of Edward Lear and Lewis Carroll is not only prejudicial; it is also inaccurate, for such works are characterized principally by a severe internal logic in development of an arbitrary assumption.

The claim of nonsense to intellectual validity is the central contention of Sir Edmund Strachey in a review article on four books of Edward Lear, all published in 1888: "Sense is the recognition, adjustment, and maintenance of the proper and fitting relations of the affairs of ordinary life. . . . In contradic-

The appendix first appeared as a review in 1946. *Man and the Sacred*, trans. Meyer Barash, was originally published as *L'homme et le sacré* (Paris: Presses Universitaires de France, 1939).

17

tion to the relations and harmonies of life, Nonsense sets itself to discover and bring forward the incongruities of all things within and without us." [9] Nonsense, then, is not simply a negative, "but the bringing out a new and deeper harmony of life in and through its contradictions." Though he does not say so, Strachey assumes a relationship of sense and nonsense. The second would scarcely be recognizable without some kind of reference to the first or a context of sense in the reader's mind, and the two seem to collaborate in the enrichment of human understanding.

In *The Field of Nonsense* Elizabeth Sewell asserts the essential freedom of such writing and thus seems to stand closer to Huizinga. She dismisses the pejorative meaning of the term by supporting the opposite, that nonsense is orderly and no more than orderly and that its constructs connect with nothing established or recognizable.[10] "Nonsense is a carefully limited world, controlled and directed by reason, a construction subject to its own laws." [11] For Miss Sewell, order is nonsense's first, and only, law, and the progression of thought that this law allows is strictly serial:

> The aim of Nonsense is very precise indeed. It is by means of language to set before the mind a possible universe in which everything goes along serially, by one and one. This serial order must not be upset by indistinctness of the units or by fusion of the whole. . . . The original references must not develop, and there must be no final manifold. The aim, an essential one if the conditions for play are to be fulfilled, is the preservation of distinctness, each unit a distinct one . . . and the whole a collection of distinct parts.[12]

From this Miss Sewell derives certain consequences. When nonsense is expressed in verse, the result is apart from what is actually thought poetry. Specifically what is absent is the "dream

9. *Quarterly Review*, 167 (1888), 335.

10. Compare Huizinga's statement: "Here we come across another, very positive feature of play: it creates order, *is* order. Into an imperfect world and into the confusion of life it brings a temporary, a limited perfection. Play demands order absolute and supreme" (p. 10).

11. *The Field of Nonsense* (London: Chatto and Windus, 1952), p. 5.

12. Ibid., p. 56.

element in poetry, its ambiguity, its imagery by which . . . fusions may take place" (p. 23). The nonsense writer must avoid fusions, fluidities, personal associations and intuitions of relationship—all the nonrational intimations that evoke a superrational richness of experience in reading. "Kubla Khan," *Alastor, Le bateau ivre,* to name only a few, would be by Miss Sewell's principle the antithesis of nonsense. She demands further the "strict avoidance of Beauty in Nonsense." Beauty must be excluded because it promotes a wish for something desirable, perhaps even goodness, whereas nonsense is without affective tendency or ethical value. To the demand that nonsense remain outside emotion Miss Sewell permits one exception: it may convey a feeling of isolation, but this is all. Beauty, moreover, is more often than not a result of perceiving agreeable proportion, and nonsense, if it is to keep its identity, must eschew the kind of total design that enables a reader to discern with pleasure the harmony of parts with each other and with the whole. To the contrary, nonsense often represents disproportion.

Let us examine a passage of nonsense writing that seems to embody Miss Sewell's requirements, though it is one she herself does not cite. It is a piece perpetrated in 1755 by Samuel Foote, designed to vex the fading actor Charles Macklin, who had boasted publicly that a single quick reading would suffice for him to memorize any text, whether or not it made sense:

> So she went into the garden
> to cut a cabbage-leaf
> to make an apple-pie;
> and at the same time
> a great she-bear, coming down the street,
> pops its head into the shop.
> What! no soap?
> So he died,
> and she very imprudently married the Barber:
> and there were present
> the Picninnies,
> and the Joblillies,
> and the Garyulies,
> and the grand Panjandrum himself,

> with the little round button at top;
> and they fell to playing the game
> of catch-as-catch-can,
> till the gunpowder ran out at the heels of their boots.[13]

This might be a fragment of narrative, perhaps, as Leonard Forster suggests, the ending of some mad fairy tale.[14] The logical trick of the passage is simple: an unasserted pretense that events follow by causal sequence when they clearly do not. The first "so" connects with nothing; thereafter the time sequence is generally a progression of separates, according to Miss Sewell's prescription. Once the reader has accepted the gambit, the notion that anything can cause anything to follow becomes the norm. The "truth" of the presentation is never opened to doubt, and the consenting reader may supply for himself details that are omitted, such as the appearance and disposition of Picninnies, Joblillies, and Garyulies, and perhaps the rules of the game of catch-as-catch-can. This is nonsense as pure as one can find in discourse by language.

At first sight, it may seem that Foote's performance shows the defeat of Miss Sewell's principle that relationship of parts does not occur in nonsense. Whatever they may be, Picninnies, Joblillies, and Garyulies bear such names as make them seem in some way coordinate. The grand Panjandrum is some kind of inflated being. His name has a sound opposed to the diminutives that help form the identity of the three; moreover, the reader cannot help thinking of it as a burlesque of some honorific oriental title. This prompts an association or reference that the reader brings to the piece because of his prior knowledge. It is even possible that "the great she-bear" alludes to Dr. John Shebbeare, an older contemporary of Foote known for the irascibility of his anti-Hanoverian writings. Dr. Johnson, who was also scornful of Hanoverians, had accepted a royal pension in 1762; Dr. Shebbeare's pension was bestowed in 1764. If Boswell's memory can be trusted, there was "a ludicrous paragraph in the news-

13. See *Quarterly Review*, 95 (1854), 516–17.
14. *The Poetry of Significant Nonsense: An Inaugural Lecture* (Cambridge: University Press, 1962), p. 6.

papers that the King had pensioned both a *He*-bear and a *She*-bear." [15]

In Foote's *jeu d'esprit* alone there seems to be a negation of the discreteness of elements, the sheerly serial progression, and the avoidance of fusion that Miss Sewell insists on as essential to the order that is nonsense. And apart from any text it is impossible to think of words as nonreferential, pure counters. For this reason, play with words is more difficult than with objects, numbers, or sounds, though the two latter present difficulties of their own. Miss Sewell does not try to deny that words, in themselves and in syntactical arrangements, have intrinsic referents. [16] Rather, she incorporates this quality and other synthesizing potentialities of language into the game as opponents, for without an opponent there could be no game. The object of composed nonsense is to make the unity-by-unit order of a closed verbal system triumph over the mind's tendency to use words for creating fusions. "The force," she writes, "towards disorder in the mind must be inhibited, both as regards the mind's tendency to produce and develop trains of dream-like and personal associations in connection with words and phrases, and as regards its tendency to run collections of images together into some new unity" (p. 56).

Nonsense, then, opposes all that makes dreams, poetry, beauty, feeling, and ethical value. Against these, nonsense attempts to establish absolute clarity, complete control, pure order, unassailable internal logic, and to do this with means more easily used by the competitor. Herein is the answer to one who might ask why the most successful nonsense would not be a page from a telephone directory or a list of words set down at random. The order in the first is mechanical and in the second whimsical; neither has internal logic. But nonsense, whether verse or prose, is obligated not only to follow syntax but to use syntax to create the opposite of what it usually produces. Most pieces of non-

15. See Boswell's *Life of Johnson* (London: Oxford University Press, 1942), 2:415. It appears that Foote's trick to catch Macklin, one of many such, occurred in 1755. The piece itself first appeared in print in *Harry and Lucy* (1825), by Maria Edgeworth, who attributed it to Foote.
16. See *Field of Nonsense*, pp. 56–57.

sense contain no violations of verbal consecutivity; this is one of the rules of the game. In all the passages from Edward Lear and Lewis Carroll that Miss Sewell examines, this rule is invariably observed. So are the rest of her requirements, except in some of Lear's songs and in *The Hunting of the Snark* and the two parts of *Sylvie and Bruno*. In these she finds "technical failure," because the authors allowed affective elements to adulterate the product. In nonsense, this is either treachery or the triumph of the enemy.

The scheme Miss Sewell elaborates is a severe one, and it establishes for play with words a freedom more self-contained than Huizinga envisioned. Indeed, nonsense might be said to end not in freedom but in isolation. "One is one and all alone, and ever more shall be." No one who reads Miss Sewell's demonstration can doubt that the playing intellect can go so far, and in doing so it reaches not lunacy, but, in terms of the product, total clarity. The product is writing in form and appearance only; essentially it is pure exercise in manipulating words as symbols. It has no rhetorical component, for it embodies no attempt to persuade or influence the reader. Ideally, nonsense does not need readers. It is the self-limited work of logic. Now few people can be, or wish to be, logicians. But they are not, because of this falling short, disqualified from the play of wit, and their productions may include elements from the "force towards disorder in the mind." Along with these impurities, they have audiences, purposes, relationships with existing concepts, and a need for rhetoric.

It has been useful to review the fundamentals of intellectual play in its ultimate manifestation. Nonsense is the end to which fantasy might go, but does not. Fantasy relies on dominant but not total logic, on play that is free but not isolated. The player who exerts himself in this area is not necessarily a logician, but what Leonard Forster calls an "ingenious person." If he expresses his game in writing, his readers will be those who can respond, in their way also ingenious persons. In nonsense the only player is the logician, deploying order against disorder; readers can do no more than watch the performance. In fantasy too there is performance, but also some participation by readers as they respond to the play of wit.

"Ingenious persons" are those who in some area, not alone learning or sophisticated taste, possess wit. It is worth remembering that in seventeenth-century critical writing, *ingenium* is often a synonym for wit. Ingenuity and wit suggest mobility of mind, impatience with routine thought, quickness to devise and explore novelties, shrewdness and daring in development, release from the vanity of dogmatizing. Play is free, and wit is free; which is the instrument of the other would be hard to say. Against the background of what they intentionally depart from, both create worlds ordered by internal logic, effective even if impure. Thus made cohesive, these worlds maintain temporarily an identity that is sufficient and plausible. Because they compete with the established, perhaps they must be the more persuasive and the more nearly perfect in structure. But as Huizinga notes, even when the activities of play—including wit—absorb the player, he still knows that he is playing by choice, that his game is factitious, and that he cannot avoid returning to the ordinary. Hopefully, however, some of the liberation will remain to enliven his participation in dailiness, and hopefully wit shows itself in activities other than its excursions. Some such happy effect as this is envisioned by Father Rahner, as he develops his thesis that play—not frivolity, which he thinks "always the sign of a secret despair"—is closely allied to wisdom and holiness. "Seriousness" alone, he holds, cannot get at the root of things; for this seriousness and speculation, by which he means free play of the mind after the manner of a creator, must combine.[17]

It will already have occurred to the reader that a talent for fantasy may derive in part from an author's endowment of fancy, which often can scarcely be differentiated from wit. Both are characteristic of "ingenious persons." Fancy, a term long familiar in critical discourse, has suffered in reputation from Coleridge's influential deprecation and from being associated with a now superseded faculty psychology. Even so, a brief in-

17. *Man at Play*, trans. Brian Battershaw and Edward Quinn (New York: Herder and Herder, 1967), pp. 26, 36, and passim.

quiry into the nature of the fancy may indirectly illuminate the kind of prose fiction with which I am concerned.

The fancy has long been thought an originator of playful intellection—restless, capricious, subversive, ingenious. In the prefatory letter to *Annus Mirabilis*, Dryden posited three poetical capabilities—invention, fancy, and elocution. Invention is, plausibly enough, the finding of the thought. Fancy continues the process by producing "the variation, deriving, or moulding of that thought, as the judgment represents it proper to the subject." [18] Elocution completes the act by putting all into felicitous language. In Dryden's formulation all three are aspects or functions of the imagination. But several criticis in the eighteenth century, most notably Addison, moved toward that separation of imagination and fancy that Coleridge completed at the end of the thirteenth chapter of *Biographia Literaria*.

It must be remembered that one of Coleridge's abhorrences was associationism, as brought to full expression by David Hartley. He saw in this a totally mechanical explanation of the workings of mind and soul, a scheme incapable of accounting for the transcendent powers of creativity. These he vested in the imagination. But he could not deny that associative activity is expressed in verse. It thus became a matter of principle and tactics for Coleridge to elevate imagination and to confine fancy to a kind of mechanical operation. So fancy is "no other than a mode of memory emancipated from time and space." It deals with "fixities and definites"; it "has no other counters to play with." It is bound by "choice" and by the "law of association." At best, it would seem, fancy may yield poetry that is startling and entertaining, at worst versified frivolity. Wordsworth was not entirely comfortable with his friend's distinction, though he never actually denied it. Wordsworth's view vacillated between considering the fancy as an immature state of the imagination and as a poetical power real enough but limited, as the imagination is not.[19]

18. *The Works of John Dryden*, ed. Edward Niles Hooker and H. T. Swedenburg, Jr. (Berkeley and Los Angeles: University of California Press, 1956), 1:53.

19. See James Scoggins, *Imagination and Fancy: Complementary Modes in the Poetry of Wordsworth* (Lincoln: University of Nebraska Press, 1966), pp. 22, 57–58, 199ff.

After these potent makers of romantic critical thought had expressed themselves, there were sporadic contributions to understanding by Leigh Hunt and Ruskin. More recently, T. E. Hulme, Sir Herbert Read, and T. S. Eliot attempted to explore the nature of the fancy, as Coleridge had not, and thus to give it its due. But with the effective proponency of I. A. Richards, the Coleridgeans have pretty much had their way about the dominance and eminence of the imagination.

This historical sketch suggests the way in which the fancy as a faculty bears on fantasy as a product. For all his partisanship, Coleridge saw that fancy is embodied in intellectual play. It is a natural ally of wit, both in the way it perceives unexpected resemblances, often of contraries, and in the way it can be mobilized to challenge inherited belief or the creations of transcendent imagination. In a descriptive sense, fancy is mischievous; it can sport with established seriousness, advance astonishing counter-propositions, and organize these into demonstrations. And this, when performed in narrative, is exactly the essence of prose fiction fantasy.

Readers and auditors are almost as important to the success of wit and fancy as are producers. The play is peculiarly dependent on the favorable responses of the like-minded, for it is impossible to distinguish sharply between response and intellectual participation. A compact between maker and participants is necessary. When Falstaff asserts, "I am not only witty in myself, but the cause that wit is in other men" (2 *Henry IV*, I, ii [11–12]), he is not only boasting but also suggesting the necessary relationship between originator and respondents. And he would see the day when the Prince refused to play his game. Many readers have been outraged at the Prince's rejection of Falstaff. Part of this anger comes from distaste for the betrayal of a friend by one who is secretly pursuing what seems a program of self-aggrandizement, but part also is an expression of refusal to tolerate the "spoilsport." Huizinga recognizes the ferocity of the play community: "It is curious to note how much more lenient society is to the cheat than to the spoil-sport. This is because the spoil-sport shatters the play-world itself" (p. 11). To those who dislike Shakespeare's principles about what a sovereign must and must not be, Prince Hal, because he entered a play compact and then withdrew, is reprehensible, even though he announced in his first soliloquy that he would withdraw and why he must.

Successful exercise of literary wit depends on community, with a rapport of understanding and taste between originator and respondents. The fact that the writer may produce, and the readers participate, in physical isolation does not deny the existence of an intellectual compact. If they move somehow toward intramural formation, they may become a coterie or cult. I hasten to add that not all such literary groups form because of sharing a taste for particular expressions of wit. Admirers of James Joyce must be held together at least in large part by the effectiveness of his wit; no one would say the same about the cult of Sherlock Holmes.

In the play produced by the exercise of wit, there are, then, a leader (or leaders) and followers, who combine to form a separate, perhaps privileged, group. This is a relationship tacitly recognized by Huizinga, though not much discussed. He is mainly concerned with the poet's superior knowledge, insight, and facility in verbal play, with what these produce in the poet's making, with the competitions of play in contests of wisdom, and with conflict as the central material of verse narrative. In some passages Huizinga treats play expressed in poetry as communal performance, a "social game" as he says, without leaders and followers. Intellectual agility and speculativeness are not inconsistent with the poet's other endowments, but he says little about them. This is understandable. Huizinga is concerned with the vatic, myth-making capabilities of the poet as player. For these the pertinent qualities are vision, mystical intuition, knowledge of the esoteric, wisdom—qualities that remain even when the expressions turn to invective or facetious contests. Wit, a lower capability, is appropriate to the rhetor or the sophist, types that emerged as the "primordial composite type," the poet-seer, disintegrated.

When play of intellect occurs, elements that were latent become prominent. The novel concepts and what develops therefrom directly challenge some established formulation. Thus play, for all its assertion of independence, becomes dependent on the established for incitement. In its pure state of nonsense, play is separate from the ordinary; in manifestations of wit, play temporarily rejects the ordinary and labors to displace it. It follows that the new proposition must be demonstrated by argument, exemplary narrative, or other means. To this end, all the devices of rhetoric are mobilized. When the developed play is ended, one of two things occurs: either the reader returns to his acceptance of the challenged norm with a sense of simply having been entertained by the departure, or (what I believe happens more frequently) he returns with his understanding modified. The first likely occurs after a reading of *Zuleika Dobson*. But after he finishes *Lady into Fox*, for example, he will know something, which he might not otherwise learn, about the relationship of the animal and the human and something about fidelity in the face of circumstances that might be expected to destroy fidelity.[20] There are, of course, variables in the causes of these residual effects. A logically weak development, even though it is agreeable enough, probably will not leave so much as a sense of entertainment. Some players with wit intend principally to enlighten the understanding, some to generate a permanently altered or modified belief, some to achieve both. I believe that David Garnett hoped to show the limits of fidelity far more than he wished to recommend extreme fidelity as a virtue. But the romances of Charles Williams do more than put aspects of Christian doctrine into illustrative action; they serve the propagation of the faith.[21]

So much for results from the skill and intention of the writer who is playing a game of sustained wit. Much depends also on the capabilities of the reader. Some intelligent readers are unable to meet the demands of a counterdemonstration of wit. If they read it at all, they do so in a state of balking and annoyance. Others may be willing enough but lack the practiced agility of

20. In a letter to T. H. White (January 10, 1956), David Garnett notes that fidelity "is a large part of the subject of Lady into Fox and of the Sailors Return." See Sylvia Townsend Warner, *T. H. White* (New York: Viking, 1967), p. 261.

21. Herbert Read asserts that any "subjective, or moralizing, intent," any strain of "subjective intolerance," in a fantasy "not only destroys its rhetorical purity but in so doing also destroys its rhetorical effect. . . ." *English Prose Style* (1952; reprint ed., Boston: Beacon Press, 1955), pp. 131–32.

mind to follow, and at best they are no more than amazed at the display. Others are oversophisticated, or sophisticated into mental indifference. Play of wit is not for Savonarola, or Joseph Andrews, or Pococurante, though Joseph Andrews might be capable of learning. The best respondents, of course, are those who are themselves witty and, more important, have an intrinsic interest and delight in mental play. With this endowment a reader may respond to propositions that had never entered his mind and play with materials that are foreign to his knowledge, using methods hitherto unfamiliar to him. Even without preparation, he will quickly consent to Judas College, Oxford, the prodigies that occur there, and the devastation that a visiting goddess works on the undergraduates. If he brings to *Zuleika Dobson* some knowledge of the mores of Oxford or of any long-established university, so much the better. But the response of the better informed reader is different in degree, not in kind, from that of an uninformed reader who has the capacity for wit play by response.

After consideration, I suggest that play of wit between originator and respondents generates an educative process. This is most lively, of course, when leader and followers meet in person. Any teacher has observed that his sessions with a small group of capable students, or even with one, often produce not the social game that Huizinga examines, but an intellectual game. This is most likely when the business at hand promotes challenge, either within the group or of the group united in an enterprise of constructing a counterdevelopment to an established idea, as prompted and guided by the professor. The results of such sessions can be most fruitful, even when they are temporary. The situation of the writer purveying wit play and his readers is obviously different, in that immediate exchange does not occur. There is a loss here of interactive stimulation and a gain for the writer in the directness with which he can deploy the components of his development. For the writer the gain overbalances the loss, for he can anticipate the responses of his readers and meet them with his tactics without the distraction of their presence and helpful voices. It is not, however, the circumstances of learning that are decisive. Simply because the writer who plays with wit propounds a sustained intellectual discourse on a dissenting theme and because readers engage themselves in a response that follows a construct even though it may not assent, the pleasure and enlightenment of education will occur.

I cannot finish this discussion of wit and play without considering briefly the suggestions Freud advanced. My consideration will be negative, not because of any disrespect or mistrust but because Freud's thought on these matters does not illuminate the ways in which wit and play may be mobilized to yield prose fiction fantasy. Even so, a statement of what I surmise to be his different direction may by contrast assist an understanding of my subject.

It is worth noting again that Huizinga expresses dissatisfaction with hypotheses about play proposed by physiologists and psychologists. They are all seeking an intrinsic purposive element and thus deny the freedom that he thought the primary condition of play. At best, he holds, they reach partial solutions. Also, as might be expected, Elizabeth Sewell simply omits any mention of depth psychology except in her chapter on those "technical failures" of Lear and Lewis Carroll that resulted from their intruding affective elements into nonsense. But even here she shows no interest in using the poems to study personality.[22] Neither Huizinga nor Miss Sewell actually rejects Freud's conclusions; they seem simply to recognize that his aim was different from theirs, in that he was concerned with wit and play as media through which the personality can be ascertained and described. Play itself and the cultural or logical products of play are apart from his purpose. It is unsatisfying to "know the dancer from the dance," but for analysis necessary.

For Freud, play, whenever and however it occurs, is an attempt to regain the natural euphoria of childhood. He does not recognize play as an objective activity appropriate to adults who

---

22. Quite the opposite is to be found in a work by Deborah Bacon, "The Meaning of Non-Sense: A Psychoanalytic Approach to Lewis Carroll" (Ph.D. thesis, Columbia University, 1950). Central in her argument is the proposition that nonsense "consists almost entirely of the writer's expression of the unconscious part of his own personality" (p. vii). I am sure that Miss Sewell would dissent or at least would say that this understanding of nonsense is radically different from her own.

willingly participate in it and expend various kinds of energy. In Freud's understanding, the motive to play is the reduction of energy that must be expended against various tensions or limitations—inhibition, ideation, feeling. This reduction or saving is what he means by economy. Play acts on the pleasure principle, the earliest disposition of the psyche, which in turn "is a tendency operating in the service of a function whose business it is to free the mental apparatus entirely from excitation or to keep the amount of excitation in it constant or to keep it as low as possible. . . . The function thus described would be concerned with the most universal endeavour of all living substance—namely to return to the quiescence of the inorganic world." [23] The reality principle, a result of the "ego's instincts for self-preservation," necessarily presents inhibitions to what it displaces and hence causes unpleasure, but it is not the only source. Also effective are "contests and dissensions . . . in the mental apparatus" as the ego matures, and tensions produced by "unsatisfied instincts" and by the perception of danger. Whatever the cause, pleasure consists of relief, and consequently an economizing of energy, from those pressures or threats that produce unpleasure.

So far, the principle of play in Freud's thought seems to be an escape from tension to a relaxed state. This is the opposite of play as a willfully entered activity characterized by construction and discipline with no directly sought reward to the participant, as I have previously outlined it. Let us test this assertion against Freud's speculations about phantasy making and about wit. The first may be found conveniently outlined in a familiar paper (1908) translated under the title "The Relation of the Poet to Day-Dreaming" ("Der Dichter und das Phantasieren"). Here he observes what is common knowledge, that a child playing creates a phantasy world, which he takes seriously even though he distinguishes it from reality. Surrendering this activity unwillingly, the adult continues the freedom of play by secretive daydreaming. But adult phantasies are motivated by unsatisfied wishes: "Every separate phantasy contains the fulfillment of a wish, and improves on unsatisfactory reality. . . . Either they

23. *Beyond the Pleasure Principle*, trans. James Strachey (1920; reprint ed., New York: Bantam Books, 1963), pp. 107–8.

are ambitious wishes, serving to exalt the person creating them, or they are erotic." [24] They gratify "His Majesty the Ego"; they impart to the dreamer a power that experience and self-knowledge deny. Freud continues to demonstrate that imaginative writers disguise the naked ego-building of daydreams and put its gratifications into acceptable aesthetic forms without essentially altering them.

But we need follow this line no further. Already it is evident that this and the forms of play I have discussed previously are markedly different. The latter are objective from the start; they need no artist to reshape the material. And in material they are by no means confined to ambition and erotic success. Though winning in competition is desirable, and esteem (from self and others) is accorded to a winner, gratification of some unfulfilled wish to serve the ego is scarcely a prime motivation. If there is any competition in this aspect of play in Freud's formulation, it is differently centered—on the vain and devious attempt of the ego to overcome reality of self and circumstances.[25] Play of this sort is involutional, as the other is not. Finally, daydreams also work according to the principle of economy by releasing or returning the dreamer to an easy satisfaction that avoids the tensions ordinarily facing him. In the other kind of play, including the play of wit, expenditure of all kinds of energy is willingly sought as part of the game.

Similarly, when Freud analyzes wit, the nature and course of play that he educes seem to me fundamentally at variance with that play which can produce prose fiction fantasy. There is a preindication of the difference in Freud's title *Der Witz und seine Beziehung zum Unbewussten* (1905). Perhaps developed play of wit has some impetus from the unconscious; it might even be argued that the conventional formulation that wit rebels against is a figurative inhibition. But assuredly the inception of the dissent and its development are essentially rational, and remain so even when material is imported from the unconscious or another

24. "The Relation of the Poet to Day-Dreaming," in *On Creativity and the Unconscious: Papers on the Psychology of Art, Literature, Love, Religion* (New York: Harper and Row, 1958), p. 47.

25. Freud hints at this in saying, 'The opposite of play is not serious occupation but—reality." Ibid., p. 45.

nonrational source. Early in Freud's exposition and throughout, it is evident that he is concerned not with those insights of wit that lead naturally into demonstration by argument or narrative, but with play in which inception and completion are simultaneous, with no need for development. Such a manifestation of wit, for which I think "joke" is an inadequate term, can have an immediate brilliance that no other expression matches, though Freud's examples do not always show it. And because it works almost instantaneously, even when not at the peak of excellence, it is an effective device for release through the now familiar principle of economy.[26]

The differences between a play of wit that requires development and seeks expenditure of energy and one which renders development otiose and seeks to reduce expenditure are so sharp that, with all respect to Freud's work, I need consider it no further here.[27]

26. In the final paragraph of his book Freud focuses his whole study on economy: "The pleasure in jokes has seemed to us to arise from an economy in expenditure upon inhibition, the pleasure in the comic from an economy in expenditure upon ideation (upon cathexis) and the pleasure in humor from an economy in expenditure upon feeling. In all three modes of working of our mental apparatus the pleasure is derived from an economy. All three are agreed in representing methods of regaining from mental activity a pleasure which has been lost through development of that activity. For the euphoria which we endeavour to reach by these means is nothing other than the mood of a period of life in which we were accustomed to deal with our psychical work in general with small expenditure of energy—the mood of our childhood, when we were ignorant of the comic, when we were incapable of jokes and when we had no need of humor to make us feel happy in our life" (p. 236).

27. F. L. Lucas, though he does not accept Freud's description of the process that yields a witticism, gives an altogether just summary of the sequence as Freud conceived it to be: "(1) idea in the Preconscious awaiting expression; (2) childish desire to play with words or nonsense; (3) inhibition of this desire by adult censorship; (4) mysterious juggling in the Unconscious which turns nonsense into sense after all; (5) emergence as witticism; (6) laughter from release of energy previously employed to inhibit childishness." *Literature and Psychology* (1951; reprint ed., Ann Arbor: University of Michigan Press, 1957), p. 163. This condensation does not reflect the full pleasurable result of economy and does not attempt to represent the ingenuity of Freud's general and particular analyses.

Contributions to a theory of prose fiction fantasy have been scanty and dispersed by lack of a common understanding. Some critics mention it only to dismiss it as unworthy of a serious person's attention.[1] Some make it an oddity within a larger genre. Some make it the subject of a single observation or two so discerning that the omission of any development is disappointing. Some discuss it in a generalizing paragraph and pass on to matters of more interest. Others fasten on a single feature, usually having to do with material or content, and force this to explain the whole. This simplification can be detected in the titles of several periodicals, such as the *Magazine of Fantasy and Science Fiction*, and in a catalog, *The Checklist of Fantastic Literature*, compiled by Bradford M. Day and issued by Science Fiction and Fantasy Publishers in 1965. The presumption suggested by these titles is that fantasy and science fiction are indistinguishable except for the nature of the material.

In effect, Kingsley Amis accepts this proposition in his differentiation between fantasy and science fiction: "Science fiction . . . maintains a respect for fact or presumptive fact, fantasy makes a point of flouting these; for a furniture of robots, space ships, techniques, and equations it substitutes elves, broomsticks, occult powers, and incantations." [2] The unstated principle in his discrimination, which despite its starkness is useful, is that the

1. Louis Macneice comes close to this kind of intolerance when he writes as follows: "The greatest traditional myths, such as those of Orpheus and Eurydice or the Rape of Persephone, are . . . works of Imagination; the myth, that is, appears inevitable and fulfills a need in the reader that he may or may not have been aware of. The fantasies of mere Fancy, on the other hand, seem not inevitable but arbitrary; they have surface but no depth; they amuse but they do not nourish; they are almost a form of doodling. These two kinds are often found in the same work." *Varieties of Parable* (Cambridge: University Press, 1965), p. 78.

2. *New Maps of Hell: A Survey of Science Fiction* (New York: Harcourt, Brace, 1960), p. 22.

material makes fantasy a violation of "fact or presumptive fact." I wish that Amis's subject and personal taste had allowed him to discuss nonscience-fiction fantasy more fully. But he excludes it, saying only that he recognizes "the existence of a body of work that can be called fantasy, from *Beowulf* to Kafka . . . but my business is not with that." He admits that he does not like fantasy.

Making material, or any other single element, the sole factor of a definition has a curious double effect. One of these is suggested by Amis's range, from *Beowulf* to Kafka. There is too much room; fantasy can be anything as long as it deals with the evidently unreal. The other effect is opposite, that of restricting fantasy to what is unreal by category and failing to perceive that the unreal can be established by manipulation of seemingly ordinary material. The central stuff—the active beings, events, and settings—of George Macdonald's *Lilith* are extraexperiential, though it is not this alone that makes it a fantasy. But to cite a contrasting example, the core of Richard Hughes's *A High Wind over Jamaica*—a group of children captive on a pirate ship—is not in itself beyond conceiving. The fantasy in this work results from the violation, as seen in the action, of a standard belief about the nature of innocence. There are a number of ways, not just one, by which a fantasist may challenge the presumptively real and demonstrate his counterproposition in narrative.

Still other commentators fail to apply the well-known discrimination between fantasy as a psychic phenomenon, whether self-serving or no, and fantasy as a literary form, sometimes, though not always, shaped from the emanation but disciplined as this never is. When this error occurs, fantasy is left hanging between "dream stuff" and an artistic-rhetorical product. There is some excuse for this mistake, for twentieth-century prose fiction abounds in direct representations of extraconscious experience. The snow dream of Hans Castorp in *The Magic Mountain* is an excellent example.

Other works present even longer sequences of seemingly unmodified psychic experience, to the point where such becomes the dominant representation. This can be found in the surrealist novel and stream-of-consciousness novel, and with the added control of formal patterning of imagery, in what Ralph Freedman identifies as the lyrical novel. Fantasies always show sharper forming, clearer external objectification, and more evident rhetorical tactics than these explorations of the psyche in its apparently inchoate wanderings.

Actually, most fantasies give the reader a sequence and consequence of events, so clearly reported that there seems no doubt of their veracity. If, in the process, "dream stuff" is used, it too is rendered with the same clarity. A successful fantasy conveys an impression of circumstantial reality no less convincing, though not always so detailed, as that which Defoe relied on in *Robinson Crusoe*. This is true of so lyrical and "dreamy" a narrative as *Green Mansions*.

The failure to think in accordance with the distinction between fantasy as a psychic phenomenon and as a literary form is a variant on definition by a single element. In both errors a part is made the equivalent of the whole.

Enough of complaints against inadequacy. Far more important is to assemble the thoughtful and constructive suggestions of the authoritative persons who have attended to fantasy as a matter for critical discourse. These are H. G. Wells, Sir Herbert Read, E. M. Forster, C. S. Lewis, J. R. R. Tolkien, George P. Elliott, and Tzvetan Todorov. All but Todorov have written fantasy, though Forster's and Elliott's contributions are in short fiction. Of Forster's novels, only *A Room with a View* is incompletely of the kind.[3]

H. G. Wells's views are offered in a brief introductory statement to a collection of his early scientific romances.[4] He first explicitly distinguishes between his own work and that of such writers as Jules Verne. The latter are concerned "almost always with actual possibilities of invention and discovery," and appeal to a practical interest. Wells associates his own work with the line that includes Lucian's *Vera Historia*, *The Golden Ass* of Apuleius, Chamisso's *Peter Schlemihls wundersame Geschichte*, *Frankenstein*, and *Lady into Fox*. Like these, he proposes, his own fantasies present impossibilities and aim at the same credence as occurs in "a good gripping dream." The focus of in-

3. See James McConkey, *The Novels of E. M. Forster* (Ithaca: Cornell University Press, 1957), pp. 55–61.
4. *Seven Famous Novels by H. G. Wells* (New York: Knopf, 1934).

terest must be not on the marvelous events for themselves but on the human involvement in them. As to method, in Wells's view, simplicity is essential. There must be one decisive miracle, established early in the reader's belief and "domesticated." Then follows development of the "magic trick" by narrative of its consequences, within the range of the ordinary and with "touches of prosaic detail." The one hypothesis must dominate alone. If "any *extra* fantasy outside the cardinal assumption" is introduced, the whole invention will seem irresponsible and silly.

Wells's generalizations are useful. It often does happen that the decisive principle is established early, by fiat, as in the opening sentence of Kafka's *Metamorphosis*, or by concealed persuasion through detail, as in the careful elaboration of the revisited village at dusk and the stream that flows the wrong way in Sir Herbert Read's *The Green Child*. By "domestication" one may guess that Wells means showing not only the impingement of the marvel on ordinary human affairs but also the assertion through events of a norm that previously had not existed. If my understanding of his metaphor is accurate, the results he had in mind are often found in fantasy. A "magic trick" is, of course, mandatory. But it is not always pulled off early; sometimes it becomes evident after a run of seductive development, and sometimes there is no perceptible point of establishment. Also the marvel is not always made to play on ordinary human affairs; even when it does, the effect may be to transform the ordinary into the marvelous. The total milieu of Lowes Dickinson's *The Magic Flute* is anything but ordinary; in Charles Williams's *The Place of the Lion* the Hertfordshire countryside remains unchanged, but the apparition of the beasts of Neoplatonic lore makes the environment seem a land of wonder. As for the "extra fantasy" that he forbids, it is difficult to make an arbitrary working distinction between this and major stages or changed directions within development.

Wells's theory, for all that it illuminates, is limited. Though he seems to assume that his propositions and prescriptions are generally applicable, his preface is a sketchy rationale of his own practices in these early works.

The main features of Sir Herbert Read's notes toward a theory of fantasy are contained in a brief chapter, entitled "Fantasy (Fancy)," in *English Prose Style*. Fancy he takes to be the "mental process" and fantasy the result. For the essence of his understanding, one need go no further than the following statement:

> Fantasy is extraverted feeling: imagination is introverted feeling. If in pursuit of the extraversion of feeling, the mind turns to speculation, the result is fantasy. When, however, feeling is introverted, the product of speculation is imaginative. The distinction follows the lines of discursive and non-discursive logic. Fantasy may be visionary, but it is deliberate and rational; imagination is sensuous and symbolic. Each mode has its characteristic style, but the style of fantasy is analogous to that of exposition, while the style of imagination is analogous to that of narrative.[5]

Actually Sir Herbert seems more intent to express judgments on practices in fantasy and on examples than to form a theory. And his pronouncements are more interesting, though often somewhat unaccountable.

Perfect performances in the fairy tale, his choice for the form to which fantasy should be assigned, are, he holds, rare; almost all that are not "traditional" fail. Kingsley's *Water Babies* "lacks objectivity." *Alice in Wonderland*, though "nearer to perfection," relies in part on "a suppressed background of culture which a true fairy tale never has," and it purveys satire. *Animal Farm* might be approved if the satire could be ignored! More's *Utopia*, *News from Nowhere*, *The Dream of John Ball*, *Erewhon*, *A Crystal Age*, and *1984*, are all corrupted by "some ulterior satirical or moral aim." H. G. Wells almost had an understanding of the requisite purity, but he employed a "pseudo-scientific logicality." Passages in *Ulysses* come close, but they are incoherent and call for a reader of intellectual attainment and "a temper of metaphysical disillusion." Parts of *Finnegans Wake* come closer, but again deny access to most readers by their complexity and sophistication.

5. *English Prose Style* (1952; reprint ed., Boston: Beacon Press, 1955), pp. 125–26.

In respect of fantasies, Read is more than hard to please. His wholehearted approval is reserved for *The Thousand and One Nights*, of which *Vathek* is a "counterfeit" that nonetheless deserves praise. Beyond mentioning the "magnificent apparatus of genii and afrits" in Scheherazade's tales, he does not discuss his own example of excellence. Are we to understand that it is a fairy tale–fantasy because of its material?

I confess that I find all this confusing. Is a work not a fantasy at all if it contains some subjective element, or is it simply a fantasy that is flawed in tactics and execution? May any piece be called a fantasy that is not, by Read's criteria, perfectly so? Why must a fairy tale be innocent of cultural content or reference? I cannot divine answers to these questions. When Read passes to more sophisticated examples, he still reproaches the utopias and anti-utopias for lacking the purity that he sees in traditional fairy tales. What makes him believe that the two great works of Joyce have any central resemblance to fairy tales, beyond his exploitation according to convenience of folk material and devices, I cannot imagine. Nor can I guess why he holds that *The Thousand and One Nights* is great partly because of its unsophistication.

So Read's taste in fantasy as revealed in *English Prose Style* excludes almost all exemplars. Lest it seem that he disapproved of unusual fiction throughout, I must mention a passage in his autobiography in which he writes of "one type of book" he admires and would like to imitate. He names *A Sentimental Journey*, de Vigny's *Servitude et grandeur militaire*, Merimée's *Carmen*, *Undine* of de la Motte-Fouqué, Mörike's *Mozart auf der Reise nach Prag*, Jacobsen's *Niels Lynne*, *Le grand Meaulnes* of Alain Fournier, and Voltaire's *Candide*. Within these he notes a range from works originating in known history to "pure phantasy." They are short, "deliberate"; they fuse the objective and the reflective but avoid a psychological approach. Some, like *Candide*, have "a moral or satirical motive," which here he accepts without demur. They do not represent "constructive art forms"; they are "rather projections of an idea, of an incident, of a phantasy, intellectually conceived, but exhibited in a fresh texture of a personal style and the brightness of a concrete imagination." [6]

It would be ridiculous to hold Read to tidy classification when he is recalling books that gave him pleasure. And if any evidence were needed, this list would prove that Read's taste was wide and discerning. But he speaks of them as "one type," "a prose form," and he generalizes about them as I have indicated in the preceding paragraph. He does not call them fantasies, but he attributes to them qualities—that they are deliberate, that they are intellectual projections—which are more nearly consistent with his prescriptions for fantasy in *English Prose Style* than the works he names in the illustrative part of that chapter. *Undine* alone has a close resemblance to a fairy tale. The others are a miscellany of narratives, except for *Servitude et grandeur militaire*, which is just intermittently a story. Read's titles might be used to support the thesis of Robert Kellogg and Robert Scholes that narrative is the genre and the novel one mode within it.[7] But Read's comments reveal also that his thinking about fantasy was idiosyncratic and sporadically illuminating, and that there is no continuity from his theory to his application of theory. I suggest that when Read came to writing *The Green Child*, a glowing fantasy that is part fairy tale and part fanciful historical reconstruction ideologically held together by an anti-utopian attitude,[8] he fortunately put his speculations aside.

Even before reading the lecture entitled "Fantasy" in *Aspects of the Novel*, the reader knows that he will not find systematic discourse; Forster does not wish to fasten "the claws of critical apparatus" on what has little substance. Instead of trying to define fantasy, he illuminates it with allusions, metaphors, illustrative comments, invitations to share his understanding of various books. So he plays about his subject with his wit and

6. *Annals of Innocence and Experience* (London: Faber and Faber, 1946), p. 218.

7. *The Nature of Narrative* (New York: Oxford University Press, 1966), pp. 3–9 and passim.

8. See Richard Wasson, "*The Green Child*: Herbert Read's Ironic Fantasy," *PMLA*, 77 (December, 1962), 645–51.

sensibility and shows what fantasy is as a mental exercise, how it may infuse itself into fiction, and what it requires of a reader. It is soon evident that by fantasy he does not mean a subgenre of narrative, even though his examples are all chosen from works of fiction. Rather, it is a playful spirit and what that spirit makes; he does not try to distinguish the faculty from the product. Almost all his representations suggest that fantasy is primarily active. It is a power that "penetrates into every corner of the universe, but not into the forces which govern it." [9] Always a devotee of animism, he associates it with a congeries of small geniuses: ". . . all beings who inhabit the lower air, the shallow water, and the smaller hills, all Fauns and Dryads and slips of the memory, all verbal coincidences, Pans and puns, all that is mediaeval this side of the grave" (pp. 161–62). Add to these Muddle, the little god that dominates *Tristram Shandy* and much of the known world.[10] But if only one god be allowable, "let us call upon Hermes—messenger, thief, and conductor of souls to a not too terrible hereafter." [11]

What does fantasy do? Again Forster does not differentiate between what it effects generally and what it effects in fiction. It causes little disturbances and provides unexpected enlightenments; the image of fantasy as a beam of light pervades his lecture:

> The stuff of daily life will be tugged and strained in various directions, the earth will be given little tilts, mischievous or pensive, spot lights will fall on objects that have no reason to anticipate or welcome them, and tragedy herself, though not excluded, will have a fortuitous air as if a word would disarm her. . . . Novels of this type have an improvised air, which is the secret of their force and charm. They may contain solid

9. *Aspects of the Novel* (New York: Harcourt, Brace, 1927), p. 162.

10. Forster permitted himself a fondness for muddle, which he saw everywhere in human affairs and did not regret. He called London a Muddle; it "is an untidy city, and ought not to be cleaned up." Elsewhere he offhandedly described fantasy as "muddling up the actual and the impossible until the reader isn't sure which is which. . . ." *Two Cheers for Democracy* (New York: Harcourt, Brace, 1951), pp. 354, 222.

11. *Aspects of the Novel*, p. 163. In the introduction to his collected stories (1947), which contains all of his undoubted fantasies, he suggests that the volume might be dedicated to Hermes Psychopompus.

character-drawing, penetrating and bitter criticism of conduct
and civilization; yet our simile of the beam of light must remain. . . . [Pp. 162–63]

In Forster's usage, light has the power to reveal but not to
create or alter. He is not concerned here with that light which
was the first creation and the necessary condition for all the rest.
Fantasy cannot make anything of intrinsic worth, and cannot
disturb the universe. Only "prophecy" is within this range.

Of the reader fantasy asks something extra, an act of credence
beyond and different from that asked by a work of art. The latter requires "curiosity for the story, human feelings and a sense
of value for the characters, intelligence and memory for the
plot" (pp. 158–59). Fantasy requires further an acceptance of
the not-real. Some readers gladly pay; some will not; some cannot. Those who fail to respond are not for this reason simply
stupid or philistine. The implication is that fantasy and its
purveyors are imperious. Forster makes no suggestion that, more
or less concealed in the narrative, is a strategy of persuasion and
the supporting tactics. He is the first writer about fantasy who
considers the reader's part, but he says nothing of what seems
to me central, the continued interplay between the representation and the reader's credence. It is this that makes it necessary
for the fantasist to embody in his work a rhetoric that will secure
persuasion and make the reader's acceptance a part of the
pleasure.

Throughout most of his lecture, Forster is shy about discussing methods in fantasy, largely, I surmise, because he does not
wish to confine his manifestations to literature. But he does at
last, with an air of unwillingness, list some devices that have been
used. One of these is parody or adaptation. I mention this now
because in a later chapter I shall exploit the suggestion. This is
a peculiarly rich source, and in the fantasies thus grounded the
necessary rhetoric can be discerned with unusual clarity. Forster
says little about the abstract nature of parody, only that the "fantasist here adopts for his mythology some earlier work and uses it
as a framework or quarry for his own purposes" (p. 175). *Joseph
Andrews* is "an aborted example." He suggests further that

41

parody or adaptation is advantageous to gifted writers "who do not . . . take easily to creating characters" (p. 176). Accordingly, G. Lowes Dickinson found what he needed for *The Magic Flute* in the world Mozart created.[12] Similarly, Joyce exploited the *Odyssey* for *Ulysses,* a successful engraftment on the original mythology, though Forster finds the result monstrous and repellent.

Forster's discomfort with *Ulysses* seems to derive from its material and the indignation he sees as pervasive in the book. *Ulysses* is "an attempt to make crossness and dirt succeed where sweetness and light failed" (p. 177). This tells us something not surprising about Forster's taste, and, more important, it reveals again his assumption that in its proper enterprises fantasy is limited to the sportive and the agreeable. He says as much, in effect, earlier when he calls it a "sideshow." Except for *Ulysses,* all of his illustrative works and those mentioned in passing either are, or are placed by Forster, in the category of the entertaining. He omits any intimation that *Tristram Shandy* and *Gulliver's Travels* reveal a substratum of seriousness.

Forster's slighting of fantasy is inescapable, for he commits himself to placing it lower in his scale of values than prophecy. I see no reason to state fully here the qualities of what he considers the ultimate excellence in the novel, achieved by only a few—Dostoevsky, Melville, D. H. Lawrence, and Emily Brontë. But a few of the contrasts with fantasy are enlightening. Prophecy is unitive rather than diverse, serious rather than frivolous, mystical or intuitive rather than calculative, universal rather than bound. The prophet's mythology is transcendent rather than mundane. The prophet is, indeed, something of a bard, the fantasist a discerning mountebank. The language Forster uses about prophecy resembles that with which Coleridge and others exalted imagination at the expense of fancy.

Finally, however, Forster confesses a "reservation about this prophetic stuff." The price exacted is more drastic than the something extra that fantasy asks of the reader. It is humility and what is worse, " a suspension of the sense of humour"; he

12. Forster does not mention Emmanuel Schikaneder, the librettist.

might have added to this stated price a requirement that the reason he valued be rejected. One might guess that works of prophecy extort respect from Forster and all readers who are not of a somewhat vatic disposition. Fantasy is costly but not exorbitant.

J. R. R. Tolkien's considerations bearing on fantasy are contained in a long study, "On Fairy Stories," which was published in a collection of essays honoring Charles Williams after his death. It is not solely an examination of the fictional subgenre. Tolkien's main discourse on fantasy comes in answer to his question, "What is the use of them [fairy stories]?" It is the first of four values, the others being Recovery, Escape, and Consolation. Even so, Tolkien conceives of fantasy as a capability, a rational activity, a "subcreative" art aimed at making a "Secondary World . . . commanding Secondary Belief," the result of which in the reader is Enchantment.

In his talk of the Secondary World and Subcreation, Tolkien probably wishes the reader to think of the Coleridgean distinction of imagination as the capacity for making images. And it is no more; it does not have " 'the power of giving to ideal creations the inner consistency of reality.' " Fantasy, however, as he proposes to conceive it, names not only the subcreative art itself but also "a quality of strangeness and wonder in the Expression, derived from the Image." Further, the image or images are the more effective because they are free of any required correspondence to observable fact, that is, to the "Primary World." Accordingly, he announces his own evaluation: "Fantasy (in this sense) is, I think, not a lower but a higher form of Art, indeed the most nearly pure form, and so (when achieved) the most potent." [13]

Fantasy, then, is a combined spirit, method, and expression that is best embodied in narrative. In painting, "the visible presentation of the fantastic image is technically too easy. . . . Silliness or morbidity are frequent results" (p. 68), results rarely encountered in narrative fantasy. Drama and fantasy are natural enemies; in drama the Secondary World already exists,

13. *Essays Presented to Charles Williams* (London: Oxford University Press, 1947), p. 67.

directly reaching the eyes and ears. Any attempt at a "tertiary world" is too much. Tolkien says flatly that drama is "fundamentally distinct from Literature."

As Tolkien continues, he defends and praises fantasy more than he describes it, but from his evaluating comments understanding may be inferred. Enchantment, that result of fantasy in both the reader and the work, is better than magic. Magic is a technique designed to achieve power in the primary world; enchantment is a condition that fosters both art and faith. "Fantasy is a natural human activity." As such, it is the ally, not the enemy, of reason. A clear reason is needed to make successful fantasy and to prevent the abuses by which fantasy can deteriorate into its opposite, "Morbid Delusion." Moreover, it helps maintain a keen perception of what is real and what is not. It recognizes facts, but refuses to be enslaved by them. "If men really could not distinguish between frogs and men, fairy-stories about frog-kings would not have arisen" (p. 72). Further, as a natural human activity, fantasy asserts the right of man to be a maker, within the limits of his power, which is an expression of his having been made in the divine image. And what he makes, if he remains true to fact and nonfact, will not only do much to mitigate his fallen state but will also form an opposition to the ugliness and unnaturalness brought into the world by those who seek power for the wrong reasons.

The foregoing sentences suggest that toward the end, or peroration, Tolkien's essay takes on a tone associated with Roman and Anglican neo-orthodoxy. The unique quality in successful fantasy is joy, and this is imparted by "a sudden glimpse of the underlying reality or truth" (p. 83). This is the real blessing of what he calls the eucatastrophe, the happy ending of a fairy story, which is far more than gratification of the reader's immediate wishes. It is no less than "a far-off gleam or echo of *evangelium* in the real world." Thus the fairy story or fantasy (Tolkien tends to use the terms interchangeably) shares in its way the function of Christian *logos*, doctrine, story, mystery, and revelation, past, present, and to come.[14] His final words be-

14. For a fuller restatement of Tolkien's position, see William Ready, *The Tolkien Relation* (Chicago: Regnery Press, 1968), pp. 177–79.

stow on fantasy a dignity beyond anything Forster assigns to prophecy:

> The Evangelium has not abrogated legends; it has hallowed them, especially the "happy ending." The Christian still has to work, with mind as well as body, to suffer, hope, and die; but he may now perceive that all his bents and faculties have a purpose, which can be redeemed. So great is the bounty with which he has been treated that he may now, perhaps, fairly dare to guess that in Fantasy he may actually assist in the effoliation and multiple enrichment of creation. All tales may come true; and yet, at the last, redeemed, they may be as like and as unlike the forms that we give them as Man, finally redeemed, will be like and unlike the fallen that we know. [P. 84]

It seems ungracious to disturb such eloquence by asking how it is that there are non-Christian fairy tales. One may infer that Tolkien thought the question impertinent. Fairies and faërie itself, the Perilous Realm, are not exclusively Christian possessions, and many of the tales he cites as examples were pagan in origin. In *The Lord of the Rings* Tolkien shows himself to be a notable syncretist, and this habit of thought shows itself also in his essay.

The most generous contributor to the theory of fantasy was C. S. Lewis. He wrote about it in his autobiography, in various essays literary and nonliterary, in those of his works devoted to the propagation of "classical Christianity." Thus his thoughts must be assembled, but fortunately they are clear and internally consistent.

Lewis understood that fantasy is a psychic phenomenon and a literary manifestation and that the first can prepare for the second. But he never confused the two. In the psychic phenomenon he distinguished opposed motivations. One is self-indulgent, therefore morbid; it can yield nothing but alienation from reality. The other is purely inventive and objective; self has no part in the construct, and it can yield rich results of creativity. In his autobiography he recalls his fabrication of Animal-Land. This was play, of a kind Huizinga would recognize, carried on alone except when Lewis's brother was at home from school. It started as stories but soon led to historiography and geography, complete with maps. A serious undertaking, it called for system and the exercise of the same effort that occupied much of Trollope's attention. From reflection on these early experiences, Lewis derives some foreseeable conclusions about creativity:

> It will be clear that at this time . . . I was living almost entirely in my imagination. . . . But imagination is a vague word, and I must make some distinctions. It may mean the world of reverie, day-dreams, wish-fulfilling fantasy. Of that I knew more than enough. I often pictured myself cutting a fine figure. But I must insist that this was a totally different activity from the invention of Animal-Land. Animal-Land was not (in that sense) a fantasy at all. I was not one of the characters it contained. I was its creator, not a candidate for admission to it. Invention is essentially different from reverie. . . . In my day-dreams I was training myself to be a fool, in mapping and chronicling Animal-Land I was training myself to be a novelist. Note well, a novelist, not a poet. My invented world was full (for me) of interest, bustle, humour, and character; but there was no poetry, even no romance, in it. It was almost astonishingly prosaic.[15]

In *An Experiment in Criticism*, Lewis elaborates this standard discrimination and assigns to the various manifestations of fantasy overt values of mental, and even moral, health. Psychic fantasy may be systematic delusion, which is not pertinent to literature. It may be "Morbid Castle-Building," nondelusional but unwholesome because offering deceptive nourishment to the starved ego, it tends to occupy the whole man and render him incapable, even though he does not mistake his dreams for reality. "Normal Castle-Building" is the "same activity indulged in moderately and briefly as a temporary holiday or recreation, duly subordinated to more effective and outgoing activities."[16] Here there is a subdivision by motive into "the Egoistic and the Disinterested." The former is an inescapable human indulgence, essentially harmless but unproductive; only the latter can yield

15. *Surprised by Joy: The Shape of My Early Life* (London: Geoffrey Bles, 1955), pp. 21–22. It may be recalled that the constructs of the young Brontës—Angria, Gondal, Glasstown—and the stories centering on them were circumstantial in all the ways Lewis mentions and yet highly romantic, if not poetic. See Fannie L. Ratchford, *The Brontës' Web of Childhood* (New York: Columbia University Press, 1941).

16. *An Experiment in Criticism* (Cambridge: University Press, 1961), p. 51.

literature, because only the latter is objective and fictive. And there can be a movement within the person from the egoistic to the disinterested, though here Lewis does not trace it.

He makes some suggestions about this progress in a paper read at Westfield College in 1941 though not published until 1962. In this he takes as his point of departure the final paragraph of the twenty-third of Freud's *Introductory Lectures on Psychoanalysis*, in which Freud finds the origin of art in wish-fulfillment fantasies. These the artist can purge of the disagreeable personal tone and make into stories that are appealing because the material and the gratifying result are familiar to all readers. Lewis chides Freud for not recognizing the disinterested daydream, which is intrinsically pleasurable, as the egocentric cannot be because of "its extreme surface realism, its deliberately prosaic temper, and above all its *nagging* character, the stealthy insistence with which it recurs again and again like an anxiety." [17] But Lewis concedes that even this kind of daydream, poor stuff though it must be, can be the source of literature if the maker takes himself out of it by an act of the will. So far there seems to be no serious disagreement between Freud and Lewis. The difference lies in their views of the significance of the change in itself and in its results. Lewis assumes Freud's meaning to be that the elaboration and excision or concealing of the personal are tactical maneuvers, a kind of exploitation, and that the literary product must bear a substantial resemblance to its original. For Lewis the change, taking out the self, is radical.

Still, Lewis is dissatisfied that Freud omitted to mention that daydreaming which is free of ego gratification is an inception of art. It is only this kind that can develop by what Freud calls "elaboration." Wresting a gratification away from the ego, he implies, is not easy and often does not occur. Even when it does, the product at best will be "realistic" fiction, which here seems to include nonheroic romance, capable of evoking only tepid interest.[18] But the free activity is already halfway toward art, and

17. "Psycho-analysis and Literary Criticism," in *They Asked for a Paper: Papers and Addresses* (London: Geoffrey Bles, 1962), p. 123.
18. In *An Experiment in Criticism* Lewis distinguishes between "realism of presentation" and "realism of content" (pp. 58–60). The two may coexist or

the final work is only the ordering and perfecting of its nature, without any need to deracinate. The product of this is "what may be roughly called the fantastic, or mythical, or improbable type of literature . . ." (p. 125).

Lewis makes overt in this paper what may be inferred from many passages scattered through his writing, that he came close to rejecting the Freudian concept of art and accepted the formulations of Jung. In discussing the "meaning" of symbols, as outlined in the tenth introductory lecture, he remarks, "I am sometimes tempted to wonder whether Freudianism is not a great school of prudery and hypocrisy" (p. 129). His complaint against the interpretations that the Freudians provide is not that they are shocking. They are not at all; rather, they are disappointing and inadequate.

But the accountings of Jung, followed out by Maud Bodkin and E. M. W. Tillyard among others, not only are "more civil and human" but also do justice to the primordial, poetic, and intrinsically exciting matters that they explain. And these, for Lewis, are at the heart of what fantasy deals with.

In his thoughts about fantasy as a mode of fiction, Lewis usually reveals an interest in the material, what the story is about. He can make statements, which, removed from the context of his whole view, might be misleading. "As a literary term fantasy means any narrative that deals with impossibles and preternaturals." [19] Here, for example, he seems to express that simplistic understanding that I rejected early in this chapter. But actually his interest in material is not self-limiting, not the interest of the antiquarian or collector exercised on literature. What a story is about is for Lewis an embodiment or a conveyor of a state, quality, idea, or existence that can scarcely be apprehended directly. This is anything but unusual; attending to the manifest is a normal means of objectifying the imperceptible, helpful even when the result is an imperfect knowledge. Thus to consider "gods, ghosts, ghouls, demons, fairies, monsters, etc."

may be separate. He seems to allege that the fiction which may originate in wish-fulfillment dreams is realistic in the latter sense, either solely or preponderantly. The justice of this in relation to Trollope can be understood, but I am not satisfied that Charlotte Brontë's fiction should be so regarded.

19. *Experiment in Criticism*, p. 50.

either speculatively or via a story about them is not merely to in-
dulge in the sensational or to excite curiosity, but to reach for
some understanding of mysteries that are beyond us. Not that
curiosity is a motive Lewis would despise. What is it like on
the moon, in Hades, at the antipodes? What will happen on the
last day, or what did happen on the first? To pursue these and
like questions is to liberate the understanding from dailiness and
to extend experience.

Lewis's assumption that the material is a servant of speculation determines his view of other external aspects of fiction. The
surface excitement of a story, produced by the adventure as such,
is of no great importance; as Joseph Conrad complained, it may
lead the reader away from what is central. The valuable effect
is that which is generated by the author's embodiment of and
the reader's response to an idea or vision. Lewis had little use for
a passive reader; not only must a reader respond, but he must
also supply a part of the idea or vision. Likewise plot is instrumental. The articulated sequence of events composing a unity
of action is little of itself, "only really a net whereby to catch
something else . . . something that has no sequence in it, something other than a process and much more like a state or quality.
Giantship, otherness, the desolation of space. . . ."[20] Even his
view of myth shows the same kind of thinking. Myth, he concludes, is preliterary and prelinguistic. It is originally "an un-
focused gleam of divine truth falling on human imagination."[21]
Its first embodiment is in some way historical, and after this
comes literary representation. One sees in this hypothesis a con-
flation of ideas from Jung and from Lewis himself.

All this points to one fact about Lewis as a critic of fiction.
The craft did not much engage him for itself. He had little to
say about characterization, order, structure, techniques, style,

20. "On Stories," in *Essays Presented to Charles Williams*, p. 103. Lewis
notes that for his chronicles of Narnia and for his trilogy of space romances, the
inceptions were not sequences of imagined events but "pictures," whose origin he
could not explain. "It All Began with a Picture . . . ," in *Of Other Worlds*
(London: Geoffrey Bles, 1966), p. 42.

21. C. S. Lewis, *Miracles: A Preliminary Study* (New York: Macmillan, 1947),
p. 161n. See also *George Macdonald: An Anthology* (New York: Macmillan,
1948), p. 15. Here he puts Macdonald in the select company of modern myth-
makers, along with Novalis and Kafka.

or form as a shaper of content. Perhaps we should believe him when he hints as his reason that these have been "abundantly discussed," but that story, "the series of imagined events," has been neglected or subordinated to the representation of character. In Lewis's judgment, only Aristotle, later Boccaccio and others who constructed an allegorical theory, and Jung with his followers have directly attended to story.[22] His statement here conveys an implication that these generative efforts have yielded a paucity of critical writing, though elsewhere he shows a saving awareness that the results have been rich and influential.

The value of story may be ascertained by scrutinizing the effect of excitement. The most accessible form of this is "the alternate tension and appeasement of imagined anxiety." It comes from the surface of action and is often promoted by a narrator's version of gross and violent stimulants. Its hold on the reader, whether through an episode or through a book, is short-lived; books that have no more are quickly forgotten. Lewis suggests that excitement of this kind may be "hostile to the deeper imagination." He offers no term differentiated from "excitement" to name that lasting and desirable engagement that may be conveyed through events with or without the surface effect. But he means to suggest a gripping and an enrichment of the "deeper imagination" by an idea or vision already present but dim in the reader's mind. Such a result has been called discovery—discovery in the story and in himself. This makes apparent one of the reasons that Lewis found certain principles of Jungian psychology congenial.

Discovery can be effected by a wide variety of stories, all of which were within the range of Lewis's taste: epic, heroic, romance, *Märchen*, certain kinds of science fiction,[23] and fairy stories. He labeled his own romance *That Hideous Strength* a "modern fairy-tale for grown-ups," and repeatedly expressed the view that classification of books as adult or juvenile is false, be-

22. *Essays Presented to Charles Williams*, p. 90.
23. In an essay entitled "On Science Fiction" he specifies a preference for such examples as are "speculative," or "eschatological," or supernatural. *Of Other Worlds*, pp. 59–73.

cause it represents a misunderstanding imposed on readers and reading. Like Tolkien, Lewis uses "fantasy" and "fairy tale" as near synonyms. Because of his concern with story as an access to vision, Lewis is casual about discriminations of literary form, as he is not in *The Allegory of Love*, *A Preface to Paradise Lost*, and his volume in the *Oxford History of English Literature*. In discussing fantasy itself, he often lists together works that are formally heterogeneous. Early in one essay he groups *The Ancient Mariner*, *Gulliver's Travels*, *The Wind in the Willows*, *The Witch of Atlas*, *Jurgen*, *The Crock of Gold*, the *Vera Historia* of Lucian, *Micromégas*, Abbott's *Flatland*, and *The Golden Ass* of Apuleius.[24] It is, moreover, of little moment to him whether a work be entirely or just partly fantasy. There is no doubt that to Lewis fantasy means the fantastic, however embodied. In turn, the fantastic is pretty much synonymous with the mythic and the mythopoeic. In his lists he rarely names books like *South Wind*, *Penguin Island*, or *The Orphan Angel*, which provide less evident ways, if any way at all, to archetypes and mysteries.

Throughout his writing Lewis recommends the fantastic. Some of the reasons for his partisanship have been suggested in the preceding paragraphs. Beyond these is the value of a wholesomeness that such reading can foster. He asserts this proposition chiefly as a refutation of the familiar charge that "fairy tales," whether for children or adults, promote escapism. With Tolkien, he is willing to hold that escape may be intelligent rather than retrograde. But more pertinent here, Lewis argues that the "realistic story" can do damage to the psyche, whereas the fantasy improves its health. Lewis is a cogent debater, and his application of this general principle to "school stories" versus fairy tales is instructive:

> Let us again lay the fairy-tale side by side with the school story.
> . . . There is no doubt that both arouse and imaginatively sat-

24. *Experiment in Criticism*, p. 50. In another list, too long to reproduce here, he includes "parts" of the *Odyssey*, the *Kalevala*, *Huon of Bordeaux*, *Heinrich von Ofterdingen*, all of Eddison's *Worm Ouroboros*, David Lindsay's *Voyage to Arcturus*, and Mervyn Peake's *Titus Groan*. *Of Other Worlds*, p. 71.

isfy, wishes. We long to go through the looking glass, to reach fairy land. We also long to be the immensely popular and successful schoolboy or schoolgirl, or the lucky boy or girl who discovers the spy's plot or rides the horse that none of the cowboys can manage. But the two longings are very different. The second, especially when directed on something so close as school life, is ravenous and deadly serious. Its fulfillment on the level of imagination is in very truth compensatory: we run to it from the disappointments and humiliations of the real world: it sends us back to the real world undivinely discontented. For it is all flattery to the ego. The pleasure consists in picturing oneself the object of admiration. The other longing, that for fairy land, is very different. In a sense a child does not long for fairy land as a boy longs to be hero of the first eleven. Does anyone suppose that he really and prosaically longs for all the dangers and discomforts of a fairy tale—really wants dragons in contemporary England? It is not so. It would be much truer to say that fairy land arouses a longing for he knows not what. It stirs and troubles him (to his life-long enrichment) with the dim sense of something beyond his reach and, far from dulling or emptying the actual world, gives it a new dimension of depth.[25]

This is an argument for the constructive value of *Sehnsucht*, and it rests on his discrimination of fantasies, which I have already discussed enough. Lewis did not hesitate to direct the same argument to more sophisticated literary modes. Moreover, his esteem for sophistication was limited. Far more to be desired is what satisfies the capacity for wonder, and because fantasy does this, it offers riches to children and to adults. Unlike Tolkien, Lewis does not make fantasy a means to religious revelation. But nothing in his discourses counters such a conviction, and it is frequently present as an overtone.

I come now to a few pages that illuminate fantasy without an attempt at systematic discussion. They begin an essay by George P. Elliott, some of whose stories in *Among the Dangs* illustrate

25. "On Three Ways of Writing for Children," in *Of Other Worlds*, pp. 29–30.

what happens when fantasy merges with other practices of post-realistic fiction. He starts from the premise that fantasy obeys "the obscure laws of dream and of story at once, in such a way that his words will stimulate the same fantasy in the reader." [26] So it is both like and unlike a dream, and through its fabrication it reaches truth. It is like a dream in having images and people that are "vivid and particular" (though the images convey a suggestiveness) and in constructing a coherent "invisible world" from oddly assorted materials of the visible. The whole is so plausible that even absurdity seems "immanent destiny," and the simplification of motives and results is judged by its own standards rather than those of the muddled world. Here again appears that clarity and order which relate fantasy to play. But the differences from dream are decisive—distance of teller and hearer (or reader) from the fiction and embodiment in a language that emerges from and maintains community. A dream usually remains private; "to dream is to be a solipsist." A narrator may not keep this luxury and may remake language into a private instrument only at the risk of remaining alone. *Finnegans Wake* gives Elliott a telling example. Joyce insisted on having his own way with language because of his conviction that "the more real one's knowledge, the more private it is, and the less one can communicate it with common words in normal syntax" (p. 6). But the penalty, though likely Joyce did not feel it as such, is that the community, apart from his admirers, will think his vision just virtuosity that may be ignored.

In describing fantasy's access to truth, Elliott is less explicit, understandably enough, for it is a vexed matter. He does propose, however, that when a fantasist has a message, it will be conveyed only as well as it has been fused with the story. Fiction is no more a means for truth that can be abstracted into a formulation than it is for the imparting of sheer information. Truth must be present in such a way that the reader "enjoys a play of speculation about the story's meanings" (p. 7), and this enjoy-

26. "A Defense of Fiction," in *Types of Prose Fiction* (New York: Random House, 1964), p. 4. This essay first appeared in *Hudson Review*, 16 (1963), 9–48.

ment is fused with the profit. This is a classical doctrine particularly applied.

Throughout his brief discussion, Elliott cites many examples
of dreams transformed into fiction without losing the quality of
dreams—*Pilgrim's Progress, The Thousand and One Nights* and
especially the story of Qamar az-Zaman, *Don Quixote, Gulliver's
Travels, The Trial, The Castle, The Lord of the Rings,* and
others. Again it is evident that the principle of cohesiveness here
is material and that Elliott is not concerned with fantasy as a
form but rather with the fantastic as a combination of substance
and spirit that dominates a wide variety of fiction. His terms
confirm this judgment. Allegory, story, fiction, fantasy, romance,
and tale he sets down freely; he never uses the word "novel."
This interchanging is no mark of carelessness. His purpose in
these pages is not strictly analytical, but to convey a sense of how
the dreamlike or the fantastic invests fiction of various kinds. In
being concerned with the substantive rather than the formal,
Elliott here resembles C. S. Lewis.

A most illuminating study by the prominent structuralist critic
Tzvetan Todorov is titled *Introduction à la littérature fantastique*
(Paris: Editions du Seuil, 1970). From Todorov's exposition may
be drawn a distinction, essentially like mine, between fantasy
and that more extensive and diversified kind of writing which he
properly calls *littérature fantastique,* such writing as is dominated
by the strange and wonderful. But Todorov does not restrict himself to describing the nature of the fantastic as material. He is
much more concerned with the psychic and imaginative effects
of those events that in narrative presentation contravene fact,
natural law, daily experience, or some other convention. These
generate in the reader an interplay of responses as to belief and
thus a complex of fluid relationships between the reader and the
text. Some of Todorov's key words and phrases are revealing:
"l'hésitation du lecteur," "l'ambiguïté," "la perception ambiguë,"
"incertitude." The reader is caught in conflicts caused by the
disparities among what he is of himself, the marvel of the narrated events, and credence (sometimes firm, sometimes shaky) in
those characters who report the events or participate in them.
"Le fantastique, c'est l'hésitation eprouvée par une être qui ne

connait les lois naturelles, face à un événement en apparence
surnaturel" (p. 29). When Todorov arrives at formulated definition, he posits three essential conditions for the fantastic:

> D'abord, il faut que le texte oblige le lecteur à considérer le
> monde des personnages comme un monde de personnes vivantes
> et à hesiter entre une explication naturelle et une explication
> surnaturelle des événements évoqués. Ensuite, cette hésitation
> peut être ressentie également par un personnage; ainsi le rôle du
> lecteur est pour ainsi dire confiné à un personnage et dans le même
> temps l'hésitation se trouve représentée, elle devient un des
> thèmes de l'oeuvre; dans le cas d'une lecture naïve, le lecteur
> réel s'identifie avec le personnage. Enfin, il importe que le
> lecteur adopte une certaine attitude à l'égard du texte: il re-
> fusera aussi bien l'interprétation allégorique que l'interprétation
> "poétique." Ces trois exigences n'ont pas une valeur égale. La
> première et la troisième constituent veritablement le genre; la
> seconde peut ne pas être satisfaite. Toutefois, la plupart des
> exemples remplissent les trois conditions. [Pp. 37–38]

The fantastic, then, creates a complex and dynamic relationship
of reader and text. No wonder Todorov posits further that the
fantastic resides not only in the narration of strange events but
also in "une manière de lire" on the part of a reader who is
divided for the time between his essential self and himself as
participant in the narrative. This relationship is, moreover, a
manifestation of an engagement, producing lively and sometimes
profound emotional effects, with wonder and mystery.

Central in Elizabeth Sewell's description of nonsense is her
insistence that in his devotion to order and clarity, the writer
must avoid whatever might result in poetry, including wonder,
fusion, and dreaminess. Somewhat similarly, the writer of fantasy avoids prompting those hesitations, uncertainties, and perceptions of ambiguity that Todorov takes to be essential in the
experiencing of *littérature fantastique*. In successful fantasy all
is clarity and certainty, as far as presentation goes. Thus fantasy,
though often using the same material, moves in a direction
opposite to that of *littérature fantastique*. Between the two is a
radical difference in the primary point of engagement: in fantasy
the intellect, in the fantastic the imagination. It is idle to inquire

which provides the more rewarding experience. Suffice it to note that they are different.

This concludes the review of the contributions of those few critics who have given sustained attention to fantasy.[27]

27. After this book was in press, a work by C. N. Manlove appeared under the title *Modern Fantasy: Five Studies* (Cambridge: University Press, 1975). He leads with a modestly offered definition of fantasy: *A fiction evoking wonder and containing a substantial and irreducible element of the supernatural with which the mortal characters in the story or the readers become on at least partly familiar terms* (p. 1). After he scrutinizes some fictions by Charles Kingsley, George Macdonald, C. S. Lewis, J. R. R. Tolkien, and Mervyn Peake, Manlove concludes that "not one of the people we have looked at sustains his original vision" (p. 258). It is evident that for Manlove the essence of fantasy is in its content.

What, then, emerges from this consideration of the critics' work? Principally that they were most attentive to that spirit which seeks liberation from phenomena and finds its pleasure in the nonreal, the fantastic. In tracing this quest they have done no more than expatiate, however instructively, on what always has been recognized as a never-ending human effort to find satisfactions more congenial than those that finitude provides. Even so, they have offered a sufficient understanding of the fantastic in general; except in elaboration and in reference to specific works I need not add anything. They recognize the fantastic components in a wide variety of literary forms, ancient, medieval, and modern. But none of them, except Forster and Todorov, is much concerned about the degree to which these components determine the total character of the work. Concentration of the fantastic in a few incidents, a scattering of elements throughout, such sustained presentation as to make a main and substantial tendency—they seem indifferent to the importance of these varying degrees.

Briefly, though all of them acknowledge that prose fiction fantasy exists, none grants it consideration as a distinguishable literary mode. All make valuable suggestions about the origin and nature of fantasy, such as Forster's perception that it can be allied to parody, about what it requires of writers and readers, and about what it can effect as a critique of experience. But these suggestions remain incidental, unorganized insights. Therefore, in order to complete an understanding of what prose fiction fantasy is, certain questions must be considered: What is the nature of belief or conventional expectation against which fantasy plays? What are the principles and the devices of the rhetoric by which fantasy temporarily displaces the formulation it opposes? What are the characteristics of the illusion that prevails in fantasy? What are the effects of illusion and rhetoric on style?

These questions cannot be answered in such a way as to isolate prose fiction fantasy from those other modes that often in important respects share with it some embodiment of the fantastic. If a strict taxonomy were possible in literature, its effect would be more destructive than clarifying. But fantasy can, I believe, be perceived as a distinguishable mode in prose fiction, more than the infusion of certain kinds of material into a variety of narrative modes.

In considering these questions, I start with the proposition that from the outset a fantasy is governed by the requirements and devices of rhetoric, much more than of art. Though artistry is liberally deployed in a fantasy, the dominant method is from rhetoric. This determines the nature of the illusion, the conduct of the narrative itself, and the style.

Happily, the time is past when partisans of purity used rhetoric—often "mere rhetoric"—as a term of reproach against a work of literature that they found contaminated by some attempt of the author to manage his readers' responses. For the restoration of sanity we may thank a number of critics, especially Wayne Booth. I need not argue the case for "impurity," long a fact of fiction, again. But by rhetoric Professor Booth and I mean strategies that are noticeably, though not completely, different. He states as his subject "the technique of nondidactic fiction, viewed as the art of communicating with readers—the rhetorical resources available to the writer of epic, novel, or short story as he tries, consciously or unconsciously, to impose his fictional world upon the reader." [1] The governing concept here is communication. By rhetoric Booth does not mean a scheme of external or imported persuasion but those internal means of showing and telling by which the writer enables the reader to envision his fictional world. I wish that he had not spoken of "imposing." The writer does have authority, and he "makes his readers," but he does so by his sustained effort of creation, which is an act of artistic generosity, not of tyranny. The writer, then, does use methods of persuasion, but these are essentially internal and so directed to the making that tactics and substance fuse in realization.

1. *The Rhetoric of Fiction* (Chicago: University of Chicago Press, 1961), p. v.

The rhetoric that I see as central in fantasy does exploit many of the internal means that Booth specifies, but there is a fundamental difference of purpose. A symptom of this may be seen in the fact that whereas Booth may concentrate on nondidactic fiction, I may not so limit my inquiry. This means more than that certain fantasies are didactic, even propagandistic, no matter how much one wishes to dodge the conclusion. It means that fantasies are controlled by a proposition or an understanding, usually not stated but easily formulated, which counters and temporarily displaces the norm. This invention contravenes a known or accepted fact; thus its essence is noncontroversial as to value. Secondarily, the development in narrative may attempt to persuade the reader of a subversive value or belief beyond fact and thus to become the demonstration of one side in an implied controversy, but this addition is not necessary. *The Eve of St. Venus*, by Anthony Burgess, based on a tale in *The Anatomy of Melancholy*, asks the reader to believe that a forged statue of Venus, in an English garden, comes briefly to life. Though the results are first tumultuous, then beneficent, and though the statue's actions are an emblem of the power of Venus, the essence is a displacement of what the reader knows to be possible. No argument or influencing of belief is suggested.

But Lord Dunsany's *The Blessing of Pan* first shows by action that Pan as a physical being can reassert his sovereignty over human society and then proceeds to such representation as is intended to persuade the reader that restored pagan society is a happier state than the Christian civilization it overpowered. Without the first reversal, in this instance gradual rather than sudden, of presumed fact, there would be no fantasy. Doubtless the skillful development of the subversive "fact" facilitates a reader's consent to the subversive value. But this consent is not necessary to the success of the fantasy as such. I believe that fantasy does offer tendentious writers an advantage, in that the alteration of fact may be so put into action that the deviant belief seems inseparable and totally realized in a context of an already established departure from a norm. Sir Herbert Read asserts that a fantasy is ruined, or simply ceases to be, if "a subjective, or moralizing intent" insinuates itself, for this destroys objectivity. His contention seems to me an untenable purism, denied by the weight of examples against it and by the fact that in applying it he reduces the canon to almost nothing. Moreover, the "objectivity" required in fantasy is not the objectivity of abstention but that of execution.

To return to the main matter, Professor Booth details a rhetoric that operates within the work of art to help form it and make the work itself as a creation persuasive to the reader. The rhetoric of fantasy has a different purpose, to persuade the reader through narrative that an invention contrary to known or presumed fact is existentially valid. The established fact and consequences thus displaced may never be mentioned or directly represented. No more than any other artist does the writer of fantasy honor simplistic fairness. Besides, the established is already strong because it is established, however joyfully readers may welcome its being replaced. But even when the contravening narrative is completed without a glance at what it opposes and thus becomes an entity, it cannot be intellectually other than reflexive. This is to say that the possibilities of creating within fantasy are limited by the conditions of production, and thus the rhetoric is directed to asserting and maintaining the impossible.

Whether or not obvious, intellectual rejection is indispensable to fantasy, though not the whole of it, for the simple reason that construction requires activity beyond denial. Moreover, in the inception of a fantasy, rejection does not always occur at the same point of a time sequence. Even so, there will be some enlightenment from examining the nature of what fantasy denies, that is, conventions as to fact or understanding. This could be made the subject of a searching and difficult inquiry. I do not, however, feel obligated to ask "What is truth?" and attempt a philosophical answer. For the most part, fantasies do not seem committed to this kind of intellectual discipline, and readers of fantasy are not seeking such discourse. For the present purpose it is enough to rely on common knowledge, observation, and experience. Moreover, in this examination I shall look only at the nature of conventions concerning the possible and the impossible in fact, though there are other orders of convention that the fantasist may deny.

Everyone has what he may call "a sense of fact," which enables him to discriminate without consideration between the possible and impossible. Skeptics since the time of Pyrrho have been telling people that this is a treacherous possession, that even when the defects of misinformation and ignorance have been remedied, insofar as they can be, such confidence may be illusory. But it persists. It expresses itself in many ways, among them an enormous collection of routine affirmations and denials, any of which can be elicited as an immediate response. Is the death of an organism a specific event? Yes. Is there such a phenomenon as personal identity? Yes. Will the sun continue to rise each morning? Yes. Can animals learn to use human speech? No. Could there be a human society ruled by horses? No. Can baser metals be transmuted into gold? No. Some readers may object that these questions are stated carelessly, and that at least two of them do not relate strictly to fact. Exactly so; I have made an effort to this end, because unconsideration in questions, as well as answers, is the common way and thus the kind of presumptiveness against which the fantasist plays. I venture to say further that an ingenious and knowledgeable skeptic could make a case, disturbing if not quite successful, for challenging every one of the answers given above. Yet I am confident that the answers I have posited would be the ordinary responses.

It will have occurred to the reader also that the routine answers to many questions of possibility will be contingent on some variable, whether of the general state of genuine or presumptive knowledge at a given period of history or in a given culture, or of some other. This is a matter that bears on much science fiction.[2] There are other questions to which the foreseeable reply has changed from yes to no or no to yes, but with enough nonconvictive remnant of the former response to keep an ambiguity sufficient to disable a fantasist.

In several of the answers I cited above, there are two sources

2. In a Ph.D. thesis James R. Shively worries about this problem and concludes with this definition of all fantasy, not just science fiction: "I shall consider fantasy to be those works of fiction which contain some occurrence, **situation, or** setting which at the time of original publication of the work would have seemed to the ordinary reader to be actually impossible." "Fantasy in the Fiction of H. G. Wells" (University of Nebraska, 1955), p. 8. This definition surely overemphasizes historical conditioning.

of what passes for certainty as to fact—evidence of senses and reliance on authority, individual or collective, so generally trusted as to produce consensus. The latter may include divine beings, sages and savants, institutions, traditions, and the heritage of common experience. That both sources can be fallible is a familiar argument of skeptics, and I need not stop to discuss it here. But the answers to the questions about the sun and about the rule of horses rely on presumptions projected from fact. We expect the sun to rise tomorrow because it always has within our experience, throughout reported past experience, and supposedly before there were any human beings to report experience. Whatever is expectation of future events and surmise about events in a past beyond recall or record is regarded as factual. This kind of reasoning is extended to situations of cause and effect. As to horses, we are cognizant of no occurrence of their ruling a human society, and we presume that as nonrational beings they could not, in the past, present, or future, rule rational beings or any other kind. In these cases of projection from fact, probable and improbable are regarded as if they meant possible and impossible.

The conclusion from all this is simple: that the ascertainment of fact relies little on incontrovertible evidence and much on acceptance of authority, stable or changeable consensus, and normative expectation. The gap between these approximations and assurance is filled by a kind of faith or arbitrary confidence, and thus convention becomes intellectually satisfying. As a result, there are many questions of fact that will be answered almost unanimously "yes" or "no," though most persons doing so could not begin to justify their answers.

I have not imposed this discourse on readers because I believe that they need fragments of a course in straight thinking or need more insight than what the daily scene gives them on the habits of *homo sapientiae capax*. My purpose is to suggest how basic and of what general concern are the questions of the possible and impossible in fact with which the fantasist starts, choosing always to assert the contrary.

As I noted, conventions as to factual possibility and impossibility are not the only kind that fantasists deny. There are also beliefs, interpretations, and understandings seemingly based on fact and widely enough accepted to have the status of conventions. One group of fantasies demonstrates in narrative that the "innocence" of children and other nonadult beings is radically different from what the standard notion of innocence presumes. Another group offers societies that are outside the range of those principles and organizations conventionally thought possible in human society. In these fantasies and others the narrative denies a norm of understanding derived from the "factual" rather than the factual itself. There is also a category of fantasies by adaptation or extension, in which the writer wishes not to reject the accepted formulation but to say in effect that it does not represent the sole and complete truth. Such is T. H. White's Arthurian tetralogy, *The Once and Future King.* In some such cases of this kind, the norm is a book or several books. Because both the books themselves and the conclusions they foster are the referents, the fantasy is both technical and conceptual, and approaches parody.

I am almost done talking about the fantasist's denial. Even if one could know when in the inceptive process it occurs, the knowledge would be without significance. Such an act of mind is indispensable, because it is the writer's means of freeing himself from the accepted so that he may conduct his game of the impossible. Thus denial contributes to forming the fantasy but does not determine it, for after development begins, the main business is making a coherent and persuasive narrative, which, though it will play against the rejected norm more or less overtly, must become itself an entity.

A fantasist chooses to invent a narrative embodying this or that impossibility, and in this choice, if he is prudent, he will be governed by a discrimination between potential advantage and disadvantage. This is to say that he will from the outset think as a rhetorician. Thus, for example, if one answer to a question about possible fact has been superseded by its opposite, a play against the new conviction promises well only when there is no persuasive residue of the old. It follows that the best strategy is to controvert an answer for which there is no prospect of reversal. One may guess that Ovid discovered this advantage in myths of metamorphosis.

The example of Ovid suggests another consideration of choice.

Recall two of the six questions and answers I perpetrated earlier: Is there such a phenomenon as personal identity? Yes. Can animals learn to use human speech? No. To attempt a narrative countering the answer to the first would be a commitment to frustration, for it would be trying to fabricate results where the absence of results has been established. A positive answer to the second question, however, is rich in potentiality, as Olaf Stapledon illustrates in his fantasy *Sirius*. A third question was: Will the sun continue to rise each morning? Yes. A narrative demonstration against this positive answer might succeed. The question refers to future occurrence, and by the maneuver of replacing "no" with "let us guess what would happen if it did not," the way to constructing a story is cleared. The principle of strategy illustrated in this paragraph is obvious enough to make formulation unnecessary. To return to the beginning, Ovid in *Metamorphoses* regularly took the easiest way to success, that of countering the assumption that change of total form cannot occur.

The fantasist also must think of what is likely, and not likely, to engage the reader's interest. The impossibility that is developed must have some claim to importance; triviality is a luxury no fantasist can afford. A story might be written on the fanciful notion that a man could detach one of his hands and send it to the post office to mail a letter. But no reader would attend to such a tale, and a writer would have to be perverse, contemptuous, or addled to undertake it. Such a play, like many puns and facetious departures from the actual, is good for no more than a moment's amusement in conversation. For a story, much better to assert, for example, that Shelley really did not drown off La Spezia but was instead rescued by an America-bound merchantman and survived to make a romanceful journey across the continent. At first sight, even this may seem momentous only to lovers of Shelley, but Elinor Wylie imbued *The Orphan Angel* with a far more extensive interest and significance. The corollary is clear: the fantasist need not confine himself to what is of immediately self-evident importance.

The final principle of advantageous choice is that it must center on human involvement. One might develop the assertion that there can be wasps the size of partridges, but if he restricted his story to the consequences of this monstrous condition in an unpopulated area, it would offer no more than brief entertainment over the incongruity, and this would be worn out long before the end. Book II of *Gulliver's Travels* presents a system of such enlargements, all in proportion. A story about the fauna, flora, and other natural phenomena of Brobdingnag is unthinkable. Even the inclusion in this of the giants would be inadequate. It is Gulliver who effects the human involvement.

Regrettably I cannot claim that a fantasist will weigh the considerations of advantage and disadvantage just as I have outlined them and, thus guided, reach his invention. But I have observed in the successful fantasies I have read that whatever preliminary cerebration may have occurred, the effect of an advantageous choice has been achieved, and thus that the value of an intelligent rhetorical maneuver has been secured. From this point on, the strategy and tactics of fantasy may be more clearly seen or reliably inferred.

In order to approach these, let me discuss how the writer must regard his readers and what general responses he must draw from them. At the outset, he might as well accept what Forster and others have observed, that some readers will reject his work, perhaps within the first few pages, not because of his inept presentation but because of their own incapability or unwillingness to tolerate a narrative of the impossible. Even if they finish his story, progressing with the vexation that Edmund Wilson clearly felt as he read *The Lord of the Rings* so he could review it, they cannot be expected to emerge converted to satisfaction. So the writer may perform for those who are predisposed to join his play and those—probably a larger group—who are willing to be drawn into it. In these readers he must establish and maintain credence, from this secure participation in his fiction, and provide under control opportunities to see contrasts and skewed comparisons between his developed invention and the norm it counters.

If, as in 1984, he wishes the reader to accept certain value judgments that are intellectually apart from his invention, he must so realize these in his story that the reader will need no exhortation from himself or from any character who acts extraneously as a spokesman. Such is the strategy of a fantasy, or to state the matter otherwise, the general aim of its rhetoric. Like any strategy, it is ideal, and never executed perfectly. Nor is it like the usual play of direct argument, in which one phase of the development is completed before a succeeding one is undertaken. The credence a fantasy elicits may be imposed promptly and with undisguised arbitrariness, or it may be encouraged in the reader by a presentation in which the impossible is taken for granted, because it exists, and nothing else does. Thus, to say that the reader's participation in the narrative depends on his credence is neither to require a sequential maneuver nor to suggest that acceptance once established can be thereafter ignored. Credence and participation are interdependent, and these two have the same relationship with the reader's controlled play against the displaced norm and with his consent to the major value judgments, if such be part of the writer's total purpose.

No one will be surprised, I trust, when I say the credence fantasy generates is playful. The willful entering of a nonserious activity, as Huizinga described it, is exactly what a fantasy invites the reader to do. The reader's "belief" is one of the rules by which the game is played, even though each instance requires its own act of consent, immediate or protracted. Now, no one capable of playful belief, as a certain Irish bishop was not when he doubted the veracity of *Gulliver's Travels,* confuses it with the center from which it departs. The temporary eccentricity is governed by "as if." Among children, as we are frequently reminded, the same attitude is expressed by "let's pretend" or "let's make believe." Embarrassed by such ordinary language, the academic person prefers to call it "speculative" and "factitious."

It would be a mistake, then, to think of the emphasized demand for credence in fantasy as a means of seriously and permanently refuting the "truth." Quite the opposite. Without certitude, there can be no fantasy. Accordingly, Tolkien remarked, "For creative Fantasy is founded upon the hard recognition that things are so in the world as it appears under the sun; on a recognition of fact, not a slavery to it." [3] For fantasies and

3. *Essays Presented to Charles Williams* (London: Oxford University Press, 1947), p. 72.

cooperating readers this is orthodoxy. Here is the crux of discrimination between fantasy and romance. With apologies for
quoting what many people could recite from memory, I must
cite Henry James's statement: "The balloon of experience is
in fact of course tied to the earth, and under that necessity we
swing, thanks to a rope of remarkable length, in the more or less
commodious car of the imagination, but it is by the rope we
know where we are, and from the moment that cable is cut we
are at large and unrelated. . . . The art of the romancer is, 'for
the fun of it,' insidiously to cut the cable, to cut it without our
detecting him." [4]

In the present context this is a deceptive passage. It might
seem that James is, through his extended metaphor, describing
the inception of fantasy, especially when he speaks of somebody's
fun at cutting the cable. But the result is that the reader is "at
large and unrelated"; a romance effects a total separation from
experience. It follows that romance is not an intellectual game,
and that it fosters a credence different from that which fantasy
requires. In a romance the reader is induced to lose his sense of
fact; in a fantasy he is persuaded to play the new system of
"facts," which he has willfully and speculatively accepted, against
the established facts, which he only pretends to reject. Don
Quixote's wits were overturned by believing in romances; not
even *The Lord of the Rings* could have so affected him. Of
course, materials from the fantastic are ever-present in romance,
even in the domestic and social versions. One encounters the
term "romantic fantasy"; as a name for a literary mode this is
inaccurate; it should be "fantastic romance." I have already demonstrated that the fantastic infuses many literary forms. But
material alone, however rich, does not make a fantasy, dominated
as it is by rhetoric and requiring the credence accorded to play.

What are the general methods of inviting this kind of belief
and maintaining it? One is either to omit any reference to the
norms the fantasist will counter, or to advert to them in so brisk
and disadvantageous a way that initially they seem of little moment and easily overcome. I do not know how to illustrate an
omission. The slighting representation may be seen in a pas-

4. *The Art of the Novel* (New York: Scribner's, 1934), pp. 33–34.

sage that, though not strictly narrative, nonetheless shows the rhetorical efficacy, the mounting of the Queen Mab speech in *Romeo and Juliet* (I, iv, 53–96). Romeo, never a match for Mercutio in wit combat, is troubled because he had a dream. We do not learn what he dreamed; we can only guess that it was vaguely monitory. The mental state of Romeo early in the play is such that almost any kind of softheadedness may be expected of him. Against this compounded feebleness Mercutio mobilizes his counterdemonstration, which is as rapid, assured, detailed, and engaging as Romeo's wanderings were the opposite.

There are variants on commencing with the normal. In one the opening situation has the external signs of an ensuing realistic narrative, until it becomes evident, without any departure from the sober tone of presentation, that the situation is actually fantastic. So in C. S. Lewis's *The Great Divorce*, a number of quarrelsome people board a bus standing on a dreary street of a dreary town. But the bus is destined for Heaven, and the passengers are the dead. There can also be a genuinely prosaic opening with a series, usually not long, of expected events, the last of which delivers the action over to the impossible. The classic instances here are the first chapters of Books I and II of *Gulliver's Travels*. Shipwreck and abandonment on shore by frightened comrades are plausible occurrences in the life of a seafarer. To these introductions I shall return in a consideration of the fantasy-illusion. Another means is that of intrusion upon what seems ordinary enough, as exemplified in *The Elephant and the Kangaroo* by T. H. White. Here the household of Mr. White [5] in County Kildare seems odd though not startling. The mad performance sets in abruptly when Mrs. O'Callaghan reports something in the kitchen. It is the Archangel Michael: "There the Archangel was, just as she had said, in front of the middle damper. It hung against the dark background of the range in a nimbus of its own light, looking straight between his [Mr. White's] eyes, with awful splendor." [6] After this the household,

5. The name of the central character, who approximates T. H. White himself.

6. *The Elephant and the Kangaroo* (New York: Putnam, 1947), p. 16. In the first draft the visitant was the Holy Ghost. David Garnett insisted on the archangel, and after some resistance White yielded. Sylvia Townsend Warner, *T. H. White* (New York: Viking, 1967), pp. 198, 214–15.

the village, the county, and all Ireland move into farcical convulsion.

All these are methods of quiet assertion, whereby ordinariness is either shown to have been illusory from the beginning or is demeaned by appearing less potent and interesting than what easily supplants it. Spectacular assertion occurs in the opening, which may be called the fiat, even though the manner of this is usually neither noisy nor flamboyant. "Als Gregor Samsa eines Morgens aus unruhigen Träumen erwachte, fand er sich in seinem Bett zu einem ungeheuren Ungeziefer verwandelt." This is the first sentence of *Die Verwandlung* of Kafka. No argument; just a statement of fact. What the disturbed dreams had to do with the change, if anything, we never know. From his being named, we assume that Gregor Samsa had been a man; he is expelled without explanation from humanity, though residues of humanness soon emerge to torment him. The effect of the fiat is not to circumvent, obscure, or transform the real but to call attention to it so that it may be overpowered by its opposite. It is a bold stroke, risked against the certainty that some readers will go no further, intended to achieve the central need at once. Very much the same maneuver is executed in Winifred Ashton's *The Arrogant History of White Ben,* in which a scarecrow comes to life, though not in the first paragraph. An instance of delayed fiat may be found in Virginia Woolf's *Orlando.* Through the first chapter an unwary reader may believe that the book is what she says, a biography, but with the opening of the second chapter the feminine central person is a young man.

Other openings, though less spectacular, are equally arbitrary. The reader simply finds himself in A.D. 1995 or 39000 or the Stone Age or in New Crete without any literary equivalent of the four chords with which Mendelssohn conveys the listener to fairyland. There are no authorial exclamations about how astonishing all this is, and even the remarks of the narrative character or characters, if they have entered the new time or place from different customary lives, are usually straightforward observations, expressing interest rather than amazement. The same is true, as I have suggested, in the reverse case, when the fantastic enters and overwhelms the ordinary. The one kind of opening rarely found in fantasy is the leisurely approach. Because the novelist does not face a need for prompt and strenuous persuasion, he may permit himself such diffuse openings as Scott enjoyed. The fantasist has no such freedom. What's to do must with dispatch be done. And the tactical reason is easily surmised: the reader, however joyfully he accepts the fantasist's gambit, brings with him enough attachment to the ordinary; the time to encourage his playing the old against the new is later.

In most fantasies, then, the opening maneuver is decisive. Whatever the method, all have one purpose, early and total persuasion. Once this is achieved, the narrative is mounted for a persuasive continuation, and in considering this I must discuss the working of rhetorical tactics through the fantasy-illusion.

Already I have pointed to the major characteristic of the illusion that the developing narrative establishes and conveys. The style is generally sober and straightforward, the images, descriptions, events, and characterizations pervaded by what is often called circumstantial realism. That talent which, rightly or wrongly, Sir Leslie Stephen thought Defoe's great capability, a talent for "grave, imperturbable lying," is steadily put into execution by the fantasist. Fantasy heeds the demands of what C. S. Lewis calls "realism of presentation" and ignores direct obedience to "realism of content." In the chapter that develops the nature and values of these two realisms, Lewis comments on this aspect of the fantasy-illusion: "No one can deceive you unless he makes you think he is telling the truth. The unblushingly romantic has far less power to deceive than the apparently realistic. Admitted fantasy is precisely the kind of literature which never deceives at all." [7]

The amount of such circumstantiality varies widely from fantasy to fantasy. In *Lady into Fox* there are few details, carefully chosen, each one remarkably efficacious; it is a rich book. In *The Lord of the Rings*, the details of fauna, flora, nonhuman beings, weather, customs, diet, history, language, beliefs, songs, weapons, topography, and more are so generously given that one wonders

7. *An Experiment in Criticism* (Cambridge: University Press, 1961), p. 67. This chapter in Lewis's book is as much polemical as expository. He mistrusts realism of content, or perhaps the misreading it permits. As a result he conceives of this kind of realism in a manner that seems to me unjustifiably narrow.

if Tolkien's inventiveness could ever be exhausted. And not content with all this, he provides appendixes and maps. The author's choice of spareness, lavishness, or something between is —or should be—ruled by a rhetorical consideration, "How much specified experiencing does the reader need to form the persuasive illusion I wish him to have?" That is, how much need be given to him and how much of what serves the fantasist's purpose may he be relied on to provide for himself? *Lady into Fox* presents one fundamental, decisive change in an otherwise familiar situation. Hence more than a little highly skillful detailing would be wearisome, perhaps distracting. But *The Lord of the Rings* takes the reader into a totally new world, and accordingly he needs a generous provision of what might be called documentation.[8]

This instrumentation of rhetoric is not confined to fantasy. It accounts in part for the paucity of physical description and psychological explanation in *Tom Jones*. But in respect of this matter the writer of realistic fiction has a latitude of choice not open to the fantasist. The total representations in *Pamela* or *Clarissa*, for example, were no less familiar to Richardson's readers than the representation in *Tom Jones* was to Fielding's. The detailing that Richardson elaborated most, the slow intricate changes in psychic and emotional states, is not esoteric and not beyond a reader's constructing in his own unaided imagination. Lovelace's delusionary diabolism, adapted from a long-standing tradition, offers no mysteries. Even Clarissa's endless *Liebestod*, which is also a history of willful apotheosis, composed on the coffin of the life to which she must die, contains no surprises; it is effective largely because it is familiar, for every reader of *Clarissa* has experienced the luxuries of emotional self-indulgence. The fact that many readers have found this, and many other features of Richardson's fiction, ludicrous or intolerable or both points to a permanent strain in taste; it is impertinent to the question of whether or not Richardson needed all that for persuasion. Of course, he did not. Richardson was shrewd enough, I think, to divine that many readers would find their greatest pleasure and

8. See W. R. Irwin, "There and Back Again: The Romances of Williams, Lewis and Tolkien," *Sewanee Review*, 69 (1961), 571–76.

edification in what others could not tolerate. The history of his reputation confirms this judgment.[9]

A fantasist cannot ignore the tastes of his potential readers; like any other writer of fiction, he exploits them as shrewdly as he is able. But in the matter of realism in presentation the issue is not taste. Rather, it is the persuasiveness than can be exercised by means of an illusion that is and remains credible throughout the narrative. This continuing plausibility, which helps to hold the reader in participation, pervades the usual components of a narrative—action, setting, and character. All must be presented, in articulation, according to the requirements of the general strategy.

As to action, the steady operation of the rhetoric may best be seen in the fantasist's abstention from certain liberties that other writers of fiction allow themselves, often to the great profit of their books. The events of a fantasy may be as remote and exotic as imaginable, but they are, separately and in sum, rendered objectively. What happens must be clear, because it could not happen. This is only an application of the principle of presentational realism. That mistiness or uncertainty as to fact which other writers sometimes use to advantage rarely occurs in fantasy. Did the scarlet A appear branded on Arthur Dimmesdale's breast? We do not know. Did Clyde Griffith, at the crucial moment, willfully murder Roberta? We do not know. And such uncertainties of fact, though disastrous if not perfectly executed, sometimes enrich their novels as no clarification ever could. But the logic of fantasy denies any privilege of ambiguity, and some of the technical failures result from an incomplete obedience to this demand. In Chesterton's *The Man Who Was Thursday* there is a grave flaw, because though we learn that Sunday somehow symbolizes the peace of God, the action never reveals his literal identity.

Other freedoms enjoyed by the novelist and romancer but closed to the fantasist must be discussed more briefly. Subplots

9. It is worth reminding readers that Fielding, after he had produced those "lewd and ungenerous engraftments" *Shamela* and *Joseph Andrews*, formed a high opinion of *Clarissa* as it was being published serially, and like many others, wrote to Richardson begging him to rescue his heroine with a happy ending.

rarely occur in fantasy. Narrative excursions that prove, after they are completed, to advance the main action also are rare. Seldom does a fantasist attempt any means other than cohesive sequential narration to unify his action. *Tristram Shandy* reveals a rich infusion of that spirit of play which is central in fantasy, but the unification of the work through a complex of recurring and significant images puts it in some other category. Any fantasist who attempted to unify his work by the daring indirect devices of Faulkner, or according to something like the Chinese box structure of *Wuthering Heights*, would founder. Those digressions into essay writing that persist in English and American fiction are forbidden. And I cannot think of a fantasy that comes to a surprise ending.

These forced abstentions, likely irksome to some fantasists, are not reasonless negatives. They derive from the rhetorical demands of fantasy and specify practices that would reduce or destroy the efficacy that obedience to the rhetoric makes possible. In one way or another such devices impair realism of presentation, even as they may promote realism of content of a kind more expanded than what Lewis had in mind. Like any other writer, the fantasist must pay for the advantages of his chosen form.

The principle and results I have just been outlining govern also the representation of settings in fantasy. A wide variety of possibilities may be found, as well as a range from the sparse to the highly detailed. But the same external realism, order, and clarity are imperative, and for the same reason.

When one considers the characters of fantasy, some further interesting practices and limitations reveal themselves. Of course the range of possibilities is almost, not quite, unlimited. The inclusiveness of the "gods" involved by Forster is just a beginning: "all beings who inhabit the lower air, the shallow water, and the smaller hills, all Fauns and Dryads. . . . all that is medieval this side of the grave." [10] Add to these all residents of the spirit realm whether benevolent or malign; the dead, quiet and unquiet; all beings from nonhuman, animate nature; any hybrid or monster. And further all ordinary and many extraordinary

10. *Aspects of the Novel* (New York: Harcourt, Brace, 1927), pp. 161–62.

human beings. But I must exclude, because they are not to be found in fantasy, all beings, human and other, whose nature and attributes cannot be apprehended by the reason and whose essence therefore cannot be rendered objectively.

This discrimination calls for an explanation that will not be easy. Let me start by saying what I believe most readers will intuitively accept, that fantasy cannot contain beings that are intrinsically heroic and those whose essence is either psychic, spiritual, or passional. A fantasy would be destroyed by the presence of Odysseus, Captain Ahab, Raskolnikov, or, to depart from fiction, of Julius Caesar, Mary Magdalene, or Saint Teresa of Avila. But why? Forster hints at a reason when he speaks of the invocation to the "gods" of prophecy that might be uttered: ". . . it will have been to whatever transcends our abilities even when it is human passion that transcends them, to the deities of India, Greece, Scandinavia and Judaea . . . and to Lucifer son of the morning." [11] This is no precise statement, and I might dissent from some implications of it. But the criterion, "whatever transcends our abilities, even when it is human passion that transcends them," is helpful. We must go further. The heroic, the psychic, the spiritual, and the passional—separately or in combination—may be approached by reason, anatomized, explained, understood, illuminated, but they cannot be so apprehended in their fullness. When one finds these qualities at the center of a being, whether grand or humble, reason can assist, but the real apprehension comes from a kind of divining.

By the same token, a method of fiction that relies upon rhetoric to establish and maintain its illusion cannot comprehend beings of these qualities. It is significant that Forster mentioned Lucifer son of the morning. He would have no proper place in a fantasy. But Satan, ultimately foolish and defeated despite the power he has through time owing to human folly, could be a character in a fantasy and does so appear in Mark Twain's *The Mysterious Stranger*, though here he is a nephew of the Enemy, little Satan.[12] There is nothing intrinsically heroic, psychic, spiri-

11. Ibid., p. 162.

12. Satan as a character was a favorite with Mark Twain, as evidenced by "That Day in Eden," "Sold to Satan," "Dialogues with Satan," and "Young Satan in Hannibal."

tual, or passional, and there is no mystery, in evil. The quality itself and those who embody it may be plumbed to the depth by reason. Milton understood this routine principle of moral theology, and this was part of what moved him to portray Satan objectively. In *Paradise Lost* he made no such attempt to objectify God, and little to portray the Son of God, who in *Paradise Regained* is properly shown because he has become the incarnate Christ. Milton's giving the angels physical reality in the war in heaven was a disadvantageous, though unavoidable, consequence of his general method.

A more egregious error of this kind occurs in a fantasy entitled *Unclay*, by T. F. Powys. Here John Death loses his parchment and with it his ability to claim lives, to "unclay." So for the time of his impotence he lives as an agreeable citizen of the village of Dodder. He is charming, particularly accomplished at seducing maidens, daughters of Eve who cannot resist him. All this is in favor of a sex-love-death equation that Powys exploits even more than Wagner did in *Tristan und Isolde*. The only reason that this character does not explode the story is that death is trivialized and divested of mystery, that is, loses its two major qualities. The control of reason is maintained only by violating the essence of the concept. Death, as rendered in much medieval iconography and in "Der Tod und das Mädchen" of Matthias Claudius, keeps what Powys discarded. But in these death is a personification, not a character. Moreover, the poem, as well as Schubert's well-known song, presents a two-stanza confrontation, not a realized narrative action.

There is another symptom of the confinement of characters in fantasy to portrayals that can be comprehended by reason. Generally, readers who have no idiosyncratic rapport with them watch and follow, as if the characters and their actions were a display or a performance rather than a living history in which one cannot avoid participating. This occurs not only when the characters are strange creatures doing strange things in exotic settings. One watches Gulliver in the same way, and Winston-Smith in 1984. Naïve identification by a reader with any character in a fantasy results from a failure to perceive the representation accurately. Apart from this, any closeness of a reader to characters must be limited by the requirement that he respond critically throughout, even as he accepts the impossible construct. No doubt one could demonstrate that the variations of distance which Wayne Booth identified [13] are operative in fantasy as well as in other fiction. But the general principle of distance in fantasy is controlled by the fact that it is a demonstrational narrative dominated by intellectual persuasion.

I have now moved into discussion of the reader's participation in fantasy. Certain aspects of this are either obvious or already suggested. The reader follows the story as it develops; at any point he has certain general expectations of what is to come and certain hopes, positive and negative, though these are rarely as powerful as they can be in other forms of fiction. Altogether, between fantasy and nonfantasy, participation in the story as story differs in degree, but not in kind.

But there are two complementary features of participation that, if not peculiar to fantasy, are so prominent as to be effectively distinguishing. These are the reader's continuously renewed awareness that he is engaged with the impossible as a factitious reality, and the play of his mind as he regards the impossible construct vis-à-vis its established opposite. This facing-both-ways is a result of the already mentioned paradox of fantasy. The reader must at all times feel intellectually "at home" in the narrative and yet maintain his sense of intellectual alienation as a means of reflecting on the displaced real. His engagement with the construct is continuous for the obvious reason that this is what he is immediately attending to. His reflective activities, I suspect, are less regular. They rise and subside; they may not be complete until he has thought about the story after finishing it. They may never be as full as the ideal response would require. They may be open to revision, particular or general. They may contain affective components that the fantasy itself does not strictly justify. But until the reader has used the story for some kind of critique of what it opposes, the experience that the fantasy enables is incomplete.

This dual participation can scarcely be illustrated by general statements; later in this chapter I shall examine it as it occurs in a fantasy that is classic in concept and execution. For the mo-

13. *Rhetoric of Fiction*, pp. 155–58.

ment let me review a well-known aspect of participation in non-fantasy. A reader of *Barchester Towers* is taken into a "world" that is fictive in all its major components. But this world, far from displacing the known, intentionally resembles what is known either by observation of a cathedral city and clerical life or by otherwise possessing sufficient information about these. Once the reader's awareness is stimulated, the writer need only keep the material developing before him, without any effort to renew the sense of familiarity. Correspondingly, in comparing the fictive with the real, the reader need only think of two separate manifestations of the familiar. The paradox that fantasy imposes is absent from *Barchester Towers*. With *Robinson Crusoe* participation is different in that the strange, but still not the impossible, is made familiar. The reader's effort to perceive this is unevenly distributed; the strangeness is mainly in the environment, somewhat in the action the environment dictates, and not at all in the main character, for Crusoe remains a standard English entrepreneur, whether or not he is only economic man. Hence Defoe had to include (and the reader must understand) more in the way of detail, providing what I have elsewhere called documentation. In response the reader compares the known with the strange made known, Crusoe helps him do so and by his own reflections on the two. A great part of Crusoe's thought history consists of just such reflections, which provide an index of his progress on the island from early deprivation and distress to satisfaction with his state as ruler of a little empire, and from his initial fear that he has lost divine favor to an assurance from his prosperity that if ever really cast out, he is at least restored.[14] *Robinson Crusoe* calls for more adjustment by the reader, but it is yet far from presenting the paradox characteristic of fantasy. The same generalization would be valid for any narrative in which components initially strange are essential.

14. The balance in this sentence is not intended to imply an opinion that Crusoe's character is equally infused by self-serving individualism and Christian spirituality. Ian Watt is doubtless right in stressing the "relative impotence of religion in Defoe's novels." *The Rise of the Novel* (Berkeley and Los Angeles: University of California Press, 1957), p. 82. Possibly Robinson Crusoe is indirectly an ancestor of the many who have made substitutes for religion out of secular concerns in which they idiosyncratically find value.

I am not suggesting any such ridiculous proposition as that because one kind of challenge and response is absent from *Barchester Tower* and *Robinson Crusoe*, they are dreary reading. Actually, abstention from the game of paradox enables Trollope and Defoe to follow other lines of pleasant and profitable exploration so evident that I need not specify them.

Last there is a kind of participation sometimes elicited by fantasy, sometimes absent. I refer to the embodiment of a value judgment that the reader will, I hope, accept. The author has a motive of propaganda. This is different, of course, from the intent of describing values so that they may be impartially understood. Some fantasies call for this response with undisguised clarity, especially the utopias, in which the purpose of exercising this kind of persuasion seems the chief reason for the books' having been written. In some fantasies the value is less evidently urged, and its perception relies more on the willingness and capability of the reader to infer it.

I do not propose to discuss this kind of stimulus and response fully, because its operation in a fantasy seems to me no different from what is found in any *roman à thèse*. The rhetorical tactics, quite separate from those that make a fantasy-illusion intellectually acceptable, are likewise the same. If the message is articulated with the narrative and "proved" by the result of the action, with no need for any exhortation, the reader will consider it. But his concurrence or dissent will in part depend on the values he brings to the reading and on whether he wishes to keep or change those values. The persuasiveness by which a fantasist attempts to establish the possibility of his factitious narrative is addressed to the intellect; the persuasiveness of the propagandist may work through the intellect, but its aim is the affections.

The ways of the novel of propaganda are well enough known to need no repetitious exposition here, and I believe that the same ways are found in the tendentious aspects of certain fantasists. To decide for himself, I encourage the reader to compare the suasion in two diverse works, Mrs. Gaskell's *Mary Barton*, which intends to elicit approval of the motives and methods of the pioneers of the trades-union movement in Manchester, and Charles Williams's *Descent into Hell*, which urges that the sharing of burdens is a sacred human obligation deriving from "the central mystery of Christendom, the terrible fundamental substitution."

There remains for attention the characteristics of style in fantasy, and in this consideration too it is necessary to generalize. Even so, the practices of individual authors are not misrepresented by being viewed as conformable to certain general traits. As persons, fantasists seem no less individualistic than other writers, but in their deployment of language they generally show obedience to a discipline not imposed on them by current fashions in fiction and sometimes ignored by themselves in writings that are not fantasy. Again, a convenient access to the principles that govern style in fantasy is furnished by certain negative symptoms. Though one finds in fantasy plenty of virtuosity and often some sporting with language, radical experimenting and purposeful distortion are notably absent. *Mistress Masham's Repose*, by T. H. White, is an extension from Book I of *Gulliver's Travels*. Appropriately enough, White played at imitating Swift, especially in the speech of the latter-day Lilliputians. Late in White's *The Elephant and the Kangaroo*, the ark floats down the River Liffey through Dublin on its way to foundering in the bay. For narrating this passage and the public tumult that accompanied it, White chose to adopt a pseudo-Joycean style.

In both instances the results are skillful, even spectacular, but just the opposite of eccentric. If one compares White's Joyce with Joyce himself, the differences are obvious. One shows the critical shrewdness and facility that are the excellence of the parodic imitations in Beerbohm's *A Christmas Garland*. But nothing in White's performance approaches Joyce's practice of exploding language, perhaps thought too, in order to remake it in accordance with his extraordinary creative needs. Joyce himself was a great imitator and appropriator of phrases, idioms, syntax, and tones, but all that he gathered he possessed, so that ultimately he was imitating no one. To speak of Joyce brings to mind one in particular of his many instruments toward stylistic revolution, his constant neologizing, though this word seems inadequate to describe his practice. By contrast, even the most modest neologizing is rarely found in a fantasy. Robert Graves invents a few words for the phenomena of New Crete; David Lindsay does the same for Arcturus, C. S. Lewis for Malacandra and Perelandra, Tolkien for all the strange places of Middle Earth. But these all pertain to places unknown, as Joyce's Dublin assuredly was not, and they are simply devices for familiarization. Beyond a few instances of this kind, the diction of fantasy is remarkably straight and pure.

Similarly, surface distortions in presenting character and action are rare in fantasy. If a dream is recounted, it is a coherent narrative, showing little of the displacement and apparent inconsequence covering latent organization that Freud often described. If a character thinks to himself, he thinks in consecutive prose. There is nothing like that sustained use of the soldier's idiom which Joyce Cary made the linguistic vehicle in *Not Honour More* or the anglicized pseudo-Russian argot of Anthony Burgess's *A Clockwork Orange* or the brilliant apocalyptic visions of a dying Prometheus in Golding's *Pincher Martin*. One might continue nothing phenomena of style that never appear—or do rarely—in fantasy, but I trust that the point is clear.

What causes writers to eschew methods of expression for which they have, as some of them showed in other works, the technical competence? Clearly a commitment to narrative as a means of demonstration that, addressed to the reason, requires observance of the conventions of rhetoric. One might say that they observe, and profit from, an intellectual decorum; their style is simply appropriate to their purpose. The straightforward style generally characteristic of fantasy is one more evidence of that adherence to realism of presentation that I stressed earlier.

Thus the positive manifestations in style are what one might expect: clarity, surface order, and objectivity in diction, phrasing, syntax, organization of paragraphs, and all the other aspects of language that are artificially isolated for examination in discourses on style. Now this imposes no more uniformity on writers of fantasy than the heroic couplet imposed on neoclassical poets. A range is open from the apparently dispassionate reporting of Sylvia Townsend Warner in *Lolly Willowes, or the Loving Huntsman* to the linguistic virtuosity that marks all the fiction of Ronald Firbank. Virtuosity is the display of remarkable technical skill within the confines of an orthodox discipline of art or performance. Firbank's effort was to give an imitation in language of dandyism. His style is part of his whole game, and for all that it is mannered, it is also disciplined. But even those fantasists who seem only to report in the most sober and straightforward way are also playing a game of which their deployment of language is a part. Here again we come to something quite familiar, an exploitation of the incongruity between bizarre content and a matter-of-fact expression, which seems to convey a matter-of-fact attitude. There is no rhetorical difference between this maneuver as one finds it in fantasy and the remarkable disjuncture between matter and manner in Swift's *A Modest Proposal*. This is a trick used with never-ending effectiveness by satirists, comic writers, stage comedians, cartoonists, and conversationalists. It is always a device in the play of wit, and it may be used for purposes ranging from the purely serious to the purely entertaining.

The conclusion can be stated simply. In style, as in the other components of narrative discussed earlier, fantasy accedes to the demands of that persuasive purpose which is its major law.

The generalizations of the past pages may become more plausible and meaningful by an attempt to see how they are realized in a single fantasy. Despite the impossibility of making one work represent all fantasy, I have chosen Kafka's *Metamorphosis* for careful examination. Of its kind it is a classic in concept and execution, and has the further advantage of being outside the arbitrary limits of this study.

The tactics of Kafka's first sentence I have already discussed. Within this sentence, however, the exact change is not stated. Gregor Samsa has become something verminous (*Ungeziefer*), but whether animal or insect is not clear. The details of the second and third sentences—hard back; brown, domed, and striated belly; numerous spindly legs helplessly moving as he lies on his back—make clear that he is an insect. Just what kind is never clearly established. Throughout the story, words and images pointing to traits of insects are frequently used by the unknown narrator and by the human beings who encounter the monster, never by the transformed Gregor himself. An actual naming word occurs only when the raucous old charwoman addresses him twice as *Mistkäfer*. A. L. Lloyd translated *Mistkäfer* as "cockroach," and such seems to be the understanding of the word in this context. Willa and Edmund Muir used "dung beetle," which is accurate. But dung beetles, dorbeetles or tumblebugs, are not domestic pests, and cockroaches are reputedly the most noisome of household vermin; either translation serves well enough. Likely a specialist could detect various defects in Kafka's knowledge of entomology, but he was not writing for experts in a particular discipline, and—more important—the horror, for Gregor's unwilling human associates and for the reader, is in the extremity of the change and not in the accurate envisioning of a particular kind of bug. Nor does the reader know the exact size of the metamorphosed Gregor. Perhaps simply his former size, but this seems unlikely, for when he painfully stands erect his mouth reaches to the key of his bedroom door, and gripping this in his powerful mandibles, he turns it. From this and other details—his covering a picture on the wall with his body, his difficulty in crawling under a sofa, and the like—a notion of size might be worked out. Doing so, however, would be an exercise of idle ingenuity. To the general reader any bug is disagreeable, and any enlargement of a bug is repellent.

The fiat of the first paragraph makes a fact of the impossible, and elaboration on this fact, carried out with almost flawless consistency, dominates the whole work, even those figurative and allegorical meanings that can be inferred from the story's objective representation. If the reader consents to the first paragraph, he is disposed to be persuaded by all that follows. That is, he will respond to the rhetoric that controls the developed illusion and will participate in this by carrying out the contrasts and skewed comparisons that grow from the ramifications of the established impossible fact, Gregor as insect, considered against the displaced fact, Gregor as man. Kafka led with a play of wit that is always startling: he realized a metaphor. His development from this would delight any metaphysical poet.

As a consequence of accepting this first and decisive maneuver, the reader is called upon to accept further aspects of the illusion. The change of physical form is abrupt and complete, but the changes in certain physical attributes are arbitrarily extended. From the first, it seems, Gregor's voice is drastically altered; when "speaking" he produces noise of a kind Kafka does not describe beyond noting that when angry he hisses. But not until some time has passed is Gregor aware of being extremely myopic. His taste for garbage emerges quickly, but apparently he never loses his hearing. Briefly digressing, I will observe that the reader never knows exactly what causes his death. Certainly the apple long embedded and festering in his back contributed,[15] but an immediate physical cause of death is not specified.

Despite the arbitrary slowing of certain processes of physical change, which has the tactical advantage of offering the reader vivid reminders, the overall physical change is quickly accomplished. By contrast, the alterations in Gregor's mental and emotional attributes are gradual. He retains his understanding of speech; his taste for violin music; his attachment to the furniture of his room, especially the picture of a woman wearing a fur hat, boa, and muff, which is mentioned on the first page; his concern with family affairs, in overhearing discussion of which he learns that his earnings have not saved them from destitution and that they have deceived him about their financial standing and thus about their affection for him. He retains his love for his sister, Grete, and longs to tell her of his plans for giving her an education at the conservatory. He even retains for a time a somewhat patronizing attitude toward them, a result of his mistaken belief that only he is competent to deal with demanding situations. All this is an added torture to him. Eventually he becomes what the reader has long seen as oncoming—insensitive, demanding, aggressive, indifferent to the dirt he spreads and lives in. He becomes preponderantly just the opposite of what he evidently had been.

But the responses to Gregor of those who remain human are based on a divining of what Gregor himself understands either slowly or not at all. Except for the charwoman, the response is

15. In this fact there is a tactical awkwardness. The first detail of Gregor's altered form is his armorlike back. "Er lag auf seinem panzerartig harten Rücken. . . ." But by the time his father throws the apple so that it is embedded, Gregor's vulnerability to human violence is fully established, and the occurrence is only a culmination of this fact.

one of loathing, but this has varying degrees and expressions. The father is from the first bewildered and hostile, the mother agonized and incapable of acting, the sister repelled but compassionate. All recognize at once that the change dominates their lives, denies them any freedom, and imposes on them the necessity of concealing an awful secret. Why they persist over a period of time—just how long is not specified—in providing for him is long unexplained; they do not discuss the reasons among themselves, even though their evenings are spent mainly in discussing their intolerable present. An understanding emerges finally when Grete, not the father, announces:

> He must go . . . that's the only solution, Father. You must just try to get rid of the idea that this is Gregor. The fact that we've believed it for so long is the root of all our trouble. But how can it be Gregor? If this were Gregor, he would have realized long ago that human beings can't live with such a creature, and he'd have gone away on his own accord. Then we wouldn't have any brother, but we'd be able to go on living and keep his memory in honor. As it is, this creature persecutes us, drives away our lodgers, obviously wants the whole apartment to himself and would have us all sleep in the gutter.[16]

Now it is clear that all along the crucial matter has been identity. Though the change in Gregor is complete, though they cannot understand him and believe that he cannot understand them, though their feelings are a complex of loathing and fear, up to this point they never for a moment doubt that the insect is Gregor and that he must be treated as an invalid member of the family. Their belief, incidentally, exerts a powerful influence on

16. *The Metamorphosis,* in *The Penal Colony, Stories, and Short Pieces,* trans. Willa and Edwin Muir (New York: Schocken Books, 1948), p. 125. The reader may find it profitable to regard the original text: "Weg muss es . . . das ist das einzige Mittel, Vater. Du musst bloss den Gedanken los zuwerden suchen, dass es Gregor ist. Dass wir es so lange geglaubt haben, das ist ja unser eigentliches Ungluck. Aber wie kann es denn Gregor sein? Wenn es Gregor wäre, er hätte längst eingesehen, dass ein Zusammenleben von Menschen mit einem solchen Tier nicht möglich ist, und wäre freiwillig fortgegangen. Wir hatten dann keinen Bruder, aber könnten weiter leben und sein Andenken in Ehren halten. So aber verfolgt uns dieses Tier, vertreibt die Zimmerherren, will offenbar die ganze Wohnung einnehmen und uns auf der Gasse übernachten lassen." *Die Verwandlung* (Leipzig: Kurt Wolff, 1917), p. 67.

84

the reader's belief in the illusion, for they are commonplace, decent people, like the reader himself. Immediately upon this speech of rejection, Gregor innocently frightens them again and withdraws to his room. Now he understands that he must go, and the next morning he is found dead. The slow process of self-knowledge is complete, and we are to understand that self-knowledge robs him of his will to survive and replaces it with a wish to sacrifice himself for their well-being. In a way, he is still the Gregor whose existence his sister has denied.

The story might end here. But as if to demonstrate that the metamorphosis was as important to the family as to Gregor himself, the story continues with an account of their rapid renewal of freedom. They expel the disaffected lodgers, plan to discharge the charwoman, and decide upon taking a flat better than the present one, which had been chosen by Gregor. As they ride on a train for an outing in the country, an unaccustomed peace and hope settles on them. Husband and wife see for the first time that Grete is about to become a handsome woman for whom a husband must be found. And so, with the final sentence, they anticipate a new life without a thought that Gregor's death has given it to them: "And it was like a confirmation of their new dreams and excellent intentions that at the end of their journey their daughter sprang to her feet first and stretched her young body." [17] The reader will do well to remember that the first sentences refer to Gregor's troubled dreams and to a body that is misshapen, awkward, and helpless, one that could not rise and stretch, the body of death itself.

Whether all this is designed to excite pathos or laughter, the reader's participation in the story is prompted, held together, and ordered by the intricate interplay of the fantastic "facts" as arbitrarily presented and reality as it was before the change. One might expect that Gregor, like any person who must face a disagreeable truth about himself, would perceive his insect nature slowly, in contrast with the immediate perception by members of his family. But tactically this is a maneuver to keep the inter-

17. "Und es war ihnen wie eine Bestätigung ihrer neuen Träume und guten Absichten, als am Ziele ihrer Fahrt die Töchter als erste sich erhob und ihren jungen Körper dehnte" (p. 75).

play vivid and persuasive, even beyond the occurrence of Gregor's death. Nor do the stimuli to this kind of participation decrease in number and force as Gregor loses those psychic and emotional traits of humanity that persist after the change in his physical form. The members of the family remain centrally human. This not only accounts for the best and the worst in their conduct throughout; it also keeps the displaced norm prominent in the face of the fantastic facts that are asserted by the often nauseous details of Gregor's being and actions. Thus the fantasy illusion, developed by the fusion of characters, action, and setting, is maintained whole and vivid by an extension of the method of the first paragraph, fiat. This method, in turn, both generates and controls the reader's intellectual participation, the complexity of which I have only suggested.

The prose style of *The Metamorphosis* requires little explanation. Read in German or English, the work reveals the total realization in the concreteness, clarity, order, economy, and straightforwardness of tone that earlier I stated as the stylistic norm of fantasy. The diction is in no way exotic or recondite, and the other luxuries of writing that the nonfantasist may enjoy are nowhere evident. The style is an instrument of the developed concept and the persuasive strategy; the observance of intellectual decorum is complete. All this a reader may easily see for himself.

In this discussion of *The Metamorphosis* I have abstained from interpretation and attempted to add nothing to what critics have offered about the metaphysical, moral, and psychological meanings of the story. My attention has been centered on those features that make it a fantasy—the means whereby it secures the reader's intellectual consent and participation. But the success of Kafka's rhetoric is the enablement of emotional response and interpretation. As the construct of the impossible commands belief, so the reader's feelings are engaged and further speculation becomes possible. Likely mental acceptance and emotional response operate concurrently, and interpretation may be little, if any, behind them. But I believe it a distinctive, perhaps a unique, characteristic of fantasy that mental conviction is indispensable to any other effect.

Professor Booth indirectly confirms my judgment in one respect of emotional response. In discussing the proposition that
"by seeing the whole thing through the isolated sufferer's vision
we are forced to feel it through his heart," he turns his attention
to *The Metamorphosis:*

> Physically, Gregor is as far from human sympathy as could be,
> and his redeeming qualities are by no means strong enough to
> cancel, by themselves, our revulsion. Yet because we are ab-
> solutely bound to his experience, our sympathy is entirely with
> him. . . . We are caught in this scene [of the first paragraph],
> as Gregor himself is caught, in the body of a repulsive animal;
> no other narrative device could possibly convey half so much
> intensity of physical revulsion without dissociating us from the
> disgusting object. Since the story requires this sense of being
> trapped in the disgusting, since it is, in part, a story of how it
> feels to watch other men reacting to one's own repulsiveness,
> the device is perfect for the story and indeed seems inseparable
> from it.[18]

Booth concludes that *The Metamorphosis* is "one of the master-
pieces in the effective use of an isolated narrator."

This is a just and penetrating comment, and I imply no disrespect by writing a brief extension of remarks. Why is the
reader of Kafka's story "absolutely bound to his experience" and
"trapped in the disgusting"? Why does the repulsive Gregor
excite sympathy? Because the reader, unless he is unable or unwilling, believes that the asserted impossibility is a fact. If he
does not, he experiences only an intellectual rejection that precludes any constructive response at all. But I believe that Booth's
statement about sympathy despite revulsion is too simple when
he says, "We are with him against those who reject him." If the
members of the family responded with nothing but rejection
from their first sight of the bug, this would be accurate. But
their rejection is mixed with a kind of bewildered compassion
until they decide that the bug is not Gregor. Then their attitude
becomes single and hardened, and the way is prepared for the
callousness of their greeting a new life. I believe that the reader
has also a secondary fellow-feeling with the family in its ambigu-

18. *Rhetoric of Fiction*, p. 281.

ous distress. This too derives from persuasion about the fact of change. The members of the family are witnesses, and there is no reason to judge them unreliable as observers, however inadequately they understand what they see. They certainly represent a norm of humanity in all its aspects. Their responses, then, are maneuvers in those rhetorical tactics that must succeed if the emotional affects are to occur at all.

Later in his comment Professor Booth writes: "By confining us to Gregor's vision, Kafka has insured a more sympathetic reading than any amount of traditional rhetoric could do. The result is that when Gregor dies and the technical point of view inevitably shifts, the full effect of the various metamorphoses we see in his family, based on Gregor's unwilling sacrifices, still depends on our maintaining his moral point of view as our own." [19] By "traditional rhetoric" he means evaluative commentary, whether conveyed by author, spokesman, or other means. I could not agree more heartily that Kafka's method is persuasive as no overt influencing could be. Certainly, also, Booth is right in suggesting that at the end the family undergoes what approaches a metamorphosis, with the important differences that it has a discernible cause, relief, and takes no physical form. But I am troubled by his implication that the reader has no "moral point of view" other than Gregor's. Certainly this dominates, but within the domination the reader is temporarily forced to adopt points of view occasioned by the family's perceptions of the transformed Gregor. Likely these lack sustained moral validity, but they do enable the necessary view of a complex psychic and emotional situation, which Kafka maintains as part of his strategy of persuasion.

Rarely does another fantasy achieve the quality of Kafka's story. But its formal excellence derives from highly skilled implementation of those principles that govern fantasy generally.

19. Ibid., p. 282.

This outline of the general nature of fantasy may be completed by a survey of some other types of prose fiction that often resemble it. The main purpose of examining these is to show that as they ordinarily are, they can be distinguished from fantasy, despite the appropriateness for fantasy of the material and spirit they often embody. I hope the reader will understand that I am engaged in descriptive, not qualitative, discrimination as I attempt to demonstrate that ghost stories, fairy tales, gothic romances, beast fables, pornographic stories, and works of science fiction usually are not fantasies.

The element that makes it easy to confuse any of these with fantasy has been suggested: all either must or may represent the fantastic. But as I have already established, the presence, even the dominance, of material, various though this may be, does not make a fantasy. The material must be cast into a single, continuous narrative of the impossible that persuades the reader, given his willingness to be persuaded, to grant it his credence in a spirit of intellectual play. Fantasy directs the reader to accept a paradox: temporary assent to the construct without abandonment of the convention it opposes. It is in this game of contradictory credences and the interplay they produce that these other types of prose fiction usually stand apart from fantasy. Often they generate a thrill of wonder at the marvelous that would be destroyed by an attempt at logical plausibility and systematic presentational realism. The reader's engagement is secured by the story's capturing his emotions, not his mind.

Most traditional fairy tales work in this way and are thus, in effect, antifantasies. There are many instances, especially among ghost stories, in which the construct appeals to a belief that, though officially rejected, still retains over credence a power that may be revived. Fantasy relies on a discrimination between possible and impossible that is clearly conceived, even though it may not rely on evidence. Any obscuring of this discrimination precludes fantasy; *The Turn of the Screw*, for example, cannot be so classified, whatever else it may be. The same may be said of any story which leaves the suggestion that, despite convention, the pretendedly impossible is valid and should replace the established exception. Fantasy is not in this way subversive, however much it may be so in others. There are many stories that present beings, events, or situations that are highly improbable but not arbitrarily impossible, and these too must be omitted from the consideration of fantasy. In all these nonfantasies the essential wit of writer and readers and the extended conceptual play are lacking.

These tangential kinds of prose fiction are dominated by content. Their very names emphasize this. A ghost story is centrally concerned with actual revenants or objective versions of haunting spirits that "have their origin within us." [1] A pornographic story is one in which "the subject matter is sexual activity of any overt kind which is depicted as inherently desirable and exciting." [2] And so it goes. Content alone determines classification; the form may be whatever the writer finds agreeable or advantageous. Even so, several of the nonfantasy kinds have special characteristics worth noting.

Some may have been surprised that I troubled to exclude the pornographic story. Its material is not fantastic in the usual sense, and I will observe in passing that the erotic content of genuine fantasy is so slight as to be a disappointment to any seeker of nonexperiential excitement. But a moment's reflection will confirm that pornography is based almost entirely on fantasizing of a kind that Freud and many others have recognized as central in daydreaming. Gorer states that the subject of pornography is "hallucination" and that a successful story will result in orgasm. [3] I have already established that fantasy as a psychic activity may yield the material that may be shaped into a literary fantasy. But in pornography the raw material normally remains raw, even

1. See Virginia Woolf, "Henry James's Ghost Stories," in *Granite and Rainbow* (New York: Harcourt, Brace, 1921), p. 72.

2. C. H. Rolph, ed., *Does Pornography Matter?* (London: Routledge and Kegan Paul, 1961), pp. 29–30. This passage appears in an untitled chapter (pp. 27–40) written by Geoffrey Gorer.

3. Ibid., p. 32.

in several works of the Marquis de Sade and in *L'Histoire d'O*, which use the lurid tale to illustrate a concept or an ethical position. The great welter of such writing, available more or less surreptitiously, represents the unmodified use of such gross and violent stimulants as Wordsworth never thought of. And the same is true of such works—*Fanny Hill, or Memoirs of a Woman of Pleasure;* numerous passages in *Tropic of Cancer, Tropic of Capricorn,* and *Sexus,* by Henry Miller; and Terry Southern's mock version of *Candide,* entitled *Candy*—as provide the stimulants while pretending to make a comedy of erotic fantasizing or to satirize the routine products.[4] Add to all this the fact that pornography deals not with impossibility but with a kind of improbability that ignores many facts of life in order to exploit a few, and the distance between this kind of writing and fantasy, with its concentration on an intellectual game, is evidently great.[5]

4. Many readers will dissent from my including works of Henry Miller in this brief list. The substance is likely expressed in this statement:

> We . . . point out again that the feature by which they [Miller's erotic writings] distinguish themselves . . . is their brutally self-revelatory character. It is in this quality of *self-revelation* that we see in Miller a parallel to the religious spirit in Genet's early writing: both are admittedly purging their souls by this sort of public confession, thereby throwing themselves, as it were, on the judgment of their fellow men, but also putting on them the burden of throwing the first stone.
>
> In Miller, moreover, the quality of self-revelation goes hand in hand with a more general revelation of human nature in all its weakness, and often in all its untarnished sordidness, especially in the area of sex.

Eberhard and Phyllis Kronhausen, *Pornography and the Law: The Psychology of Erotic Realism and Pornography* (New York: Ballantine Books, 1964), pp. 373–74.
I have no doubt that this describes Miller's honorable purpose, but a view that his effects are frequently comic at the expense of fantasizing seems to me neither aberrant nor disrespectful. See Peter Michelson, *The Aesthetics of Pornography* (New York: Herder and Herder, 1971), pp. 190–95.

5. I need not enter the argument about whether or not pornography may have literary merit. For interesting contributions, see Morse Peckham, *Art and Pornography: An Experiment in Explanation* (New York and London: Basic Books, 1969), pp. 28–34, 54–60, 104–8, 115–21; Michelson, *Aesthetics of Pornography*; the animadversions against *The Other Victorians*, by Steven Marcus, in Taylor Stoehr, "Pornography, Masturbation, and the Novel," *Salmagundi,* 2 (1967), 28–56; and Susan Sontag, "The Pornographic Imagination," in *Styles of Radical Will* (New York: Farrar, Straus, and Giroux, 1969), pp. 35–73.

Beast fable or epic, on the other hand, might seem of its nature to be fantasy. Indeed, several prominent fantasies are special formations from this type—George Orwell's *Animal Farm*, Kenneth Grahame's *The Wind in the Willows*, and *The Three Mulla-Mulgars* by Walter de la Mare. Sentient animals figure more or less prominently in many other fantasies. But the conventions of beast fable usually work to keep it distinctive. Ordinarily each animal embodies a human type; the animal society is a direct formation from human society; and the animals, able to speak to one another and to people, carry on a life that is a diminished but proportional version of the human. Inevitably, the tendency of beast fable is toward the satiric or the comic or both.[6] The attention and interest are directed to what is human in the conduct of the beasts, and it is easy to forget that the animals have any natural reality as such. This occurs even with such detailedly barnyard creatures as Chauntecleer and Pertelote, who are still, in accordance with the conventions, abstracts of humanity. Thus there is no ad hoc establishment of impossibility to play against the known possible. The impossibility is from the outset in the convention of beast epic. But in the three examples I cited above, the animals are so intrinsically animal, despite their being comparable with human beings, and their actions so thoroughly commensurate with their nature, that fantasy does result.

The fairy tale also seems to have an inherently close affinity with fantasy. Again several works within the scope of this study are lengthened fairy tales, and in these instances are so designated by their authors. Max Beerbohm called *The Happy Hypocrite* a "fairy tale for tired adults." The subtitle of *That Hideous Strength*, by C. S. Lewis, is "a modern fairly tale for grown-ups," and in a brief preface he equates fairy tale and fantasy.[7] George Macdonald's *Phantastes* is labeled "a faërie romance," and in this usage "faërie" comprehends the entire spirit of the realm of enchantment in which the story occurs. In a foreword, Mac-

---

6. For a fuller discussion, see W. T. H. Jackson, *The Literature of the Middle Ages* (New York: Columbia University Press, 1960), pp. 78–79.

7. *That Hideous Strength: A Modern Fairy Tale for Grown-ups* (New York: Macmillan, 1946), p. vii.

donald's son Greville records his father's view that "the fairy tale is, in so far as it is art, revelation." In the story itself a passing comment on the food of fairyland might well stand for the spiritual value of the whole: "It not only satisfied my hunger, but operated in such a way on my senses that I was brought into far more complete relationship with the things around me. . . ." [8]

I have mentioned *Phantastes*, though it is outside my announced time span, because of its evident influence not only on C. S. Lewis, who repeatedly acknowledged his debt, but also on the long essay "On Fairy Stories," by Tolkien. A systematic review of this contribution appears in an earlier chapter. Suffice it here to repeat that Tolkien makes a habit of identifying fairy tale and fantasy. Moreover, he makes the center of understanding not the diminutive beings themselves but the pervading wonder of *Faërie*, or the Perilous Realm: "Fairy-stories are not in normal English usage stories *about* fairies or elves, but stories about Fairy, that is *Faërie*, the realm or state in which fairies have their being. *Faërie* contains many things besides elves and hags, and besides dwarfs, witches, trolls, giants, or dragons: it holds the seas, the sun, the moon, the sky; and the earth, and all things that are in it: tree and bird, water and stone, vine and bread, and ourselves, mortal men, when we are enchanted." [9] The fairy story, then, depends on the nature of *Faërie*, and this he asserts cannot be defined or described. If one accepts the inclusiveness of the quoted passage, one must agree.

With the exception of Beerbohm, who left to the reader the easy task of guessing at the appropriateness of his description of *The Happy Hypocrite*, these authors have freed themselves from the established historical, analytical, and descriptive criteria for

8. *Phantastes: A Faërie Romance* (London: Dent, n.d.), pp. vii, 39. Robert Lee Wolff notes Macdonald's intention to make of *Phantastes* an adaptation of *Kunstmärchen*, reflecting particularly his high regard for *Undine*, by the Baron de la Motte-Fouqué. Wolff suggests that the lavish information Macdonald provides about the animals, flowers, plants, and other phenomena of fairyland is intended to show the oneness of man and nature in an ideal state. *The Golden Key: A Study of the Fiction of George Macdonald* (New Haven: Yale University Press, 1961), p. 55.

9. *Essays Presented to Charles Williams* (London: Oxford University Press, 1947), p. 42.

the study of fairy tales. They say nothing of the standard themes, the conventions of repetition and other formulaic devices of narration, the disparate historical and geographic origins of fairy tales, their absorption of mythic material, the frequency of an aetiological motive.[10] Macdonald, Lewis, and Tolkien used the fairy tale, understood in the widest possible sense, as an access to deep spiritual truths, and thus transformed the central concern with material that appeals to the sense of wonder into narrative demonstrations. Their purpose is most overtly stated by Lewis in his preface to *That Hideous Strength*, the third in a trilogy of doctrinal fantasies: "This is a 'tall story' about devilry, though it has behind it a serious 'point,' which I have tried to make in my Abolition of Man" (p. vii).

In its ordinary manifestations, various though these are, both the traditional fairy tale and the *Kunstmärchen* rely on material and conventions that feed the insatiable human longing for wonder. The issue of "belief" in a construct that opposes the known does not arise. Enchantment exists of itself, and the reader's participation in it is scarcely intellectual. The fantastic, within which the entire material of fairy tales may be comprehended, works directly on the reader with no need for a rhetorically dominated narrative. It was only as Macdonald, Lewis, and Tolkien in *The Lord of the Rings* adapted the fairy tale to their personal and doctrinal ends that the fantastic was formed into fantasies. Usual exemplars of the fairy tale are not so formed. Likewise when Sir Herbert Read, who maintained that fairy tales are the only pure expression of the fantastic, expanded Thomas Keightley's report of the green children found in Suffolk, he produced in *The Green Child* an extended fairy tale transmuted into a fantasy.

I come next to gothic romance and propose again that ordinarily it is apart from fantasy. The discrimination of the two could be made lengthy and complicated. Gothic romance has prompted a plentitude of historical, descriptive, and critical writing. Far from producing a work that would end discussion by being definitive, Montague Summers, in *The Gothic Quest*,

10. For a summary discussion of these and other matters, see Jan de Vries, "The Problem of the Fairy Tale," *Diogenes*, no. 22 (1958), pp. 1–15.

seems to have started a run of critical consideration that remains current. Also, gothic romance easily absorbs materials usually associated with other types of fiction. It accommodates all manner of ghost lore and supernaturality, erotica and pornography; it has affiliations with the novel of sensibility, with historical romance, even with surrealist fiction. This leads to the not at all startling conclusion that gothic romance, as its name suggests, is not essentially a form but a spirit that enters or permeates a wide variety of fiction. This spirit can show itself in seemingly unlikely places. Faulkner's novels are full of it. Naphta in *The Magic Mountain* brings the gothic with him. The best seller *Rosemary's Baby*, a story of *maleficium*, by Ira Levin, was called by one critic the first experiment in the obstetrical gothic. In order to simplify and still get at essentials, I quote a definition recently formulated by Francis Russell Hart:

> Gothic is a fiction evocative of a sublime and picturesque landscape, of an animated nature to which man is related with affective intensity. Gothic fiction is fascination with time, with the dark persistence of the past in sublime ruin, haunted relic, and hereditary curse. The cult of Gothic, suggested Michael Sadleir, projected a symbolic bond between ruined house and nobly ruined mind. Gothic depicted a world in ruins, said the divine Marquis, a world wracked by revolutionary fervor and guilt. Seen from our perspective, the Gothic signals a counter-enlightenment, climaxing an era naive in the fervor of its scientific naturalism, its rationalism, its benevolism, its commitment to the norms of "common sense." The Gothic novelist, still "enlightened" but imperfect in his skepticism, gave to fiction a post-Enlightenment preoccupation with the preternatural, the irrational, the primordial, the abnormal, and (tending to include the rest) the demonic.[11]

Hart might have added that the desired response to gothic fiction is wonder, excitement, and the *frisson d'horreur*. For good reason the corresponding term in French criticism is *le roman noir*.

Hart's language reveals the resemblances and the differences

---

11. "The Experience of Character in the English Gothic Novel," in *Experience in the Novel: Selected Papers from the English Institute,* ed. Roy Harvey Pearce (New York: Columbia University Press, 1968), pp. 85–86.

between gothic fiction and fantasy. Again these are what I have
stated before. The two kinds of fiction often embody the same
material, but the aims are sharply divergent. In gothic romance
the irrational remains unmodified and intrinsically thrilling; it
gives nothing of the intellectual game and speculative participation that are central in fantasy. If readers "believe" in the gothic,
as did Catherine Morland in *Northanger Abbey*, their belief is
the result of unthinking surrender to disturbed feeling rather
than response to a rationally conducted narrative. Undoubtedly
le roman noir has its appropriate rhetoric, but it is not that demanded of a demonstrated counterproposition.

At first sight, a separation of fantasy and science fiction would
seem to offer more difficulty than any so far encountered. Popular usage, habits of classification, and even the titles of some
publications, such as *The Checklist of Fantastic Literature*, often
make the two synonymous or otherwise couple them. Beyond
this, several works to be discussed in this study often pass as
science fiction. Confusion arises also because, as Kingsley Amis
notes, "science fiction is not necessarily fiction about science or
scientists, nor is science necessarily important in it." [12] Accordingly, this empire is sometimes extended by claim to include far
more than any but its partisans might expect. I suspect that part
of the motive for such appropriation is to counter the reproaches
of intrinsic subliterariness that were long directed at science
fiction. If there were ever a time when such snobbery toward the
whole subgenre was justified, that time has vanished.

Actually, the distinction between science fiction and fantasy is
clearer than the others I have been making. Kingsley Amis provides the necessary clarity in two statements. The first is a con-
cise definition: "Science fiction is that class of prose narrative
treating of a situation that could not arise in the world as we
know it, but which is hypothesized on the basis of some innova-
tion in science or technology, or pseudo-science or pseudo-
technology, whether human or extra-terrestrial in origin" (p. 18).
His second is a brisk separation: "For now I merely intend to
differentiate fantasy from science fiction, a task that involves

12. *New Maps of Hell: A Survey of Science Fiction* (New York: Harcourt,
Brace, 1960), p. 18.

little more than remarking that while science fiction . . . maintains a respect for fact or presumptive fact, fantasy makes a point of flouting these . . ." (p. 22). Despite the prejudicial language of the second remark, the two statements together set the matter as it is. However remote, astonishing, or astounding a work of science fiction may be, it does not represent what convention regards as categorically and irremediably impossible. If it treats "a situation that could not arise in the world as we know it," that situation still arises from a hypothesis extended, though perhaps tenuously, from what either is or is inferred to be a speculative possibility. Extrapolation moves out, often far out, from a center, but it retains connection with the center. Science fiction may strain the confines of possibility, but it does not break out and assert the thing that is not.

The difference I propose may be seen clearly by brief examination of two works, one fantasy and one science fiction. The former is C. S. Lewis's trilogy of "space romances"—*Out of the Silent Planet, Perelandra,* and *That Hideous Strength*—the latter Ray Bradbury's *Fahrenheit 451,* a well-received book that was made into a successful motion picture. Lewis read widely in science fiction, with pleasure and profit; he acknowledged a particular interest in David Lindsay's *A Voyage to Arcturus,* Eddison's *The Worm Ouroboros,* and the writings of Olaf Stapledon. The phrase "space romances," in my opinion misleading as a total characterization, he himself applied to his trilogy. But it is also Lewis who provides the hint for calling his trilogy a fantasy, despite its representation of space travel and other aspects of science or scientism. In the trilogy, he says, "the pseudo-scientific apparatus is to be taken simply as a 'machine' in the sense which that word bore for the Neo-Classical criticis." [13]

Here Lewis places a further metaphorical meaning on what was already a metaphor in the context he cites. As a definition of "machine" in literary usage, the *N.E.D.* gives "a contrivance for the sake of effect; a supernatural agency or personage introduced into a poem." Lewis's trilogy is permeated with the super-

13. "On Science Fiction," in *Of Other Worlds* (London: Geoffrey Bles, 1966), p. 68.

natural, but his space machinery is not supernatural. It relies not at all on a departure into the impossible. The center of the fantasy-illusion is rather the assumption that a cosmic conflict is in progress between the forces of good and evil, with mighty opposites both human and nonhuman. This conflict, moreover, is present, purposive, and actional, with a direct bearing on the lives and fortunes of the inhabitants of the universe. That it is a competition with a foreknown issue does not alter the conventional impossibility of the central fact. Thus the trilogy presents a curious exhibit. Lewis's theology is entirely orthodox; his narrative means of showing this theology in action is intellectually subversive. I have no wish to steal his trilogy from those who claim it for science fiction, but it is not this aspect of the work that makes it a fantasy.

Fahrenheit 451, first published as a full-length work in 1953 and since then many times reprinted, belongs to a kind of monitory, nightmare fiction for which the now agreed upon name is dystopia. The principle of these works is stated in part by Nicholas Berdiaeff, in a passage Aldous Huxley used as an epigraph for *Brave New World:* "Les utopies apparaissent comme bien plus réalisables qu'on ne le croyait autrefois. Et nous nous trouvons actuellement devant une question bien autrement angoissante: Comment éviter leur réalisation definitive?" But the cautious hope Berdiaeff later expresses, that an effective retreat from utopia to nature may be possible, the anti-utopian writers categorically deny. Their works detail the *réalisation definitive* in all its grimness and perpetuity. For these writers the utopian thinkers and a general human longing after perfection provide the origins of intolerable societies, for they collaborate in that crime of wishing for perfection, the punishment of which is fulfillment. It appears that utopian fiction can never again be written. As Mark Hillegas demonstrates, the early scientific romances of H. G. Wells both exerted an influence and prompted a rejection that has resulted in a continuous history of anti-utopias.[14]

For the present purpose there is no need to detail the action of

14. *The Future as Nightmare: H. G. Wells and the Anti-Utopians* (New York: Oxford University Press, 1967), pp. 80–162.

Fahrenheit 451. It follows the line of a rebellion, more nearly successful than those that usually occur in anti-utopias, against a society rendered happy and conformist by the dominance of its gadgets, its well-organized book-burners, the Mechanical Hound, and all the other machinery that suppresses individuality and thought. The "success" of the rebellion consists largely in the fact that the outcast rebels, who have passages of books in their memories, are the only survivors of a nuclear explosion that atomizes the city. My point is that all the devices by which tyranny is secured either exist at present or may be foreseen as probable technological developments of the near future.[15] Even the Mechanical Hound puts no strain on belief; it is a not very daring instance of the malevolent robot. And we are all used to robots. I feel safe in saying that no machine that possesses super-animal or superhuman capabilities can prompt a reader to say "impossible." Even Epicac XIV, the superior electronic mentality that dominates all life after the Second Industrial Revolution, as envisioned by Kurt Vonnegut in *Player Piano*, seems an extension of what is already in operation. This and the other devices of the work, which is richer in science fiction features than *Fahrenheit 451*, are in no way beyond belief.

Thus I come again to my already stated conclusion. Science fiction deals with the amazing, sometimes with the highly improbable, but not with the impossible, as does fantasy. The two kinds of narration operate according to quite different intellectual principles and call for quite different responses. No amount of actual or seeming congruity of material should lead to their being identified as to generic classification. And the rationale for distinguishing fantasy from science fiction also separates fantasy from the normative manifestations of ghost story, fairy tale, gothic romance, beast fable, and pornographic story.

Fantasy resists tidy classification. Working independently, the writers have had diverse interests, capabilities, purposes, and knowledge, and their productions are accordingly diverse. Thus

15. It is worth remembering that in a foreword to a 1956 reissue of *Brave New World*, Huxley said, in effect, that he would revise his forecasts only by suggesting that the conditions of A.F. 632 are nearer in time than he first thought.

I am forced to organize the discussion of representative fantasies according to flexible associations, held together by resemblances of method. Even these will reveal the imposition of order on material that is almost unmanageable.

There are five such groups: the fantasies based on impossible personal change; those that show incredible societies; those that center on an unorthodox notion of innocence; those that originate in literary parody, extension, or adaptation, or in contravention of established ideas about historical fact; and those that represent a dominance of supernatural powers in some part of the known world or in a fictive world. As one might expect, many fantasies, such as Sir Herbert Read's *The Green Child*, show affinities with more than one group. Despite this ambiguity and others, all fantasies do illustrate, more or less completely and skillfully, those general characteristics of concept and method that I have described in the preceding chapters. Because those fantasies that originate in incredible personal change are conceptually the simplest and often the most clearly realized, I shall discuss this group first.

Think of a woman changing suddenly into a vixen, a young man made of glass, a scarecrow coming to life and political power. These impossibilities exemplify the maneuver or *donnée* that yields an important subtype of fantasy. The narrative demands that the reader accept a single personal change, beyond the reach of presumed natural causes, so fundamental as to determine total being and attributes. The drastic changes within natural possibility—reversal of fortune, injury, illness, even death—are inadequate as efficient causes for such fantasy, though they may occur as accompaniments or consequences. Likewise, circumstantial changes and decisive effects upon other persons in the narrative may result from the one transformation, but these too are effects and developments; they support, but do not make, the fantasy. The single arbitrary change, occurring sometimes within the represented action and sometimes before it, is the cause from which all else follows.

Metamorphosis, as it has been understood in mythography and literature since the time of Ovid, is a simple matter. Variations within the physical transformation are possible. The change may be immediate or gradual. Sometimes it is abhorrent to the sufferer, a punishment or an effect of malice, as in witchcraft; but it may be a release or a protection. It may be from a lower form of life to a higher, though the reverse movement is more common. The new form may have an appropriateness, a discernible relationship to the original. Sometimes the metamorphosed being retains the consciousness of his one-time embodiment and adds to it the psychic capability of the new; sometimes the change induces oblivion of the former state. But whatever the accompanying effects, the basic fact is total alteration in form, which gains its power from the widespread assumption that form is a determinant of identity, even of being. Few people can accept, outside of a sacramental context, a fundamental dissonance between substance and form.

The classic fantasy of metamorphosis in modern literature is *Die Verwandlung* of Kafka, discussed in a preceding chapter. In this the change is announced in the first sentence. In David Garnett's *Lady into Fox* the transformation of Silvia Tebrick from wife to vixen is the first event of the story. There is no cause or explanation; it simply happens. From this event a pathetic history progresses with the inevitability of doom. Despite all of Mr. Tebrick's efforts at control and keeping her tame by love, she becomes increasingly animal. In painful contrast to the metamorphosis itself, this is a slow process; the vixen seems as intent as her husband on retaining her humanity. For a time this seems hopeful, but no effort can arrest the course of her new nature. Finally she goes wild, takes to the woods, bears a litter of cubs, and is torn to pieces by hounds. It is not until this event that Mr. Tebrick leaves off trying to reclaim her.

Integrated with the slow bestialization is the history of Mr. Tebrick's struggles, which, though desperate and futile, never become despairing, even when she bites him or proudly shows him her litter of cubs. He dedicates himself to living as though the vixen were still his wife. As he goes through ever more heroic acts of devotion, she becomes more fully an animal. And so the alienation becomes wider. His love and stubbornness make him irrational; in the extreme stages he is briefly as nonhuman as she.

In support of the metamorphosis David Garnett uses a few contributory methods. The unnamed narrator makes no concealment or apology for the incredible. He is puzzled by it and gives the event his credence only after his doubts are overcome by incontestable evidence. As befits such a narrator, the presentation is scrupulous, objective, sufficiently detailed for cohesiveness and credibility, but not overwhelmed with detail. A less disciplined artist than David Garnett could have written a much longer book. The narrator does not hesitate to trace the thoughts and feelings of Mr. Tebrick directly. Mad though this husband becomes under pressure, he remains centrally human. The emotional history of the vixen, however, is a different matter. Here the narrator assumes a more tentative approach; he seems to suggest that human understanding of the animal psyche can be guesswork at best. Even when the vixen is showing a conflict between her animal nature and vestiges of the human, Mr. Tebrick overinterprets all signs of remaining or returning humanness, and the contrast between his irrationality and the narrator's intellectual poise is most revealing.

An objective, candid, economical narrator, whose account assumes the style of his attitude, is a strong instrument to a convincing metamorphosis. But an instrument only. As the reader proceeds, he is little aware of narrator or of the writing. The metamorphosis alone, and its consequences, dominate his consciousness. It is the decisiveness of the change that gives the story its persuasive power. This is true also of Kafka's story. The chief difference between this and *Lady into Fox* is that Gregor Samsa retains human attitudes and values despite his altered physical form and functions. He thus perceives himself as others cannot, and is painfully aware that in different ways both he and the rest of the world are correct. Because Gregor Samsa is a sentient being, *Die Verwandlung* has an effect of horror and a symbolic suggestiveness absent or far less noticeable in *Lady into Fox*. I suspect that David Garnett avoided both these possibilities in order to achieve cleanly an ironical contrast between animal and human and an exposure of the sentimental folly that allows confusion of the two orders of nature.

Sylva, by Jean Bruller, is *Lady into Fox* reversed, the story of a fox transformed into a girl. That the author had Garnett's novella in mind is clear from several direct references, mostly disparaging. A fleeing fox is rescued from the hounds and suddenly becomes a girl. This change begins a long process of making the human from the animal, carried out through a fully developed novel. In *Sylva* the event provokes more events, complications, and changes affecting more characters than the narrator of *Lady into Fox* allows himself. As a counterpart to the humanizing of Sylva, Bruller rehearses also the dehumanization of Dorothy, once a highly proper young lady and more or less M. Richwick's intended, from drugs after Sylva displaces her. The first-person presentation, moreover, permits a viewing of the narrator's involvement in a fearful history. Bruller maintains the consequences of metamorphosis up to the point that the narrator wishes only to marry her, despite her being pregnant by some other male. But when he beholds her firstborn, his dream is shattered: "On n'en pouvait douter: c'était un renard." [1]

With these last words of the story, Bruller indeed achieved a surprise ending and perhaps a telling demonstration that "human" and "animal" represent factitious and unstable concepts rather than reality. He did so, however, at the expense of his metamorphosis, which suddenly falls to pieces. With counterbalanced metamorphoses as the main method, with central characters who resemble each other in irrational devotedness, the two works seem schematic opposites. But Garnett's fantasy arrives at logical fulfillment, while Bruller's is destroyed as a fantasy, whatever may be gained for it as a cautionary tale, in the final sentence.

Metamorphosis is the most drastic and most completely objective of the changes that can produce fantasy. It may be seen also in *The Venetian Glass Nephew* by Elinor Wylie, a story prompted perhaps by Cervantes's *The Licentiate of Glass*; in *The Arrogant History of White Ben* by Winifred Ashton; and in *The Happy Hypocrite* by Max Beerbohm, a fairy tale reversal of *The Picture of Dorian Gray*. But changes in fundamental aspects of being are also effective sources of fantasy. In Virginia Woolf's *Orlando* the dominating device is a clear and arbitrary change in sex; *Orlando* is a biography of a person who is, throughout three centuries of scenes from English social history, both a man and a woman. The transformation occurs suddenly, without argument or fuss. It exerts a determining influence on the segment of narrative that follows and the way in which the enveloping social and historical scene is viewed, though what one might call the personality of Orlando is a constant.[2] Orlando is androgynous throughout and thus embodies that dual, intermixing,

---

1. "Vercors" [Jean Bruller], *Sylva* (Paris: Bernard Grasset, 1961), p. 285. This work was translated into English by Rita Barisse and published by Putnam in 1962.

2. John Graham would probably disagree with this statement, for he believes that Virginia Woolf fails in *Orlando* to preserve "a human perspective." Moreover, in his view, the world of *Orlando* is not coherent. Thus the book violates the two technical principles, or laws, of fantasy. "The Caricature Value of Parody and Fantasy in *Orlando*," *University of Toronto Quarterly*, 30 (1961), 345–66.

vacillating sexuality that Virginia Woolf thought the fact of every person's life, though it is obscured by physical formation, self-concept, and compliance with custom.

The arbitrary change in a single person is not, strictly speaking, metamorphic, but it is both startling and fundamental. The matter of sexual identity illustrates that general acceptance as well as sheer fact may provide the convention against which fantasy conducts its narrative counterdemonstration. For centuries the existence of hermaphrodites and other manifestations of mixed sexuality, physical or psychic or both, has been recognized. Yet the agreement persists that every person is either male or female, and classification by sex is the first act toward identification performed for any newborn baby, just as it was in the beginning the first discrimination within newly created humanity. The belief that this division represents nature or divine will or both is so potent that any deviation from it excites curiosity, amusement, scorn, or outrage. It is no wonder that when trans-sexual surgery became possible, the audience for publicity was at once enormous. Even persons who accept the evidence that sexual nature is no simple matter will find in *Orlando* a contravention of what passes for fact.

Virginia Woolf called *Orlando* "a biography," and recognizably biographical it is, whether or not one knows that it centers on Victoria Sackville-West and is, in the phrase of Nigel Nicolson, "the longest and most charming love letter in literature." [3] But I suspect that the subtitle contains also a mischievous denial of itself, for *Orlando* contravenes not only the assumption that biography must concern one man or one woman in finite time and space but also the convention that a person can be defined by any external characteristic, even one seemingly so decisive as sex. Identity and life, Mrs. Woolf believed, are not so simple and discrete.

If arbitrary change in sex be fundamental, so too is a remarkable difference in size, and this far beyond the mere physical alienation from environment. This simple fact was Swift's point of departure in Books I and II of *Gulliver's Travels*. It is likewise the initiating and dominating fact of Walter de la Mare's

3. *Portrait of a Marriage* (New York; Atheneum, 1973), p. 202.

Memoirs of a Midget. The reader does not see the central character, Miss M., transformed into a midget; she has been one from birth. Accordingly, she does not suffer the pains of lost normality, but she experiences other pains, which are at least as acute.

Thematically *Memoirs of a Midget* centers on Miss M.'s effort to be part of the world from which her size and the resulting attitudes almost exclude her. Hers is the story of the second book of *Gulliver's Travels* but set in a familiar environment and with ordinary human beings as the Brobdingnagians.[4] Walter de la Mare is far more concerned than Swift with the subtleties of sensibility. Miss M.'s size is never specified; rather, it is made clear that her smallness includes not only unremitting physical inconvenience but even more serious emotional difficulties. Her perceptions are as delicate as her person, but her affections, even for those who treat her callously, are capacious. She is often tempted to retreat into her own near uniqueness, but she sees that this is the way to the misanthropy that has claimed her male counterpart, Mr. Anon, the midget of Wanderslore. One signification of his name suggests that he has alienated himself, and his attitudes bear this out. Miss M.'s problems would scarcely exist were she capable of being permanently what she is for a time, a curiosity and a show, as Gulliver was among the giants. But this too has isolation, as well as vulgarity, at the end. And so she persists in facing her problem up to the time she mysteriously disappears, having been called away and leaving her voluminous memoir in minute handwriting to be found by her executor. She concludes her record with a farewell which hopes that she has had some success in her endeavor to be part of the human world.

The character of Miss M. is a technical and thematic triumph, to the point that one easily forgets that the story presents two midgets. Mr. Anon is indispensable, but he is a foil. It is Miss M.'s uniqueness of size and spirit that dominates the work. She lives intensely within herself and intensely within the society of her greaters, though not her betters. She is passionately specula-

4. See W. R. Irwin, "Swift and the Novelists," *Philological Quarterly*, 45 (1966), 109–11.

tive, and subjects to a clear-sighted yet sympathetic scrutiny her own peculiarity and the varied human responses this provokes. In solitude she draws pleasure from the stars and from the works of Jane Austen and Emily Brontë. Her private world is remote and complete. By contrast, the great world in which Miss M. must live and of which she wishes to be a part is in Walter de la Mare's creation as prosaic as bread and cheese. Many fantasists fabricate an environment distant in time, space, or both. In *Memoirs of a Midget* the fantasy of the central figures is imposed upon the ordinary.

This imposition succeeds largely because of the efficacy of Miss M. as a character. The paradoxes of her essentially integrated nature persist throughout the book. She is anything but dominant, and yet she dominates the action. Nothing about her is evidently otherworldly, except for her somewhat unsatisfying disappearance. Yet her delicacy and intensity of spirit seem scarcely human; she resembles a changeling atypically eager to love and be loved. Simple by nature, she speculates so subtly upon her experience that her refinement transforms the grossness of the world around her. But here is the crucial point. The author's principal effort is to make the reader accept Miss M.'s being—her person, mind, tastes, attitudes, and sympathies—as the measure of all. The result of his success is a kind of psychic fantasy, which, for a final paradox, has its physical foundation in arbitrarily altered size. This change is not so spectacular as a represented metamorphosis, and it occurs prior to the action. Nevertheless, *Memoirs of a Midget* is as impressive a fantasy as *Lady into Fox*.

Fundamental change is a method almost inexhaustible in possibilities for fantasy and advantageous because of its immediate appeal to the fancy. Few people have omitted, in their daydreams or otherwise, to entertain themselves with narratives based on a projection of their own altered form, personality, capability, or disposition. One of the penalties of identity is that it is identity; by having a personality, however capacious, one is debarred from having any other personality. And the release from this is the arbitrary abandonment of the known self for a factitious and usually more interesting or powerful self. Thus can any schoolboy become his own sports idol. Emma Bovary can be a heroine of romance, and Walter Mitty can have his dreams of glory. Somewhat similarly, the fancying of transformation or fundamental change in familiar persons outside the self is a gratifying source of entertainment, though not of daydreams. All this is common knowledge—and common practice.

Almost as easy is the fanciful alteration by one person of another or of groups and even nations. The number of metaphors, some of them so familiar as almost to have passed from figurative into literal signification, witnesses the prevalence of this mental trick. The animal equivalents, in present or past popular usage, for total human personality or aspects of personality are numerous—lion, tiger, dog, cat, rabbit, squirrel, fox, wolf, bear, goose, chicken, mouse, rat, hyena, jackal, snake. The list might be extended indefinitely. All suggest an analogical process often so direct or automatic as to be undetected. Both elevating and depreciating embodiments of the human as animal suggest a quick capability for seeing the one in the other, and this in turn suggests that fantasy based on metamorphosis is readily acceptable to the imagination.

seven   *Impossible Societies*

The change that generates and dominates fantasy may be circumstantial or environmental, rather than personal. When this occurs, the result is a narrative anatomy of an "impossible" society. Such a society is unique and to envision it requires a projection beyond what the common reader finds conceivable or foreseeable. It must be understood, however, that the center of the fantasy-illusion is the society itself and not the means or processes that are posited as having produced it. The agency of change can often, though not always, be accepted as possible, even plausible. There is no essential difficulty in imagining the endless warfare of three power spheres that has occasioned the totalitarianism of 1984 or the bomb that has produced a populace of mutational monsters in *Ape and Essence*. Yet the societies that result violate a convention, which says, in effect, "It can't happen here" or "It can't happen to me." This convention derives from that limited imagination which renders most people incapable without incitement of believing in a society and a style of life much different from what they know. Thus there is an impediment to the envisioning not only of general misery but also of any felicity that is more inclusive than the desiderata of personal daydreams. Whether this construction results from inertia of thought or represents a means whereby the psyche maintains its poise against threats of disturbance I need not argue. But it does establish a mental condition counter to which the social fantasist may play his game.

One version of this game is the narrative utopia. It is generally understood that utopian thinking develops the impossible. Utopia literally is nowhere, and its total felicity cannot exist except in dreams. This remains true even when within the formulation are policies and practices that may profitably be adapted to an existing society. For this reason utopian narratives normally posit some disjuncture—of time, place, or other fundamental circumstance—from the known.

The standard utopias of modern fiction are well known and require no description here. Edward Bellamy's *Looking Backward: 2000–1887*; W. H. Hudson's *A Crystal Age*; William Morris's *News from Nowhere*; Butler's *Erewhon*; H. G. Wells's *In the Days of the Comet, Men like Gods*, and *The Shape of Things to Come*; James Hilton's *Lost Horizon*—these are familiar titles, and they tell a familiar kind of story. As reports from a remote felicity conveyed to an unhappy world, they foster a *Sehnsucht* much like that generated by fairy tale and romance.

Over the past forty years, however, such constructs of the impossible have often represented societies that would be intolerable. More and more, utopia seems desirable only when dreamed of from far off; too near, it becomes ominous. One is reminded of the maxim of La Rochefoucauld: "Nous désirions peu de choses avec ardeur, si nous connaissions ce que nous désirons." George Woodcock asserted in 1956 that the orthodox utopia had almost disappeared and would soon become a relic of an optimism no longer possible for any except the naïve. He points to H. G. Wells's *Men like Gods* (1923) as the last, and suggests that the novel by Evgeny Zamiatin that was translated as *We* (1924) set a pattern toward anti-utopia, also called dystopia.[1] Apparently Woodcock's article was in production before the appearance in 1955 of the first edition of Richard Gerber's study that examines English utopian fiction from 1900 to 1950, for Gerber cites anti-utopias from early in the twentieth century and straightforward utopias after the year of *Men like Gods*.[2] Even so, his review supports Woodcock's generalizations by showing an increase of the negative.

Anti-utopias share some features worth noting. The occurrence of the societies that they show represents to a small controlling elite the achievement of perfection, a complete social control. But to one or just a few rebel characters, and to the reader, this perfection is abhorrent. An anti-utopia is monitory, for the means of its realization, unlike that of an orthodox utopia, is plausible. Usually the time of an anti-utopia is not far

---

1. "Utopias in Negative," *Sewanee Review*, 64 (1956), 82.
2. *Utopian Fantasy: A Study of English Utopian Fiction since the End of the Nineteenth Century*, 2nd ed. (New York: McGraw-Hill, 1973), pp. 143–62.

in the future; the course to it, whether through technology or by other developments, may be foreseen. Even so, the structure of the new society and the motivations of its controllers are outside the reader's belief, and it is this fact which makes the fantasy. The attitude toward the perfection is independent of the means by which it is realized. The developmental process carries the reader into the future, but with or without encouragement from within the narrative, the standards by which the society is judged are those of the reader's present time. Straightforward utopia creates a discontent with his immediate circumstance and a longing for the new; in anti-utopia only the present seems felicitous, even though the shape of things to come makes it precarious.

It is instructive to consider the means whereby these drastically altered societies have become established. In *Ape and Essence* a bomb—"The Thing"—of World War III has occasioned a population of monsters, dominated by the theocracy of Belial, in southern California. In *Brave New World* total control of artificial life processes provides the basis for an ordered society. In 1984 the reader is kept aware of continuous warfare, chiefly aerial, though it is remote from the action. In all three, technological "improvements" are important instruments. But not in *Animal Farm*, which starts with a straightforward, somewhat primitive revolution, and not in *The Aerodrome* by Rex Warner, in which the military elite is formed by the organizational will of a single man, the Air Vice-Marshal, a high-minded, fanatic Big Brother. The conclusion from this is simple: anti-utopias may, or may not, show an important component of technology, and when they do, it is instrumental rather than central. Thus there is no essential association of anti-utopias and science fiction, as there is often presumed to be. This points to a well-known though frequently forgotten, truth, that tyrannies are made—or permitted—by people, not by machines.

Between utopia and anti-utopia there is, in addition to the self-evident discrepancies, a difference of persuasive method. The reader is simply translated to utopia without explanation, and the whole emphasis is on the novel social order. In anti-utopia there is always related a development that leads to the impossible

111

society, a history that is usually brief and sometimes rehearsed by dispersed retrospect. It is necessary that this means be credible without countering any convention of belief, so that it supports the social fantasy without being part of it. The tactical reason for this disjuncture is not obscure. Within the present there must be a real potentiality, in technology or elsewhere, for evolution toward the abhorrent future. Though the reader may consider it reluctantly, the potentiality is unescapably there. Were it not, "the future as nightmare," to adopt the eloquent phrase of Mark Hillegas,[3] could scarcely be made alarming. But the reader, as he views the results of the disheartening progress, judges by the standards of his present state, and these criteria are often reinforced by the similar judgments of characters who rebel against the impossible society in which they are caught. The result, however, of maintaining a stance of the present is not the usual imaginative involvement in the action of a novel. It is rather the reader's contemplation of a spectacle of a disaster that may be believed only if he arbitrarily accepts as fact conditions and events otherwise unbelievable because he is intellectually imbedded in the present. One has no trouble projecting himself into the action of most novels and many romances, and to do so does not indicate that uncritical response known as naïve identification. But this same sense of participation does not operate for anti-utopias and other fantasies of an abhorrent future. George Orwell was careful to make Winston-Smith and Julia characters easily understood, but it does not follow that the reader feels involved in their activities and their fate. Rather, he witnesses these, as if the whole development were a hideous display, a nightmare of a time, place, and persons in which he takes no part.

I have already hinted that the impossible order of the future is not confined to anti-utopias. The latter have received much attention, largely, I believe, because they represent spectacular contrasts between an ideal and its perversion. Thus they play on the distress many have felt in the twentieth century from the failure of democratic ideology, that promise of approaching

3. See *The Future as Nightmare: H. G. Wells and the Anti-Utopians* (New York: Oxford University Press, 1967).

felicity, to prevent the threat of tyranny. But there are several fantasies in which the impossible society results from some natural or military disaster so devastating as to produce a basically altered world. No doubt the authors started with a question in the "what if" form. Their answers provide the frame, to be filled willfully but logically, of the narratives.

Typical of these is *The Hopkins Manuscript* (1939), by Robert C. Sherriff. In this it is pretended that centuries after the event there is discovered a unique memoir of the final days and the consequences of a cataclysm that ruined western Europe and opened it to oriental conquest. There are actually three related catastrophes: the moon, thrown off course, moves toward the earth, strikes a glancing blow in western Europe, and subsides in the mid-Atlantic; it is discovered that the new landmass is rich in natural resources, and the European nations mobilize their remaining power to fight for them; encouraged by European disunity, an Eastern horde, led by Selim the Liberator, prepares to subjugate the West. As the story ends, the forces of Selim have swept through feeble opposition, occupied Vienna and Berlin, sacked Venice and Milan. They have passed the Rhine, and their guns can be heard in England itself. Probably they have gone on to occupy the mid-Atlantic moon, while a ruined London waits on the convenience of their conquest. This is the nightmare not only of Edgar Hopkins but of many who have lived in fear of another swarming of hordes from the East.

There is finally a group of fantasies derived from showing societies that, because of prevailing values, attitudes, and styles of living within a group of persons, are exotic beyond credibility. The fantasy society is created not by external conditions, but by the existence and interaction of some small and concentrated community of persons who share strange values, whose total outlook and communication are determined by extreme snobbery, preciosity, affection, ennui, or the like. So complete is their eccentricity that they rarely need discuss it. It is simply an accepted norm among them. Moreover, it is a peculiarity of these fantasies that no more widely disseminated, competing norm is represented. The asserted exposure of comedy and satire rarely occurs in these fantasies. Yet they are predominantly comic, partly because the reader may be trusted to judge the eccentricity by his own standards and partly because they are usually rich in scenes in which the characters expose themselves by their excesses. It is axiomatic that few sights are intrinsically more ridiculous than those in which people are caught taking themselves too seriously. This is a repeated, almost a steady, occurrence in the fantasies of bizarrerie. So absorbed are these social groups in their own orchidaceous ways that their idiosyncrasy is self-evident. Comment, or even climactic scenes in which sense triumphs over the ridiculous, would be otiose.

The most persistent practitioner of such fantasy was Ronald Firbank, who wrote no other kind of fiction, and Norman Douglas contributed brilliantly to it in *South Wind.* Most of Firbank's work belongs to the tradition of the conversation novel as established in English by Peacock. But whereas Peacock isolates his performers in a country house, the isolation of Firbank's characters results from their tastes and mind sets. He does not utilize arranged opposition of ideas as does Peacock. Though Firbank's people bicker among themselves and talk maliciously of those not present, they are fundamentally at home together in an exotic community of pose and modishness, which may be called dandyism. Peacock's interest was mainly ideological, Firbank's psychological, though in no disciplinary sense. Ernest Jones rightly observes: "The tradition of the contemporary novel now closest to our sensibility is that established by Joyce and Virginia Woolf. To this tradition, in his own eccentric fashion, Firbank belongs." [4]

It is difficult to describe Firbank's method because there appears to be little of it. Plot lines and causal development are scarcely observable. Thematic centers, if they exist, can only be inferred. In most fantasies there is an early establishing of the impossible made fact, and the perverse illusion dominates the entire work. One is soon aware in reading any of Firbank's novels that he is watching an unbelievable display, but to find the point at which the exotic becomes the norm is impossible. Since events and action play little part in Firbank's fictional method,

4. Introduction to *Three Novels* (Norfolk, Conn.: New Directions, 1951), p. vii.

it is not surprising that the necessary illusion is an emanation from the atmosphere of his novels rather than an objective positing of a condition contrary to fact. The main components of Firbank's development are the talk of his characters and interspersed paragraphs of description and explanation. Few novelists have relied more heavily on dialogue, and few have made it more various and mobile. Cyril Connolly observes: "A book by Firbank is in the nature of a play where the descriptive prose passages correspond to stage directions." [5] The chatter seems to run on endlessly, and it is often difficult to say what the people are talking about. But it is a steady revelation of what they are— their vanities, hypocrisies, perversities, and infatuations are paraded in a mockery that rarely relents. Firbank is, technically, the least obtrusive of authors, but his amusement at the display is implicit throughout. Firbank never speaks in his own person, but in his descriptions there is a tone of ironical sympathy with the speakers that reinforces the revelations of the dialogue. It is customary to praise good dialogue for its authenticity, by which is meant partly that the recorded speech is what one would expect of the characters and partly that it is generally familiar to or accessible to the imagination of the reader. In both respects it puts no excessive demand on him. By this standard the dialogue of Firbank is unnatural. This no doubt alienates some readers at the outset and often annoys those who read him with approval. It is actually necessary that Firbank's dialogue be exotic, for this is his principal means of defining the inhabitants of the fantasy world that was his material.

To ascertain Firbank's methods more closely, it will be advantageous to examine *The Flower beneath the Foot* (1923). This is certainly no better than his other social fantasies, but in it seems to me concentrated all that is peculiarly his. It is, moreover, somewhat more clearly organized than others, though it still shows Firbank's characteristic freedom of movement within a casual structure.

Two quotations from the pretended "confessions" of Saint Laura de Nazianzi are presented as the epigraph: "Some girls are born organically good: I wasn't." "It was about my eight-

5. *Enemies of Promise* (Boston: Little, Brown, 1939), pp. 45–46.

eenth year that I conquered my *Ego.*" The main narrative line
concerns the disappointment in love of the future saint when
her lover, His Weariness Prince Yousef, philanders his way toward marriage with the English Princess Elsie. We first see Laura
Lita Carmen Etoile de Nazianzi, niece of Her Gaudiness the
Mistress of the Robes (the Duchess of Cavaljos), in the court,
where it is her duty to read elevating tracts to an inattentive
queen, Her Dreaminess. The Prince has casually made love to
her, and she expects the best. She will be queen. But even faced
with such triumph, she does not forget the piety learned at the
Convent of the Flaming-Hood, and prays in a manner befitting
her fancied prospect: "Oh! help me, heaven . . . to be decorative and to do right! Let me always look young, never more than
sixteen or seventeen—at the *very* outside, and let Yousef love me
—as much as I do him. And I thank you for creating such a dar-
ling, God (for he's a perfect dear), and I can't tell you how much
I love him; especially when he wags it! I mean his tongue. . . .
Bless all the sisters at the Flaming-Hood above all Sister Ursula.
. . . and be sweet, besides, to old Jane. . . . Show me the
straight path! And keep me from the malicious scandal of the
court. Amen." [6] But she learns that her prince has been playing,
with the Marquesa Pizzi-Parma, with a dancer, with the wife of
the Master of the Horse. His marriage is announced. She retires
to the convent of her childhood, and from the vantage point of
the wall watches the nuptial procession: "Oblivious of what she
did, she began to beat her hands, until they streamed with blood,
against the broken glass ends upon the wall: 'Yousef, Yousef,
Yousef . . .' " (p. 256). With this the novel ends, and presumably here begins the life that led to sanctification and the composition of a spiritual autobiography.

So far *The Flower beneath the Foot* may seem a burlesque of
court life and the pious maiden who fulfills the convention of
taking the veil in her disappointment. And it is such; burlesque
and parody, even when there is no direct object of imitation,
can be used to create fantasy. But his main narrative line is repeatedly interrupted, sometimes apparently forgotten, as Firbank
fills the novel with the vagaries of fashionable life in Kairoulla,

6. *Five Novels* (Norfolk, Conn.: New Directions, 1949), p. 151.

which makes Cockaigne seem by comparison as exotic as Gopher Prairie. These deviations from the main line occur casually, at any point, with no apparent cause, then disappear in favor of other diversions, only to recur as capriciously later on. The attentive reader, however, can easily see in them a full and somewhat Shandean rendering not only of an environment but of an entire bizarre style of living, which is the essence of Firbank's fantasy.

Most prominent of the noncentral presentations is the fashionable and self-indulgent Roman Catholic piety, an extrapolation from the aestheticized religiosity that became prominent late in the nineteenth century with Ernest Dowson and Lionel Johnson. Aberrant forms of religious observance recur frequently throughout Firbank's work. In *The Flower beneath the Foot* there is the Convent of the Flaming-Hood, a church coterie at court, a group of priests used to cosseting their charges, and Mlle. de Nazianzi herself. The general tenor of Pisuergan spiritual life is well expressed in this passage:

> And in this difficult time of spiritual distress, made more trying perhaps because of the blazing midsummer days and long, pent feverish nights, Mademoiselle de Nazianzi turned in her tribulation towards religion. The ecclesiastical set at court, composed of some six or so ex-Circes, under the command of the countess Yvorra, were only too ready to welcome her, and invitations to meet Monsignor this or "Father" that, who were constantly being *coaxed* from their musty sacristies and wan-faced acolytes in the capital, in order that they might officiate at Masses, Confessions, and Breakfast-parties *à la fourchette*, were lavished daily on the bewildered girl. Messages, and hasty informal lightly-pencilled notes, too, would frequently reach her; such as: "I shall be pouring out cocoa after dinner in bed. Bring your biscuits and join me!" . . . or a rat-a-tat from a round-eyed page and: "The Countess's comp'ts and she'd take it a Favour if you can make a 'station' with her in chapel later on," or: "The Marchioness will be birched tomorrow, and *not* today." Oh, the charm, the flavour of the religious world! Where match it for interest and variety! [P. 202]

The passage is consonant with Firbank's representation of religious preciosity throughout the novel and in such other works as

Vainglory and *Valmouth*. The probing of a deviant prince of the church in *Concerning the Eccentricities of Cardinal Pirelli* is more profound and in part compassionate.

Firbank uses two standard devices to portray a fantasy society. Many of his people bear characterizing names, in accordance with a long-standing tradition of formal satire and stage comedy, which came early into prose fiction and has maintained its influence there. Some of these names have already been mentioned. Others are Countess Medusa Rappa, Lord Limpness (Lord Tiredstock's third son), Mrs. Chilleywater, April Flowers, Father Nostradamus, and Count Cabinet. Such is the effect of these, and of the general extravagance, that even the names that might conceivably be found in a telephone directory or a court gazette take on a similar characterizing coloration. Such naming was one of Firbank's habits. Examples abound in all his novels, always with the same effect.

Firbank had a flair too for the small scene, sometimes in dialogue and sometimes not, which ends in a satirical bit or a special revelation of the bizarre. Of the many instances in *The Flower beneath the Foot* the following is typical:

> Lying amid the dissolving bath crystals while his manservant deftly bathed him [the Hon. "Eddy" Monteith], he fell into a sort of coma, sweet as a religious trance. Beneath the rhythmic sponge, perfumed with *Kiki*, he was St. Sebastian, and as the water became cloudier, he was Teresa . . . and he would have been, most likely, the Blessed Virgin herself but that the bath grew gradually cold. "You're looking a little pale, sir, about the gills!" the valet solicitiously observed, as he gently dried him. The Hon. "Eddy" winced. "I forbid you ever to employ the word gill, Mario," he exclaimed. "It is inharmonious, and in English it jars; whatever it may do in Italian." "Over-tired, sir, was what I meant to say." "Basta!" his master re-replied, with all the brilliant glibness of the Berlitz school. [P. 178]

The cap line scores perhaps on an easy target, but such almost self-contained tours de force occur frequently in Firbank's novel and give points of focus within his normal diffuseness of presentation. This scene emphasizes physical and sexual decadence. Homosexuality, androgynism, and other deviations from the norm drift through Firbank's novels like a mist of comic perfume. Ordinary heterosexuality is rare, and when it does occur it is afflicted with an etiolation that renders it less than serious. There are few exceptions; Firbank is not the author for sexual passion treated straight.

Sufficiently in *The Flower beneath the Foot*, but even more in other novels, Firbank exploits the dedication of his vainglorious groups to obscure culture. Of Firbank's own knowledge Sir Osbert Sitwell remarks: "He was not, I think, a deeply read man, but his reading was very different from the rather blowsy pastures so well cropped by the ordinary 'literary man.' French novels, French poetry and eighteenth-century memoirs of every European country composed the bulk of it, and in these matters he was excessively well-informed, yet often in his books there flashes out an allusion to some subject or another on which one would not have expected him to be an authority, but which this reference proved him to have mastered." [7]

"An authority" I beg leave to doubt, but that Firbank had a facility in wide and sometimes esoteric knowledge is indisputable. This is not so much the point as is the use he made of it in anatomizing his societies. His characters are busy name-and-title-droppers, generous providers of allusions and quotations. They live in an ambience of superficial culture; it is part of their small talk, his version of cocktail party conversation. And this milieu, as he presents it, is not at all demanding. Those who do not understand an allusion or do not recognize a quotation have only to pretend or to counter with something else, and their position remains secure. Penetrative discussion of anything would be *demodé*; it does not occur. Thus Firbank uses a kind of cultural patter to define another dimension of his groups.

We have grown used to the direct presenting of knowledge in prose fiction. By way of Des Esseintes, Huysmans has instructed generations of readers in the subtle delights of precious stones and Silver Latin authors and French poets. Several of the novels of Thomas Mann, especially *The Magic Mountain* and the Joseph tetralogy, are compendia of learning and intellectual history. To know as much as Joyce requires would cost a life-

7. Introduction to ibid., p. xviii.

time. But in these cases, as in others that might be cited, the presentation of knowledge is substantive. In Firbank it is different. The cultural talk of his characters is a patina only. For them to skip lightly from one reference to another is a way of their revealing membership in a coterie dominated by chic. In this respect, as in others, Firbank creates and anatomizes social enclaves of such preciosity that they could exist in fantasy only. Indeed, he made a career of such anatomies. He is one of the few authors who devoted himself to fantasy.

The exotic society of *South Wind*, a novel better known than Firbank's, is less spectacular. In it the sense of place is kept before the reader's attention, and the fantasy-illusion is effective in part because of the comparisons he repeatedly makes between the real and the invented. We have Norman Douglas's word for it that Nepenthe is "a composite place," "two-thirds imaginary, and the remaining third distilled out of several Mediterranean islands." The physical details of the island—climate, sea, cliffs, foliage, sunshine, the fountain of Saint Elias, and a hundred other natural features—are kept vividly to the fore. This is part of Douglas's demonstration that pagan man and nature live in intimate rapport.

Important as setting is—more important than in any novel of Firbank—*South Wind* is a fantasy because again it displays a bizarre society in action. Douglas's method is more clearly organized than Firbank's. Into Nepenthe, beset from time to time by the sirocco, comes the young missionary bishop of Bampopo in Africa. He is the youngest bishop of the Church of England and has done the work of his immense diocese with such zeal that he is exhausted, unfit ever to return. He has, moreover, found something in the savagery of the natives that is appealing; he is no longer convinced that they must be Christianized. Hence Mr. Heard, as he prefers to be called, is ready to have his values changed. But only ready; what he will find on Nepenthe is yet alien to the muscular Christianity that retains a hold on him. And so he comes, this man of goodwill and present uncertainty, into contact with such paganism and amorality as he has never seen before. At the end the bishop is educated, in accordance with a program of life that likely Douglas himself advocated:

There was something bright and diabolical in the tone of the place, something kaleidoscopic—a frolicsome perversity. Purifying, at the same time. It swept away the cobwebs. It gave you a measure, a standard, whereby to compute earthly affairs. Another landmark passed; another milestone on the road to enlightenment. The period of doubt was over. His values had righted themselves. He had carved out new and sound ones; a workable, up-to-date theory of life. He was in fine trim. His liver—he forgot that he ever had one. Nepenthe had done him good all around. And he knew exactly what he wanted. A return to the Church, for example, was out of the question. His sympathies had outgrown the ideal of that establishment; a wave of pantheistic benevolence had drowned its smug little teachings. The Church of England! What was it still good for? A stepping-stone possibly towards something more respectable and humane; a warning to all concerned of the folly of idolizing dead men and their ghosts. The Church? Ghosts! [8]

Something like this E. M. Forster meant in remarking, "The Mediterranean is the human norm." And variations on this theme, in which Anglo-Saxons find truth-with-serenity somewhere between the Bosphorus and the Pillars of Hercules, pervade the rich literature of neopaganism in the twentieth century.

It is his experience of two weeks with the exotic society of Nepenthe that educates the young bishop and provides the developmental substance of the novel. This society is an amalgam of native and foreign, civilized and barbaric, enlightened and fanatic, genuine and fraudulent, benevolent and malicious. The foreigners are mainly refugees. The government, such as it is, of the island is in the hands of known rascals. The community is full of conflicts and hatreds. The fanatic parish priest, often called Torquemada, can scarcely endure Don Francesco, the fat youngish monsignor who has cheerfully adjusted his morality to the ineradicable paganism of Nepenthe. Mrs. Parker occupies herself in inventing slander concerning the whole population. The governing officials are outraged by Miss Wilberforce's habit of drunkenness and public undressing; they almost convulse themselves to get her taken off to a sanitorium. The local club,

8. *South Wind* (1917; reprint ed., New York: Modern Library, 1925), p. 432.

run for his personal profit by Mr. Parker, is the scene of frequent riot and breakage of furniture. But somehow the place and the whole society can absorb these violences and remain unified. Nepenthe can absorb any kind of adulterant, however depraved or eccentric, and remain essentially the same. And the genius of the place so works on those who understand it—and if he will accept the invitation, the reader—that they perceive moral values undistorted. To those who can see with the clarity of the local sunshine, Miss Wilberforce is no menace and the girls who give their favors to those who pay for them are no vessels of uncleanliness. They are simply living according to their natures. The severest test for Mr. Heard comes when he sees his kinswoman, Mrs. Meadows, murder Mr. Muklen. There is enough priest and Englishman left in him that he has a fearful struggle of conscience before he can decide that her action was right, the only defense she could take against the threat, to herself and her child, of an evil force. So far has he come, and he could have done so only in Nepenthe.

Norman Douglas displays this society to the reader in all its fullness. Many persons are given individual attention. Nepenthe is full of people—Mr. Keith, Mr. Martens, the Count—who will hold forth concerning their beliefs. Social gatherings, public functions, processions abound, and again the society reveals itself for the curiously unified diversity that it is. Since it is a place with a past as well as a present, Douglas intersperses chapters of its history—the legends of Saint Dodekanus and Saint Eulalia, the career of the good Duke Alfred, his enumeration of the fountains, now all but one dry.

South Wind is the fullest of all the anatomies of exotic society, and the most dominated by the propaganda of neopaganism. Concern with the propaganda may be postponed. The anatomy is conducted in all ways—conversations, monologues, descriptions, historical and archaeological digressions, penetrations into the minds and secret histories of the characters, and a persistent enough line of action to keep the narrative moving. All is presented, moreover, with a compassionate irony and candor that are not far from the spirit of the place itself. A completer construct of a fancied society would be hard to conceive.

Impossible societies are portrayed in many other fantasies, societies of the past, the future, of other planets, and unknown places of this earth, in dream projections, and the like. This is only to say that in fantasy, as in other kinds of prose fiction, one can scarcely place characters in relation to each other and to some kind of environment without fabricating at least a rudimentary society. Those discussed in this chapter, however, differ in several respects from the societies generated in the course of fantasies based on essentially other methods. Here I have been concerned with societies that are the direct and primary result of an effort to present their impossibility in its fullness. The anatomy has been the fantasists' evident purpose. Sometimes, but rarely, the representation itself is the limit of purpose. Often the author had, whether he obscured it or not, a programmatic motivation. By a combination of the fiction per se and the comparisons the reader will make from its stimulus, the author hopes to persuade by pretendedly objective—or if not objective, then defensible—illustration. Most social fantasy is thus basically earnest. There are happy exceptions in the submethod practiced by Firbank and Norman Douglas. It must be noted, however, that Douglas too makes his values and his partisanships clear; it is one of his triumphs that in doing so he yet maintained the comic tone of *South Wind.*

"What is life like in an elsewhere remote enough to be beyond any factually based imagining?" This question, which can take many forms, is intrinsically engaging to human curiosity. Whatever his motive, the social fantasist exploits this interest.

eight

Organized Innocence

Among most people who have attained majority but have not yet retired from steady employment, there is a tacit agreement that only they are competent to conduct the affairs of the world. Those who claim this competence possess a power that they justify by calling themselves practical, experienced, sensible, enterprising, responsible, and the like. Whether by intent or presumption, they exclude from their status children, adolescents, the aged, artists, dreamers, prophets, saints, drunkards, eccentrics, animals, and other types too numerous to mention here. This agreement as to worth I call the "adult convention."

It has some features worth noting. Although the term "adult" signifies a position somewhere within the age span I have suggested, it also implies a state of mind or an elevated self-appraisal. The uncritical participant in the adult convention believes or assumes without thought that he is superior to those who evidently do not qualify and to those qualifiers who have compromised their standing beyond redemption. Many people share in the convention somewhat uneasily. Their possession of the flattering notion of self may be disturbed by what they know of their own potentialities for deviation; they may even grant a sneaking approval to limited deviation. They may be aware also of such tendencies in others, who must therefore hold their honorific positions, particularly if they happen to be prominent in public life, by posturing. They may recognize that the adult convention has in it an element of presumption, even fraud, and that to make it into a sovereign standard is a short way to tyranny. And yet, as every parent, teacher, or senior executive knows, when a serious challenge or dissent occurs, even the person who has reservations about the adult convention will resort to its sanctions.

Thus a contest between adult and nonadult (of whatever kind) is one of the most familiar themes of imaginative litera-

ture, and capable of innumerable variations. It is inexhaustible
in yielding both comedy and pathos. Fantasists too have drawn
upon it, but in a way peculiar to themselves. They rarely represent the conflict directly. Rather, without argument or assertion
they attribute to some nonadult being or group the intelligence,
purposiveness, and resolution that the adult convention claims for
itself alone. This attribution is the inception point of their narrative. It is sometimes possible from the narrative to infer a
dissent from the adult convention. Sometimes the story is self-
contained, without any overtone of controversy.

In the fantasies that relate to this conflict there is a specialized
aspect. Of all the types outside the adult convention, these fantasies concentrate upon animals, upon children, or upon people
who are in some significant respect childlike. All three are shown
as having the heightened capabilities that the convention claims
for adults alone. Closely related is a thematic uniformity. In
some way these fantasies all represent innocence in action. I
would not pretend to decide what is cause and what effect in
this matter. Do fantasists choose to concern themselves with
animals and children in order to portray innocence? Or, having
without preconception centered their narrative on such characters, do they find that they have as a consequence revealed the
activities of innocence? It is possible that were the histories of
composition of all the works known, both progressions would
appear to have occurred. Fortunately, a knowledge of the cause
and effect sequence is not necessary for a critical understanding
of this group of fantasies.

It is necessary, however, to give some thought to the meaning
of innocence. In an independent note written on one of the
pages of *The Four Zoas* William Blake proclaimed: "*Unorga-
niz'd Innocence: An Impossibility. Innocence dwells with Wisdom, but never with ignorance.*" [1] It would be ridiculous to assume that the writers of fantasies centering on innocence had
this apothegm of Blake in mind or were in any way following
the sometimes darkling illumination he has offered to many since
his time. Yet most—possibly all—of them would likely agree

1. See *The Complete Writings of William Blake*, ed. Geoffrey Keynes (London: Nonesuch Press; New York: Random House, 1957), pp. 338, 380, 905.

that far from being a state of chaos, dormant will, or unawareness, innocence is an organized dynamic condition. In conformity with the moral theology of his church, Hilaire Belloc wrote: "No one can understand the value of innocence who does not understand its positive quality. The word does not mean (as its derivation might make one think) a mere absence of evil; for there would seem to be no evil in a lump of clay, yet it has no innocence. We predicate innocence of a will which might turn to evil later on, but has not yet done so. Therefore the word connotes a will in action, but a will in action for good in some degree. And since it is a will in action without any evil intent, therefore it is a will wholly good—though perhaps illinstructed. . . ." [2] A moment's reflection will reveal that this statement describes the condition of Milton's Adam and Eve before the Fall, with the exception that the discourse and answers of the archangel Raphael left them anything but "illinstructed."

Belloc concedes that the innocent may "turn to evil later." If so, it is presumably no longer innocent. It would be comforting if all the fantasists agreed with him. But they are artists, not lay expositors of moral theology, and accordingly it is not always "good" children and animals that populate their pages. It will appear, however, that even the "bad" ones, as judged by conventional standards, are in an important sense yet innocent. That is, they are inexperienced in adult presumptions and the ways of the world; this is even a possible meaning of Belloc's "ill-instructed." An understanding of this discrimination informs the pages of Blake's *Songs of Innocence* and *Songs of Experience*.

As the fantasists have explored and exploited the quality, several further properties have become manifest. To understand their practice it is necessary not only to liberate the idea of innocence from any negative connotation, but also to extend it to include naïve faith, psychic and emotional integrity, and singleness of purpose, particularly as all these can express themselves in directed energy, whether to constructive or destructive ends. Fantasists are not rigorous about where innocence may be found; they do not see

2. "On Innocence," in *The Silence of the Sea* (New York: Sheed and Ward, 1940), p. 249.

it as the possession of the pious, or the obedient, or the poor in spirit. Indeed, they are likely to show the innocent as having an opposite disposition. Many do idealize children, rustics, and animals because all three are parts of uncorrupted nature.[3] But as the fantasists represent them, children, rustics, and animals often instrument their simplicity with a shrewdness that can compete with the tactics of sophistication. Finally, in respect to literary result a commitment to a theme of innocence may yield fantasy that is rhapsodic or satiric.

The fantasies in which children, childlike adults, and animals predominate show an astonishing variety. At one pole is the idyllic rendering of innocence in W. H. Hudson's *Green Mansions* (1904), at the other the social satire of John Collier's *His Monkey Wife* (1930). Between the extremes are a number of works in which the energy and intelligence of the innocent are represented more moderately. An analysis of the extremes will reveal the limits of possibility in this kind of fantasy.

When I label *Green Mansions* idyllic and rhapsodic, the reader may at first demur that the book begins in violence and ends with a serenity that the narrator has wrested from grief and madness. Cruelty, treachery, fear, superstition, and vengeance are never far away through the course of the narrative. This is true. It is also true that the human beings in *Green Mansions* are all to some degree evil. Old Nuflo is a deceiver; the narrator, though he adores purity, cannot achieve it, and he is in his rage capable of crimes against nature. Hudson's savages are as far from noble as baseness can be. Not being wholly in nature, these people can at best stand in awe of it. But Rima embodies a different order of being. "A creation," as William Y. Tindall observes, "not of Hudson the naturalist, but of Hudson the transcendentalist,"[4] she is not wholly of human or of physical nature. I surmise that Hudson intended her to be the fusion and epitome of both with a power over both, though because of her

---

3. Hilaire Belloc would object to the inclusion of animals: "And talking of beasts, beasts also have a sort of parody of innocence about them sometimes, but it is never real innocence." Ibid., pp. 251–52.

4. *Forces in Modern British Literature, 1885–1946* (New York: Knopf, 1947), p. 367.

gentleness more vulnerable than either. Against the blackness of her human associates Rima blazes forth like a flame of purity.

I do not suggest that human and physical nature are equally blended in Rima. Her human aspect alone is not impressive. She is a quiet girl in a dull dress, living meanly with her grandfather. It is her bird personality that lifts her into vividness.[5] Immediately after noting that the Rima he meets in Nuflo's hut is "silent, shy, and spiritless," Abel compares her with a humming-bird, in flight "a living prismatic gem," but alight "like some common dull-plumaged little bird sitting listless in a cage." Thus he establishes an identity between the contrasting appearances. In her bird personality she speaks a language that, though not directly intelligible to men, is meaningful and compelling, better than the inadequate Spanish she must use with human beings. Absorbed into nature, Rima is bright in a dress of cobweb sheen, quick, agile, imperious, gay, eloquent, tender, and wasplike in anger. It is her natural part that elevates her human and creates the forest queen.

I have suggested that Rima's innocence is informed and dynamic. This makes her a force for good and an expression of beauty; throughout *Green Mansions* the good and the beautiful are identified. The creatures that have some share in her character are incapable of ugliness and evil, even when they are preying on each other. There is grandeur, but no cacophony, in the fearsome chorus of howling monkeys that deafens Abel. The hunting spider and the coral snake whose sting is the occasion of Abel's joining Nuflo's household—these and many other manifestations are both blameless and vital. Rima is of them; they will not harm her, and they depend on her protection. But she excels her subjects in penetration. She alone of the forest creatures can recognize human evil for what it is and oppose it. Especially, she will not tolerate the eating of flesh, and the Guayana Indians

5. One must consider also that Hudson often expressed his delight in birds. "Birds certainly gave me more pleasure than other animals . . . and I take the reason of it to be not only because birds exceed in beauty, but also on account of the intensity of life they exhibit—a life so vivid, so brilliant, as to make that of other beings, such as reptiles and mammals, seem a rather poor thing by comparison." *Far Away and Long Ago* (London and Toronto: Dutton, 1925), p. 205.

believe that she is death to hunters in her part of the forest. Her human component, however, is a source of her weakness and finally of her destruction. She is not only a queen of nature but also an ignorant girl longing for membership in a family. This longing leads to Rima's futile journey, the solitary return, and her falling victim to the Indians, who burn her.

My statement does not yet fully convey Hudson's emphasis. In the moral scheme of *Green Mansions* only nature is pure, and only man is vile, even Abel, who comes as near as one can to transcending the inherent malevolence of Cain and his progeny. These are the enemies of nature's innocence, and *Green Mansions* violates a convention of romance, in that Rima has neither a rescuer nor the strength to save herself. The conclusion which Hudson urges is that in the corrupt world innocence can have only a remote, precarious, and transient existence.

Appealing as she is, the portrayal of Rima, the center of the fantastic illusion, reveals serious artistic flaws. Whether a character or an embodiment, she is unresolved—as Robert Hamilton says, "neither spirit, nor bird, nor complete human being." [6] Hudson's attempt to create in her an epitome out of disparate elements did not achieve the requisite unity, as one finds it, for example, in the central figures of *Wuthering Heights*. It follows that the love which grows between Rima and Abel seems amorphous and unreal. It troubles the reader and perhaps impeded Hudson himself. So at least Hamilton surmises: "With the removal of the artificial erotic element Hudson was at last able to give full rein to his imagination. In its fierce note of fantasy and tragedy it [the culminating action of the book] is akin to *Marta Riquelme*, and is surpassed nowhere else." [7] But with Rima's death the innocence that has been the thematic center through the major part of the book disappears, and there is left only Abel's rage purging itself to quietude.

Little need be said of the fantasy setting that Hudson used for his idyll of innocence in nature. It has been praised for its beauty of imagery, for the sense of mystery that invests it. Whatever else, the forest of *Green Mansions* is certainly a world apart from

6. W. H. *Hudson: A Vision of Earth* (London: Dent, 1946), p. 67.
7. Ibid., p. 69.

known geography, just as the action is so much apart from the ways of the world that it intensifies one of them only, the workings of malevolence. William Y. Tindall aptly describes the land of *Green Mansions* thus: "This Venezuelan refuge is to be compared only to that jungle of improbable trees which Henri Rousseau arranged. A man of the pampas, who had never seen a jungle, Hudson allowed his fancy to decree a place where natural beauty is unimpaired by nature." [8]

It is not surprising that Hudson's exotic romance has claimed many rhapsodic admirers. A world that never was, peopled with strange beings who embody both loveliness and violence, is an unfailing tourist attraction.

The second polar example, *His Monkey Wife*, is a satire achieved by confronting the innocence of the central figure and the shoddiness of the world about her. The only exception to shoddiness is Mr. Fatigay, Emily's master and finally her husband, who remains until late in the action a moral neuter, dominated by his own lassitude. The reader is required to believe that a female chimpanzee is capable not only of a better than human devotion to her master, but also of learning to think, read, and write. She never learns to speak. Single-mindedly Emily serves her Mr. Fatigay, in Boboma and London, saves him from false accusation, from the disaster of marrying Amy Flint, from poverty and starvation. In the end Mr. Fatigay, delighted with the trick by which Emily has made herself rather than Miss Flint his bride, returns to Africa with a better wife than he could have found among women.

His Monkey Wife is a highly stylized novel; it will remind readers somewhat of "Saki" and of Ronald Firbank. The basis of Collier's artifice, the illusion that dominates, is simplicity itself. He carries to a logical extreme the notion that animals are more capable of devotion than human beings. Because of her devotion, Emily seeks to please Mr. Fatigay by learning all but one of the communication skills. It is awkward that Emily must express her thoughts in writing or typing, but Mr. Fatigay seems pleased with a genuinely dumb wife.

Around this simple pretense Collier groups his objects of

8. *Forces in Modern British Literature*, p. 367.

mockery. Emily herself betrays a well-meaning gaucherie; her thought processes and expression reveal the effects of unassimilated literary and moral culture. By comparison, Emily's limitations are amiable, and she serves as a means of exposing the real faults of the fashionable society that surrounds her—the egocentric triviality and hardness of Amy Flint, the emptiness of the bright young people of her set. The constricted world that Collier creates is a travesty in which excesses—whether of egocentricity, folly, or preciosity—are the norm. This environment is as effectively separate and subject to its own laws of probability as Hudson's forest, or Erewhon, or fairyland. Accepting Emily as presented takes the reader into accepting the world of the action as the only place where such things could exist and happen—such things as her becoming the Belle of the British Museum and the dancing star of a revue. One wonders if Emily is a reembodiment of the estimable Sir Oran Haut-ton of Peacock's *Melincourt*, who also is a center of sense and civility in a microcosm of folly and self-importance. But for all the uniqueness of life as the book projects it, *His Monkey Wife* suggests analogies with observable human nature and social intercourse. The effect of these analogies is to deprecate what we know of societies dominated by vanity and hypocrisy. The establishment of a unique illumination from which searching shafts of light play upon what we experience is a standard method of satirical fantasy.

In fantasies between these extremes are several works by Walter de la Mare, Kenneth Grahame, and T. H. White. Their purveyors of organized innocence are again children and humanized animals, who share a nonacquisitive, imaginative, adventurous psychology. Their narratives are hospitable to magic and marvels, which are treated as natural phenomena of their settings. These settings tend to be holiday places, more interesting and lovely than the familiar world, places where conflict and evil are either nonexistent or sure to be overcome and menace provides no worse than excitement. These are the characteristics of the river, the Wildwood, and Pan's island in *The Wind in the Willows*, the Lilliputian island known as Mistress Masham's Repose in T. H. White's novel of the same name. Even more magical is Tishnar, a creation of Walter de la Mare, the center of a dream theology and cosmogony.

A more nearly recognizable world, with seemingly familiar conflicts of good and evil, appears in several fantasies of G. K. Chesterton. But here again the central dynamic is an innocence that is variously resourceful, intelligent, strong, but always single-minded. His best-known figure of this kind is Father Brown, that whimsical embodiment of the serpent and the dove; Chesterton entitled one collection of stories *The Innocence of Father Brown* (1911). Despite the recurrent suggestion that detective fiction is a form of fantasy,[9] I cannot include it in this study. Fortunately Chesterton represented somewhat similar figures in three other works—Humphry Pump and Patrick Dalroy in *The Flying Inn* (1914), Auberon Quin and Adam Wayne in *The Napoleon of Notting Hill* (1914), and Michael Herne in *The Return of Don Quixote* (1927). They cannot be included within the adult convention; they are organized innocence, each dedicated to a single though inclusive value, and embattled against powers that threaten widespread oppression. Humphry Pump and Patrick Dalroy, publican and adventurer respectively, keep alive the last English pub, that is, the last stronghold of traditional English liberty, against the totalitarian efforts of Lord Ivywood, who in his madness is imposing a version of Islam on England.

In *The Napoleon of Notting Hill* the proponents of the right are a humorist and a fanatic. The one is "elected" king, since in the period represented (ca. A.D. 1994–2014) the hereditary monarchy has disappeared. In his whimsy he revives a medieval form of government, divides London into its constituent parts, and with elaborate pageantry puts into effect the Charter of the Free Cities. The fanatic Adam Wayne becomes Lord High Provost of Notting Hill. He takes the game seriously, and when an unspecified central authority attempts to put a road through Notting Hill, he arouses the residents to arms to defend their fastness and their rights. Their first defense is successful, but twenty years later they fail. Nonetheless, the effort of Adam Wayne, the

9. See, for example, ibid., pp. 143–44, and Pierre-Georges Castex, *Le conte fantastique en France de Nodier à Maupassant* (Paris: Librairie José Corti, 1951), pp. 402–3.

Napoleon of Notting Hill, is made to signify a victory for the human spirit against forces that would subject it to uniformity and city planning. Moreover, the two leaders—the one fanatic, the other humorous—are joined by Chesterton's euphoria in an alliance that the world needs: "When dark and dreary days come [says Adam Wayne in the concluding exhortation of the book] you and I are necessary, the pure fanatic, the pure satirist. . . . Auberon Quin, we have been too long separated; let us go out together. You have a halberd and I a sword, let us start our wanderings over the world. For we are its two essentials." [10] I doubt that Chesterton ever propounded a more ingenious paradox.

In all three fantasies Chesterton is urging the rightness of personal and social values that were more honored in the past. In all three, especially *The Return of Don Quixote*, much is said about the wrongness of the times and the need to recover a simplicity and sanity that are almost lost. Michael Herne might be speaking for his colleagues, and certainly for Chesterton, when he proclaims: "You all love change and live by change; but I shall never change. It was by change you fell; it is by this madness of change you go on falling. You had your happy moment, when men were simple and sane and normal and as native to this earth as they can ever be. You lost it; and even when you get it back for a moment, you have not the sense to keep it. I shall never change." [11]

This is an appropriate rationale for innocence of the kind Chesterton propagates. It is simple, with moral perplexities dismissed or ignored. It permits the establishment of purity and facilitates clear-cut, exciting conflicts in which the excellence of the protagonists is self-evident. In Chesterton's hands the harshness and bigotry often associated with a unilateral code and program do not emerge to alienate the reader's sympathy. Instead, he is wooed with grace, humor, verbal ebullience, and something that has at least the appearance of wisdom. The Napoleon of Notting Hill does not hesitate to call himself a fanatic, and he

10. *The Napoleon of Notting Hill* (New York and London: John Lane, 1914), pp. 300–301.
11. *The Return of Don Quixote* (New York: Dodd, Mead, 1927), p. 167.

proposes that the expression of this quality is love. Adam Wayne is so endowed by his creator that there is no suggestion in his conduct of the grimness and fury evoked by the names of the famous fanatics of history.[12] Similarly, the eccentricities of Michael Herne, Chesterton's reincarnated Don Quixote, emphasize his unique rightness and benevolence.

Fundamentally, it is innocence organized by energy, conviction, and an unfailing love of mankind that gives Chesterton's heroes their quality. Compromise does not touch them. In the end the conflict between good and evil in these romances of Chesterton becomes as uneven as Milton's war in heaven. Chesterton was not concerned with characterization as the realistic novelist conceives it. His major characters are determined by their allegiances. Thus in psychic and emotional growth they are static; in resolution, however, they are as vigorous as their begetter could make them.

One more work must be considered in this chapter, but apart from the others, for it is more complex. This is *The Green Child*, by Sir Herbert Read. It is a book difficult to classify, for in it one finds important elements of several principles of fantasy. Inasmuch as it develops a fairy tale, which Read reprints from Thomas Keightley's *The Fairy Mythology* in chapter nine of *English Prose Style*, it might be thought a fantasy of extension and adaptation. Since the green child herself is an essentially altered human being, it resembles the fantasy based on a metamorphosed condition. Richard Wasson asserts that the second and third parts—Olivero's establishment of an orderly state in Roncador and his achievement of permanent beauty in the crystalline cave—are utopian, though ironic in the sense that the events release the participants and the reader from dogmatism so that new, experiential affirmations of perfection can be achieved.[13] Wasson's argument is persuasive and the more interesting because of his exposition of the anti-utopian tendencies of Read's political thought. There are, however, difficulties in

12. For a denunciation of Chesterton's political and social principles as expressed in his fiction, see Kenneth M. Hamilton, "G. K. Chesterton and George Orwell: A Contrast in Prophecy," *Dalhousie Review*, 31 (1951), 198–205.

13. "*The Green Child*: Herbert Read's Ironic Fantasy," *PMLA*, 77 (December 1962), 645–51.

the way of justifying the term "utopian fantasy" for the whole of *The Green Child*. To be sure, the third section, which brings the work into unity, represents a realization of a stasis in which the questing spirit achieves union with beauty. But part one, despite its rendering of unbelievable events as fact, contains nothing utopian, and part two, though it recounts the reaching of the highest art in government and a felicitous condition of society, is a narrative of the improbable, not of the impossible. Roncador becomes at best a compromised utopia.

The Green Child may be best understood, I believe, as a fantasy of innocence. It is more complex than many, such as *The Wind in the Willows* and *The Three Mulla-Mulgars*, since innocence and its functions are seen as a contrast to conduct and government that are good because they are simple but short of innocent because they must employ force and fraud. Moreover, all these explorations are carried out both in the memory of Olivero and immediate actions of the two central characters. This makes possible an interplay between history and an ideal timeless condition in which even death seems to be not a termination but a realization of permanence. Also, because Olivero has an unusually precise memory, he is a person of superior reflective capability and accordingly an excellent ruler. The green child—Sally on earth, Siloen in the cave—has none of these qualities. But Olivero's accomplishments require that once in the cave he must be "disintoxicated of all his earthly sentiments," a process she need not go through. Thus are innocence and experience appropriate to different states of being, and experience, even though it has produced a virtuous man, seems of limited value.

A force hostile to innocence is prominent in the first part of *The Green Child*. No single formulation can name this force, which is concentrated in Kneeshaw, whose precocious destructiveness drove Oliver from the village thirty years earlier. Wasson suggests that Kneeshaw "represents the inherent evil of the race, the doctrine of original sin so dear to the hearts of Hulme and Eliot. . . ." [14] This is a persuasive suggestion, but if one adopts it, "inherent evil" must be understood as a personal condition

14. Ibid., p. 648.

rather than a willful dynamic. Thirty years earlier Kneeshaw had been "a boy, whose character was in general sullen and unimpressive," and his act of vandalism revealed no particular ill will toward Oliver. In their next encounter Olivero discovers him trying to force the green child to drink the blood of a newly killed lamb. It is a hideous scene, but again malevolence does not appear, for Kneeshaw says—and there is no reason to disbelieve him—that she has for weeks refused to eat anything solid. "She is wasting away and will die, because she never eats meat, and has no desire to live." [15] Throughout their years of relationship in a kind of marriage, Kneeshaw has been unable to understand her fairy nature, and he has tried to force her to act like a human being. This she cannot do, and she can protect herself from violation of her being only by flight. Throughout the story that Kneeshaw recounts, he shows himself to be dull, uncomprehending, and brutalized, but not malicious. Kneeshaw is guilty only of the grossness of human nature, but that is enough. In the progress toward realized innocence this is the first enemy that must be destroyed.

During two hours of rest after their escape from Kneeshaw but before Olivero and the green child sink beneath the surface of a pool and reach the crystalline caves that are her home, he tells her the story of his life. Being otherworldly, she cannot understand the story or even the language, but she finds his voice musical and enchanting; already her response shows that he has the potential for the pure existence he finally achieves. The story he tells is a straightforward account of one who inadvertently becomes an adventurer and reaches a worldly destiny in being the mild and enlightened despot of Roncador, a remote province of Argentina. He transforms this little area from an oppressed and starving dependency to a condition close to earthly paradise. His methods of doing so, however, are conspiracy, revolt, and ruthless elimination of enemies. He exercises virtue, constructively in building the country and destructively against whatever threatens it. But with accomplishment he grows discontented and wishes to return to the scenes of his early life, particularly to learn how the mystery of the green child was solved. Another

15. *The Green Child: A Romance* (New York: New Directions, n.d.), p. 31.

destiny is drawing him. So he stages his own assassination and escapes, leaving behind the best that political action can achieve.

From this we are to understand that virtue is excellent but short of innocence, because it is worldly, and therefore unsatisfactory. Innocence and perfection he finds in the crystalline caves. Here the life is contemplative, devoted to understanding "the laws of the natural world" and to preparing for a petrified death, which is the highest felicity because it makes permanent "their whole desire: to be one with the physical harmony of the universe" (p. 177). Thus, though the nature of this cave-universe requires much description, though the activities in pursuit of the crystalline ideal are many and gradated, though their rituals are elaborate, the essence of the place is unified and simple, as perfection must be. Siloen resumes this life as if she had never left it, for her innocence has never been disturbed by thirty years' experience in the world. But Olivero the activist must learn everything anew, and this is a slow progress, for all his willingness. Time, however, exerts no pressure in this universe in which all thought and doing are directed toward eternity and in which to philosophize is to learn how to die.

Read reverses the usual understanding of the release that death provides. It is not the soul that is freed from the prison-house of the body, but the body that is at last rid of the troublesome soul. Accordingly, when death comes on Olivero with its slow and painless possession, he feels a "peculiar joy" at the final cessation of vital functions. Siloen dies at the same time, and the two are at last united. "The two bodies were laid side by side in the same trough, and these two who had been separated in life grew together in death, and became a part of the same crystal harmony. The tresses of Siloen's hair, floating in the liquid in which they were immersed, spread like a tracery of stone across Olivero's breast, twined inextricably in the coral intricacy of his beard" (pp. 194–95). These are the final sentences of the book. The union in death of those who were divided in life despite their love is a frequent occurrence in fiction. One thinks particularly of Cathy and Heathcliff and of Maggie and Tom Tulliver. But in *The Green Child* the union comes not because the passions of personal conflict are spent, but because Olivero achieves the innocence or purity that has always been the essence of the fairy Siloen and of her home. Thus a destiny is fulfilled.

The Green Child is a triumph of fantasy notable equally for technical achievement and beauty. In other pages of this study I have complained of arbitrariness and illogic in Read's theory of fantasy. One part of his theory, that the fairy tale is the only true fantasy, he perhaps sought to illustrate in *The Green Child*. Certainly Siloen is an otherworldly being throughout, but beyond this he took such liberties with the fairy tale as to transform it beyond recognition. But this is no cause for complaint. The writer whose theory looks sick when compared with his practice is a familiar figure in literary history. The only regret that attaches to *The Green Child* is that Read wrote nothing else like it.

The display of organized innocence provides delight to most readers, so long as they feel no obligation to live according to its demands. It plays against, but does not threaten, the adult convention, which, for all its daily usefulness, is still part of the world that is too much with us. Innocence, moreover, generates a scheme of virtue simplified, the more attractive because it seems free of the potentialities for abuse inherent in other moral simplifications. Living virtuously and judging correctly require thought and careful discrimination; so busy people are always seeking to reduce the imperatives to a single, objective standard that can command emotional allegiance. Hence blind patriotism, the work ethic, and, for women, the ideal of the spotless maiden who becomes the obedient wife—all agreeably simple criteria and all rich sources of conflict and bigotry. But the innocence that is essential in these fantasies seems free of such unhappy consequences. Further, its natural expression is in energy uncompromised by divided aims. No wonder that Blake proclaimed, "Innocence dwells with Wisdom." The fantasists exploit this principle to produce ethical romances whose very purity assures that for the worldly they will never furnish patterns of life.

nine   Parody and Adaptation

In Chapter two, I discussed the principal features of nonsense writing. These illustrate a restricted manifestation of the intellectual play that is central in my subject. Nonsense resembles a kind of fantasy that originates in arbitrary and fundamental deviation from a literary text or a historical formulation and expresses itself in parody, adaptation, or extension. The fantasies previously described have a thematic center, and the play begins with a countering of some "fact" or convention that has an existence independent of literary embodiment. But those now to be considered are more closely derivative. Instead of a general understanding that is rejected, these have a specific interpretation or fictional object against which they play, and to participate fully in the game the reader should have some knowledge of this context. It follows that perception of contrasts and skewed analogies is an immediate and continuous part of the reader's experience in adaptive fantasies that violate a convention.

Little need be said to prove that the release from the accustomed in fantasy resembles that of nonsense writing, except that it is not necessarily so complete. There is a greater range possible in fantasy than in nonsense. Some fantasies are such unqualified invitations to freedom that they seem to have relevance to nothing but themselves. This may be observed in *The King of Elfland's Daughter*, by Lord Dunsany, and to a high degree in W. H. Hudson's *Green Mansions*. The analogies drawn between these worlds and the reader's derive from his own speculativeness. At the other extreme are quite purposeful fantasies, sometimes satirical and sometimes allegorical. Such are the anti-utopias and the "theological romances" of Charles Williams.

That kind of analogizing which in nonsense writing manifests itself as parody, actual or putative, appears somewhat differently in a number of fantasies. Parody requires a close and detailed adherence to the original. What one finds in prose fiction fantasy is some loose, freer, affiliation—adaptation, sequel, or renarration of established material. The works thus produced are artistically self-contained, but there is nonetheless a steady dependency on the reader's comprehension of and pleasure in the known original. Thus *The Magic Flute* of G. Lowes Dickinson relies on the reader's knowledge of *Die Zauberflöte*. E. M. Forster says this of the adaptation: "It has taken as its mythology the world of Mozart. Tamino, Sarastro, and the Queen of the Night stand in their enchanted kingdom ready for the author's thought, and when these are poured in they become alive and a new and exquisite work is born." [1] Were it not that the opera has an infusion of the fantastic, Dickinson probably could not have produced a fantasy by adaptation, because he takes Mozart's "mythology" seriously. Only when the fantasist imposes a fundamental alteration or alienation can a realistic original be carried on into a fantasy adaptation.

Most derivative fantasies are projected from congenial material and keep the source prominent. Thus C. S. Lewis's *Till We Have Faces* is an expanded redaction of the Cupid and Psyche story, and its subtitle is "A Myth Retold." C. S. Lewis's *Perelandra* is a Venusian recurrence of the conflict of *Paradise Lost*, with the difference that paradise is saved. T. H. White's series *The Once and Future King* renarrates, with the insight gained from perspective, the heritage, coming, dominance, and dissolution of Arthur and his court. White's version is factually faithful to Malory, though he omits much that Malory includes and gives an intimate, domestic, sometimes comical view of the personages and institutions that *Morte d'Arthur* treats heroically.

There are two fantasies that present sequels of a kind. In *The Return of Don Quixote* G. K. Chesterton adds another to the many literary attempts to bring the Knight of La Mancha to England. This twentieth-century embodiment, however, is a crusader and a righter of prevalent wrongs; Chesterton takes him as seriously as Don Quixote took himself. In *After the Death of Don Juan* Sylvia Townsend Warner propounds the story as it would have been if the violater had not fallen into hell during his impious banquet. After all, she pretends, we have only Leporello's word for it, and he is a dubious witness. Instead, Miss

1. *Aspects of the Novel* (New York: Harcourt, Brace, 1927), p. 177.

Warner has Don Juan return in time to Tenorio, where he meets a Doña Ana who has grieved for him and prayed spectacularly for his soul because she has always loved him, even when she was believing that his advances were outrageous. Saint and sinner discover that they are much alike, and each in his way rejects the other in despisal. Their confrontation is sharper than that which Shaw posited in act 3 of *Man and Superman*, and less informed by ideology.

These are sequels in the sense that the activities of characters are continued through events and circumstances that are at variance with the original. Such sequels as *Further Adventures of Robinson Crusoe, Pamela in High Life,* and *The Return of Monte Cristo* simply spin out more of the same overall logic as the parent works; they present no intrinsic innovations. Chesterton and Miss Warner, however, arbitrarily alter the basic formulation of "mythology." Thus they fulfill one of the conditions of parody, though not the others, and the reader's comparisons with the originals grow simultaneously from perceiving similarity and modification. Much the same is true of Lewis's version of Cupid and Psyche and White's of the Arthurian cycle.

It is in arbitrariness, objectification, and sustained intellectual control that prose fiction fantasy approaches nonsense writing. But normally it approaches only. The logic of nonsense is entirely self-contained and internal; fantasy offers a plausible reality, whose logic resembles that to be observed in external reality. Nonsense writing and fantasy, then, are alike in kind but different in the degree of departure from the standards and habits required by discursive logic.

The potentialities for fantasy of the looser discipline of continuation and adaptation can best be revealed by a careful examination of some systematic and extended examples: Elinor Wylie's *The Orphan Angel*, T. H. White's Arthurian tetralogy, and Mark Twain's *A Connecticut Yankee in King Arthur's Court*.

The fascination that Shelley, as poet, man, and embodiment of high romanticism, exerted upon the imagination of Elinor Wylie is well known. It appears repeatedly in her work, but nowhere more fully than in *The Orphan Angel*.[2] Here she pretends

---

2. See Julia Cluck, "Elinor Wylie's Shelley Obsession," *PMLA*, 56 (1941), 841–60.

that Shelley did not really drown in the Bay of Spezzia but was pulled more dead than alive from the sea onto the deck of *The Witch of the West* as she was standing out of Leghorn harbor destined for Boston. He is revived by David Butternut, an earthy young New England seaman, and renamed Shiloh because David has understood thus the murmured name Shelley, and Shiloh seems appropriate in America. So confidently does Elinor Wylie present all this that the reader, mistrusting his memory, may doubt the received account of the recovery of the bodies, the burning of the dead poet in accordance with ancient rites, and the burial of the ashes in the Protestant cemetery in Rome. But if he looks again at Trelawney's narrative and at later biographical sources, he will find their version beyond doubt. Elinor Wylie advances—and continues to advance—a fabrication of the fancy. If the reader is outraged by this, he had best put the book aside.

The story that ensues is structurally simple but rich in development. Shiloh rapidly becomes an able seaman and the devoted friend of the equally devoted David. But once in Boston they turn from the sea and begin the long search for the orphaned sister of Jasper Cross, the man whom David killed—in self-defense, but still it haunts him—in Leghorn. Their journey leads them by stages and various modes of travel from Boston to San Diego. No stranger ever had a more exciting introduction to America, and none ever responded more wholeheartedly. Shiloh is everything that Sterne's learned Smelfungus is not. The two friends experience a great adventure, much diversified by events. But their adventure is also a quest, more definite than that of *Alastor* or *Epipsychidion*, to rescue a maiden and quiet David's remorseful conscience. The quest completed, Shiloh departs from his new-found life and perhaps out of this world as unaccountably as he came.

Engaging as they are, the action and the lavish descriptions of a new land are not the center of fantasy in *The Orphan Angel*. This is rather the projection of Shelley into Shiloh. The Shelley of romanticizing tradition is still present in this new incarnation. Shiloh is accordingly high-spirited, generous, lofty of principle, devoted to beauty. But as new sights and experiences come to him, the traditional character is enriched and elevated to an even more compelling heroism. Shiloh is the opposite of "a beautiful and ineffectual angel beating in the void his luminous wings in vain." He is a swift and tireless strider through the wilderness. He faces danger with equanimity and courteously offers his protection to the weak; Shiloh cannot avoid inspiring the love of frontier maidens, even of a Cheyenne princess, but without giving pain to the smitten repeatedly disengages himself, because of his commitment, unwilling but binding, to "his own domestic bluestocking" Mary in Lerici. Indeed, there are few Americans, no matter how rough or cultivated, with whom Shiloh does not establish an effortless communication. His quick sympathy makes him a citizen of the world in time and space. With no feeling of incongruity he can in a wilderness camp amuse himself after supper by turning one of the choruses from the *Antigone* of Sophocles into English lyrical verse, and a bit later prepare to defend himself from what in the darkness appears to be a bear.

Actually, Elinor Wylie's method is simple. She makes Shelley-become-Shiloh welcome all experience, respond joyously to the beauty, freedom, and dignity of a new world in which the way of life accords with the principles he almost alone espoused in Europe. All the unattractive aspects of the historical Shelley she blandly omits. She makes him at once great-souled and common, heroic and graceful, grave and humorous. Matthew Arnold had said, "Shelley has no humour," but granted him "as quick and sharp a tact as the most practiced man of the world." In Elinor Wylie's version the tact is an expression of courtesy and love, and humor is granted him as if it had never been denied, either by Arnold or by the evidence of Shelley's known actions.

Elinor Wylie began with an arbitrary pretense, projected Shelley into Shiloh, and produced not a character in realistic fiction but a fanciful construct. But she did not stop with this. David Butternut is likewise an elaborate figure or embodiment. Even more, her reconstruction of the rich, varied, exciting life of America in the third decade of the nineteenth century is almost a dream. One acquainted with American history of the 1820s can see in Elinor Wylie's idyll, if not inaccuracies, at least overemphases and omissions. She shows very little, for example, of the harshness and ugliness of rural life of the time. To raise this as a fundamental objection, however, is to ignore or mistake the way in which she is using history. Like many another, Elinor Wylie had a kind of love affair with the American past. This, and not a concern for accuracy, is the determinant of her representation; she was willing to be accurate enough as long as factuality was not her final commitment.

Similarly with her portrait of the orphan angel. Likely Elinor Wylie too could see Shelley plain, but she did not choose to show him so. This would be the obligation of a biographer. The historical Shelley informs and supports her Shiloh, but her figure calculatedly surpasses the model and has a rightful existence as an idealization of the adventurer-poet.

All this is to say that *The Orphan Angel* is a fantasy in which the known, though indispensable, is but the beginning from which the visionary proceeds to its quite different end. It is clear from all of Elinor Wylie's work that she had abundantly the knowledge to be a scholar. But she preferred to be an artist.

Even more ambitious was the sustained effort of T. H. White in his Arthurian tetralogy, *The Once and Future King* (1958), an elaboration based on Malory's work. Its very title echoes the paradoxical formula applicable to Arthur alone: Hic jacet Arthurus Rex quondam Rexque futurus. The four parts—*The Sword in the Stone, The Queen of Air and Darkness* (a much altered but essentially similar version of *The Witch in the Wood*), *The Ill-Made Knight,* and *The Candle in the Wind*—provide not just a historical romance, but a loving, high-spirited adaptation and extension of the cycle, from the coming and self-discovery of Arthur to the dissolution by treachery of that flowering civilization that he brought out for its short glory from the muck and violence of a baronial lawlessness.

One may wonder how with several major Arthurian reconstructions since Tennyson's—those of William Morris and E. A. Robinson and the unfinished works of Charles Williams—yet another presentation can be either justified or interesting. Perhaps the material is inexhaustible and the British myth ever alluring, as Spenser and Milton found it to be. Certainly it should be noted that post-Tennyson versions are most often heroic poetry, with emphasis on the wonder and the tragedy inherent in the stories. T. H. White chose prose fiction, and without at all neglecting the wonder and tragedy of Malory's narrative enriched his own representation with suggestions of psychic and emotional motivation, with comedy and antiquarian farce, and with a fleshing out of what the daily lives and personalities of the Arthurian figures must have been. That they existed he seems never to have doubted. It is a part of his tactics of fantasy to omit, as if there were no such consideration, all discussion of the historicity of Arthur, which has engaged many scholars and speculators. For T. H. White the author, it is simple: the Arthurians lived. Now long separate, we can but dimly know them; therefore he will freely reconstruct them in their fullness. This is the purport of an epigraph to the 1939 version of *The Sword in the Stone*: "And now it is all gone—like an insubstantial pageant faded; and between us and the old English there lies a gulf of mystery which the prose of the historian will never adequately bridge. They cannot come to us, and our imagination can but feebly penetrate to them. Only among the aisles of the cathedral, only as we gaze upon their silent figures sleeping on their tombs, some faint conceptions float before us of what these men were when they were alive." [3]

To put before readers of the twentieth century "what these men were when they were alive" is the principal effort in *The Once and Future King*. For this purpose T. H. White renders them familiarly, not from the accustomed distance of heroic regard. This means that all their aspects—their foolish, petty, wayward, whimsical, bemused, fond, and jealous moments, as well as their exalted—are told, but with an affection that makes the reader both understand and love them, except for the few irredeemable cravens and villains such as Mordred. But if the reader becomes sentimental about his new-found Arthurian pets, it is his own fault, not T. H. White's, for a strain of comedy persists throughout these fantasies until it can no longer be with propriety maintained in combination with the growing elegiac emphasis.

In the presenting of "the comedy of Camelot" Nathan C.

3. This quotation is used, without specification of source, as an epigraph to an essay entitled "Ecclesiastical Architecture," by E. A. Greening Lamborn, which appears in *Mediaeval England*, ed. H. W. C. Davis (Oxford: Clarendon Press, 1924). I have been unable to trace the quotation further.

Starr considers that White's work equals the best—Peacock's *The Misfortunes of Elphin* (1829) and Mark Twain's *A Connecticut Yankee in King Arthur's Court* (1889)—and excels the efforts of Heywood Broun, Maurice Baring, and James Branch Cabell. White "has written Arthurian comedy of a very high order without losing sight of the heroic legend. . . . This reconciliation of the two worlds of humorous and heroic experience is accomplished with freshness and originality by a mind teeming with the pageantry of Arthur's career." [4] Starr might have added that White was a knowledgeable medievalist even beyond the Arthurian range, and he filled his work with details of the daily life of domain and castle. He introduced into their speech equivalents of the variety that was doubtless originally there, though these are largely ignored in heroizing renditions. Sufficient courtly speech remains on the proper occasions. But Sir Gawain always speaks like a Gael who has improved his English somewhat against his will. The children have a racy language of their own. The Saracen tutor Sir Palomides is given a farcical speech of unidiomatic pedantry. And the main characters in their intimacy are made to use an easy and unaffected modern conversational English, with a tendency toward slang. All this counters the strict veracities of linguistic history but contributes to White's greater effort, to make his material accessible to modern readers.

This effort is further served by the liberties he takes with time in relation to point of view. One may conjecture that both to promote familiarization and to suggest the transcending power of the Arthurian story, White calculatedly released it from its restricted time setting. This appears in the devices of language mentioned above. It is enhanced by the peculiar assignment of Merlyn to live backward in time. "I unfortunately was born at the wrong end of time, and I have to live backwards from in front, while surrounded by a lot of people living forwards from behind. Some people call it having second sight." [5] Merlyn's pres-

4. Nathan Comfort Starr, *King Arthur Today: The Arthurian Legend in English and American Literature, 1901–1953* (Gainesville: University of Florida Press, 1954), p. 131. See also pp. 109, 115–30.

5. *The Once and Future King* (London: Collins, 1958), p. 29.

ence and participation in the life of various ages helps to create a kind of fluidity within time. But even where Merlyn does not appear, White introduces free movement in time on his own initiative. In combination with other manifestations of magic and prodigy, fluidity within time seems entirely plausible.

The four parts of *The Once and Future King* represent a progression in time and logical development. *The Sword in the Stone* is White's version of the coming of Arthur. Its substance is the education chiefly by Merlyn of the unrevealed son, often called Wart, of Uther Pendragon. This education is unsystematic, conducted partly by magic and partly by curriculum, but mostly through the experiences of the prince who does not know who he is. He emerges fit for rule because of his unaffected sympathy with all living things and his modesty. When he draws the sword effortlessly from the stone, he is ready for his destiny.

The Queen of Air and Darkness has two centers of attention: the early career of Arthur and the unhappy nurture of the Lothian-Orkney children—Gawaine, Gareth, Agravaine, and Gaheris. For much of the story these two lines are separate, though they come to an ominous crossing at the end, when in unknowing incest Arthur begets Mordred and his own doom. Thereafter the participation of the northern clan in the fortunes of Arthur and Britain is steady. The one part of the novel presents Arthur's arrival at his principle that might must be made the servant of right, his victory over the Gaelic Confederation at the battle of Bedegraine, and the formation of an order, to include his former enemies, which is the genesis of the Round Table. The growth of the brothers, nephews in fact of Arthur, is a contest for supremacy among themselves and an attempt to gain the affection of their unreliable mother, Queen Morgana, who will presently bear Mordred.

The Ill-Made Knight concerns Sir Lancelot, the Chevalier Mal Fet, ugly of face, and throughout his life—not just after his liaison with Guenever—tormented by feelings of guilt and inadequacy. Necessarily much attention is centered on the long-continued adultery, the guilty secret known to all but suppressed until the Orkney disturbers of the peace, incited principally by Mordred, at last force it into the open. White is not at all interested in the sexual aspects of the affair; he knows that his readers will take them for granted. *The Ill-Made Knight* is the richest of all the tetralogy in psychological reconstruction. Lancelot battles with himself, his situation, his sense of honor, and the "wordless presence" of the Holy Spirit until the revelation vouchsafes him in his healing of Sir Urre of Hungary, whose wounds will go on bleeding "until the best Knight in the world had tended them and salved them with his hands" (p. 541). Arthur maintains with difficulty his profound love for an unfaithful wife and a betraying friend, on both of whom he still relies as he can on no one else. Guenever is compassionately examined, the queen whose "central tragedy was that she was childless." White's most direct pronouncement of her is clear throughout the action:

> You could pretend that Guenever was a sort of man-eating lioncelle herself, or that she was one of those selfish women who insist on ruling everywhere. In fact, this is what she seemed to be, to a superficial inspection. She was beautiful, sanguine, hot-tempered, demanding, impulsive, acquisitive, charming—she had all the qualities for a proper man-eater. But the rock on which these easy explanations founder, is that she was not promiscuous. There was never anybody in her life except Lancelot and Arthur. She never ate anybody except these. And even these she did not eat in the full sense of the word. People who have been devoured by a man-eating lioncelle tend to become non-entities —to live no life except in the vitals of the devourer. Yet both Arthur and Lancelot, the people whom she apparently devoured, lived full lives, and accomplished things of their own. . . .
>
> Generosity, courage, honesty, pity, the faculty to look short life in the face—certainly comradeship and tenderness—these qualities may explain why Guenever took Lancelot as well as Arthur. . . .
>
> Perhaps she loved Arthur as a father, and Lancelot because of the son she could not have [Pp. 497–98]

The quest for the Holy Grail receives a curious treatment in *The Ill-Made Knight*. In a way it starts with a dodge; Elaine tricks Lancelot into her bed, and the conception of Galahad results. For a time the comedy and the pathos of sex mingle, for Elaine—not the lily maid of Astolat but "the plump partridge who had always been helpless"—cannot hold her man, and she ends a suicide. White shows us little of the Galahad, and what we see is not especially attractive.

That the knights go searching for the Grail is almost a device. Arthur has created his order of perfect knights, only to find that they quickly exhaust their worldly objects and are in danger of corruption, misdirected energy, and "games-mania." They must have a spiritual object, and the Grail is a perfect answer. But of the quests themselves little is narrated, except as various of the knights return (many do not) to report their misadventures and discontents as they pushed the high purpose. It is not, I suggest, that White found the Holy Grail uninteresting; Malory himself made the quest no more than a developmental part of his total narrative. More important is that *The Ill-Made Knight* attends to Lancelot, whose knowledge of his own excellence and power must be achieved through the painful way of his sin-burdened nature, a way that the virgin Galahad could never have followed. Galahad is unique, and welcome to his uniqueness; there is a little bit, usually very little, of Lancelot in every man.

Though revealed to himself as the best of knights, Lancelot's sorrows pursue him. Nor has the turning of energy to a holy object of quest been efficacious. The divisive forces at work in *The Ill-Made Knight* continue and become more powerful in *The Candle in the Wind*; they cannot be arrested until what Arthur wrought has been destroyed. Through the several actions of this final part—the accusation of Guenever and her lover; her sentencing to be burned; Lancelot's rescue action and the death in the melee of Gaheris and Gareth, both unarmed; the grief of Lancelot for what he has done; the rage of Gawain to avenge his younger brothers—persists one determining force: the malice of Mordred. Without his aggravation the wounds to Logres could have healed of themselves. And so toward the end Arthur, in camp near what would become the battlefield of Salisbury, faces the future almost in despair. He could face defeat, face even the dissolution of the lawful society he had created. "But he had been taught by Merlyn to believe that man was perfectible: that he was on the whole more decent than beastly: that good was worth trying: that there was no such thing as original sin" (p. 665). Now he must confront the denial of all these principles. His attempt to understand the puzzles of human nature fails him, and he can only act as best he can. So he sends away from the battle scene a thirteen-year-old page, young Thomas of Newbold Revell, who wears a surcoat "with the Malory bearings." The boy, in time to become Sir Thomas of Warwick,[6] is commanded to save himself from the battle and in time to tell all who will listen of the king's ideal. Only thus can the candle in the wind be kept aflame. This done, Arthur faces the oncoming day refreshed and clearheaded. The tetralogy ends with an *explicit* and an *incipit:*

EXPLICIT LIBER REGIS QUONDAM REGISQUE
FUTURI

THE BEGINNING

Unlike Elinor Wylie, T. H. White takes few liberties with the material he found in Malory. White's account of the nurture and education of Arthur by Merlyn at the castle of Sir Ector of the Forest Sauvage is largely a backward projection, and his version of the rearing of the children of Queen Morgause is an absorption and elaboration from other sources. White casts Sir Grummore Grummursum, King Pellinore, Sir Palomides, and the Questing Beast into comic, even farcical, parts. The lengthy affairs of Sir Tristram, La Beale Isoud, and King Mark occur only by references in the conversation of the principles of *The Once and Future King.* Many other persons and associated narratives are ignored or mentioned only in passing. White's narrative ends with Arthur's preparation for the day of final battle. All that follows in Malory is left untold. There is the further important difference that in White's version Arthur awaits a battle he knows to be inevitable. No hint is given of an arranged truce and

6. White's sporting with history here should not pass unremarked. If the site known as Newbold Revell (in Warwickshire) existed in Arthurian times, it was probably called Fenny Newbold. The name Sir Thomas of Warwick suggests the relationship that Kittredge posited between the Malory family and the earls of Warwick. But the first earl of Warwick, Henry de Newburgh, was created by William II about 1088. Two earls of Warwick were named Thomas: Thomas Beauchamp (d. 1369) and his son (d. 1401). Sir Thomas Malory was a retainer of Richard Beauchamp, earl of Warwick, son of the second Thomas Beauchamp.

division of reign with Mordred, which is exploded by the mis-adventurous drawing of a sword to kill an adder.

Nor are there many additions in *The Once and Future King*. I can find no precedent—nor, I surmise, could anyone else—for the boy Arthur's instructive adventures with Robin Hood (preferably known as Robin Wood) and his crew, though a congruity of Arthur and Robin Hood—the ideal knight and the ideal yeoman—has been many times noted. The eloquent Irish Saint Toirdealbhach (or Saint Torealvac), who is also a virtuoso in heresy, and his consort Mother Morlan seem to be entertaining inventions; likewise the romance between King Pellinore and the Queen of Flanders, familiarly known as Piggy. There is no sanction in *Morte d'Arthur* for Arthur's entrusting his ideal—his candle—to a young page who will presumably be an ancestor of Sir Thomas Malory. No one named Thomas appears in *Morte d'Arthur*, and the only citation of the name by Robert W. Ackermann is of Tomas, the narrator of the story of Tristram.[7] This is White's way of suggesting a purposeful communication by Arthur to the posterity over whom he will in the fullness of time reign again, when, as in C. S. Lewis's *That Hideous Strength*, Logres is restored to dominance in Britain.

Altogether, there are few changes in material, and these occur mainly in the first two parts, which are also those most notable for fanciful comedy. But of changes in presentation, in order to make familiar the ordinary facts of medieval life, there are many. Intruding his own explanations into the narrative does not trouble White's artistic conscience. Plentiful examples of his familiarizing tactics may be seen within the first chapter of *The Sword in the Stone*. He explains that being "bladed" for a mistake in the etiquette of hunting "was horseplay, a sort of joke like being shaved when crossing the line." He makes Sir Grummore Grummursum and Sir Ector speak a kind of fox hunter's slang as over their port they discuss the education of boys. Sir Ector is hoping to engage a tutor for "Wart" and Kay. Sir Grummore wonders about sending them to Eton, though he concedes "long way and all that, you know." At this point White inter-

7. *An Index of Arthurian Names in Middle English* (Stanford: Stanford University Press, 1952), p. 230.

rupts: "It was not Eton that he mentioned, for the College of Blessed Mary was not founded until 1440, but it was a place of the same sort. Also they were drinking Metheglyn, not Port, but by mentioning the modern wine it is easier to give you the feel" (p. 4). Strictly speaking, the ability to move freely in time is reserved to Merlyn and T. H. White, but unobtrusively it is extended to others, so that when Lancelot begins drawing parallels between the quest for the Holy Grail and the Crusades, few readers will notice and fewer object. White makes a method of anachronism. But much as he familiarizes and invents, he is still primarily an adapter rather than a creator, to the point that for a reader ignorant of the general features of the Arthurian cycle, if such a reader can be imagined, *The Once and Future King* would be scarcely intelligible or interesting. This is a mark of fantasy produced by adaptation from known literary or other artistic centers.

No view of fantasy by adaptation of Arthurian material would be complete without a brief consideration of *A Connecticut Yankee*. Some readers may demur, saying that promulgation of one more version of matter already well known was not Mark Twain's major purpose. This is indisputable. The fanciful exploits of Hank Morgan in and around Camelot are, of course, directed at social criticism and an interpretation of history. But as an experiment in fantasy, *A Connecticut Yankee* is interesting not for thematic content but for its method. Indeed, this is pretty much true of any fantasy that results from parody, continuation, or adaptation. Theme and tendency may be what they are; the works are fantasies because of method.

There is no need for me to rehearse any of this well-known story. It will suffice to describe Mark Twain's means of adapting standard Arthurian material so that fantasy results. The opening gambit is a familiar one, regularly offered (in the hope of acceptance) by many novelists of the eighteenth century who wished to assert the veracity and repute of their fictions. In Warwick Castle the tourist Mark Twain encounters a mysterious stranger who can explain how a bullet hole came to be in the chain mail that once belonged to Sir Sagramor le Desirous. From this it is only a step into the first-person history, briefly oral and then written, of the Yankee Hank Morgan, who regains consciousness in the England of King Arthur, or rather Mark Twain's construct of this time and place. Thereafter the narrative proceeds by the triumph of the nineteenth century over the disadvantaged sixth century.

This triumph has several aspects. It includes the running commentary, sometimes derisive and sometimes serious, of an enlightened and practical democrat on the absurdities and offenses of Arthurian society. Hank Morgan has the same advantage as T. H. White's Merlyn, that of returning from a far-future point in time. Censure of the sixth century is slightly modified by a few approvals. Hank Morgan cannot resist a liking for Sir Lancelot; he finds King Arthur good-hearted and capable of learning. But his real affection is reserved for those who participate in his imposition of republicanism and nineteenth-century technological advances upon the unsuspecting past. These reformations constitute his greatest triumphs, or better "effects," since the showman and the altruist are about equally mixed in Hank Morgan. So successful is his destruction of knight-errantry and his introduction of modern methods that they can lead only to holocaust. In the end the conquerors are conquered by the very thoroughness of their success, and Mark Twain is obliged to bring his fantasy to an arbitrary end. But this does not occur before the events start the suspicion that he finds the nineteenth-century capability for devastation as reprehensible as sixth-century tyranny. Through the last pages of *A Connecticut Yankee* is an undertone of what became the ominous tones of *The Education of Henry Adams*.

The whole of Mark Twain's fantasy is a calculated engraftment of one time upon another. The stock on which the graft is made is the standard Arthurian material—or rather a part of it, for Mark Twain could not conveniently have represented all of it—as set forth by Malory. Whatever is genuinely medieval in *A Connecticut Yankee* is a faithful presentation of what Malory wrote or suggested. The fanciful parts are all Mark Twain—his interpretations and additions. These make up the bulk of the narrative, and they are the memorable parts. But without the support of the solid, even though simplified, Arthurian material, they would be meaningless for lack of referents.

Once again the main principle of adaptive fantasy manifests

itself: however spectacular the author's inventiveness, it has its validation from the work that provided the original and continuing impetus. Such fantasy is thus a limited creation; it shows the author's powers—often powers of the highest order—put to the service of a will not entirely his own. But before it is assumed that such service is bondage unworthy of a free creative spirit, a few considerations must be examined.

The cult of original genius has had its day and gone the way of most secular cults, but behind it remains a widespread notion that total fabrication, or creation, is one mark of the highest art. Without pausing to argue this matter on principle, I note only that many great works of literary art do not meet this test and that classical theory does not recognize it. It is a commonplace that classical theory regards the writer's assimilation of literary heritage as an irreplaceable part of his preparation; it is a means of studying nature. And if this process leads to "imitations" of Horace or Juvenal, the results are by no means therefore spurious. Rather, the modern understanding of "imitation" has improperly turned the term into a reproach. Adaptive fantasy is a special manifestation and extension of this well-known classical discipline. Such fantasists enjoy an extraordinary freedom in the material that they may assimilate and some in the recensions of it that they may produce. But these are differences of procedure rather than of principle. Adaptive fantasy belongs with those emanations from wit and judgment, in contrast to vision, that we associate principally with the great names of English neoclassicism, though the occurrence of such works spreads through a far wider range of literary history.

It is necessary finally to examine fantasy of the supernatural, a kind that has attracted more writers and probably more readers than any of the others. First, however, a tempting error must be forestalled. Many novels present a rich content of the supernatural but even so remain outside the range of fantasy. Such, for example, are *The Scarlet Letter* and *The Plumed Serpent*. Fantasy does not result when the supernatural, however seriously rendered, remains a subject matter or a display; nor when it impinges upon ordinary human life and environment without transforming them; nor when it is primarily a means of recommending conduct and values; nor when it is but a projection, even though vivid, from the psychic and emotional constitution of a character.

Fantasy results when the supernatural is shown as present and acting of itself because it is real. It brushes aside the established sense of possibility and imposes itself as the center of belief. Because of its concreteness and its intrinsic energy, moreover, the supernatural of the fantasies determines the field of action in which it dominates. Sometimes this field is self-limited (however large) and distant. For the time of reading there is no "world," for example, but "deep heaven." Such a remote place, however, is not the only possible locus. The supernatural can as well be shown visiting and dominating a known environment or some part of it. Charles Williams was fond of loosing spirit forces in some part of rural or urban England. When he does, that part is so invested that the reader feels taken into a new arrangement, which temporarily obliterates all others. And so it is with all successful fantasies of this type: whatever the supernatural possesses, it possesses completely.

Fantasies of the supernatural are essentially homogeneous; their central feature is the dominance of powers that countervail those known through normal experience and expectation. Accordingly, the rhetoric that conveys them relies on narrative assertion so assured that doubt is never recognized as a possibility. Within this overall homogeneity are three discernible, though not cleanly separable, divisions: the narratives of supernatural visitors and unseen presences; the total mythologies; the theological romances, which are often almost indistinguishable from the mythological fantasies.

Of these the narratives of supernatural visitants and unseen presences are conceptually and artistically the simplest, and I shall consider them first. The basic maneuver in such fantasies has already been specified. It is further necessary that the supernatural being bring his extraordinary power, of whatever kind, to bear upon people unprepared for his coming and that he thus alter their lives and create a causal sequence of events leading to a result that could not have occurred in the course of nature. The intruder himself may be benign, malicious, serious, whimsical, adaptable, intransigent. These and other variants in attitude are possible; the invariable is that he must exert power.

Accordingly, in *The Elephant and the Kangaroo*, by T. H. White, the Archangel Michael appears suddenly in the kitchen of a house in County Kildare, forecasts a second flood, and commands that an ark be built, filled, provisioned, and ridden to whatever new Ararat it may find. It is Satan who resides for a time in a sleepy Austrian village that Mark Twain was pleased to call Eseldorf and controls the narration of *The Mysterious Stranger*.[1] Mark Twain's Satan, also known as Philip Traum, is not the great enemy himself, but his plausible nephew, a more accomplished diabolist than the nephew who acts as a fledgling tempter in *The Screwtape Letters* of C. S. Lewis. We expect a disguised Satan to roam the earth for his appointed time, but not Death or God. Yet T. F. Powys attempted just these presences—God as an incognito wine merchant in *Mr. Weston's Good Wine*, and in *Unclay* John Death, as an agreeable villager. Both books illustrate the mistake of including in fantasy characters too potent for the illusion. But the three pagan angels—

1. Though interesting in itself, the tangled matter of there being three versions of *The Mysterious Stranger*—the Eseldorf, the Hannibal, and the Print Shop—need not concern us here. In all three a young Satan is the visitor.

Finnan, Caeltia, and Art—of James Stephens's *The Demi-Gods*
are thoroughly at home in Ireland,[2] as are Pan and Angus Óg in
The Crock of Gold.

A variant of the fantasies of supernatural visitors is that in
which the power of the great being is exerted without his physical presence. Such extension of force is by definition within the
capability of spirits. Whether the influence moves directly from
the source to its object or expresses itself by way of a human
agent makes little difference. The power will work in either case.

The triumph in this kind of fantasy is an insufficiently
esteemed work of Lord Dunsany, *The Blessing of Pan* (1928).
In this representation the disturbing but benign power of Pan is,
as his very name suggests, everywhere. It gives magic to the pipe
playing of a boy; it pervades the wooded hills and the ancient
patterned stones, the scenes in the primordial past of ritual
dancing and sacrifice. In various ways Pan calls to the Christian
villagers, reaching in them the overlaid memories of every human
heart. Nothing civilized and Christianized can effectively oppose
this power—not the efficacy of Saint Ethelbruda (a famous
pagan-chaser), and not the heroic efforts of the Rev. Mr. Anwrel,
vicar of Wolding. His labor to control the parish is untiring.
His preaching, especially the final sermon, is a most eloquent call
to faith and order, but it fails. At first stealthily and then boldly
his congregation leaves and seeks the ancient site. Presently the
clergyman himself fits up his paleolith as an axe, joins them,
sacrifices the bull, and becomes a kind of Druidic priest. At one
with nature as their unremembered ancestors were, the village
never returns to civilization; its people live now in an earthly
paradise, which is the blessing of Pan.

The excellence of this fantasy is the vivid representation of
opposing forces. The propaganda of neopaganism offers many
narrative embodiments of the advocated faith, but most are as
pale as the Galilean whom they deny. Of such poor argument
several novels of Eden Phillpotts will serve as exhibits. In *The
Blessing of Pan*, however, the spirit of the Arcadian, the deity
whose disorder is both freedom and discipline, is as immediate as

2. See Vivian Mercier, *The Irish Comic Tradition* (Oxford: Clarendon Press,
1962), p. 37.

the air itself and as pervasive. In the person of the vicar of Wolding, the opposing Christianity is no amiable weakness; he embodies the true church militant. But even this cannot win the
devotion of human nature. The vicar speaks with the finest eloquence of a faith and a church that civilize, but the blessing of
Pan comes in the original language that penetrates directly to the
blood and the passions of men. The goat-foot god himself is not
made to appear in this story, but his presence is everywhere.[3]

Supernatural powers, usually from Graeco-Roman mythology,
are plentiful in the early works of short fiction by E. M. Forster.
This was part of his attempt to gain "a liberation from the
phenomenal world—a liberation which, in the degree of its
achievement, is responsible for his particular vision." [4] These
tales are well known and need be mentioned here only in passing.
"The Story of a Panic" shows that nympholepsy, that terrifying
blessed condition of those seized by Pan, is yet a living possibility. "The Other Side of the Hedge" tells of an escape to that
green land of those who refuse to contend. "The Celestial Omnibus" tells of a visit to the immortals. In "The Curate's Friend"
a faun appears at an outdoor tea and invites a young clergyman,
who alone sees him, into a life of rapport with nature. Probably
the best-known work of this group is "The Machine Stops,"
though this fantasy does not rely on a supernatural visitor.

In these stories all the elements contributing to a persuasive
fantasy-illusion are combined with a rare skill. In his novels,
however, fantasy is usually recurrent or latent, and there is evidence of his dissatisfaction with this means of "liberation." Perhaps James McConkey is correct in suggesting that Forster
attempted to make his mythologies ascend from fantasy to
prophecy, as these concepts are later discriminated in *Aspects of
the Novel.*

In the opinion of McConkey, the only novel of Forster that
is unequivocally a fantasy is *A Room with a View.* It is also the
earliest conceived, though not the earliest published. The novel

3. For a comprehensive study of Pan revived, see Patricia Merivale, *Pan the
Goat-God: His Myth in Modern Times* (Cambridge, Mass.: Harvard University
Press, 1969).

4. James McConkey, *The Novels of E. M. Forster* (Ithaca: Cornell University
Press, 1957), p. 44.

does indeed contain devices and maneuvers found in fantasy. The main effective deity is "not the great god Pan, who had been buried these two thousand years, but the little god Pan, who presides over social contretemps and unsuccessful picnics." [5] This is the same being Forster invokes in *Aspects of the Novel* among a host of minor spirits that produce fantasy; the little god Pan is closely related also to "Muddle," the "god" of *Tristram Shandy*. This trivial being is no supernatural visitor imposing his power on an astonished world. The little god Pan is rather a symptom of Forster's growing deprecation. Forster the maturing novelist understood fantasy as a whim of the writer's individuality, and he played with it because he thought it essentially a plaything. Except in several short stories, he did not allow fantasy to determine meaning, form, and rhetoric. Soon discontented with trifling, he produced in long fiction only the one half-committed experiment I have been examining. Thereafter he moved away from it and sought to express that more formidable and serious spirit that he called "prophecy."

I have already cited, as many have before me, Forster's quest after a mythology, a means of liberating his fiction from sheer phenomenality. This was an aspect of his participation in the widespread revolution in which many novelists of the twentieth century sought in many ways to break out of a highly developed realism. The same desire also motivated Virginia Woolf and has its distilled expression in her essay "Mr. Bennett and Mrs. Brown," which rejects the total commitment to externality and circumstances that had, as she believed, become the deadening norm of the novel.

Myth, the mythic, and mythology have been the concern of many contemporary novelists, and of even more critics. These latter especially have searched for myth as assiduously and ingeniously as they have searched for symbols, without which presumably myths are meaningless. And as one might expect, they have found both in abundance, often in unexpected places. Some say that a striving for an adequate mythology has been the major effort of twentieth-century novelists. It may be so. But assuredly the appetite for myth of many readers would not be so keen

5. *A Room with a View* (New York: Knopf, 1953), p. 111.

and insatiable without these critical informants about good living. A result is that the idea of myth, never a simple one, has had many meanings injected into it and has become too complex for normative discussion. Thus is the empire of prose fiction extended.

Before this emergence from recent theory and practice, the idea of myth had at least one constant, whatever might be the variables. This was an intrinsic, not a merely decorative, presence of the supernatural. And this persisted despite the long-foregone loss of any power of a particular supernatural to command belief. In the twentieth century we have seen the prosperity of secular myth-making, of which there can be no better example than Faulkner's Yoknapotawpha County series and its affiliates. I do not mean to deprecate these. I simply say that for all their deep explorations of the personal and communal psyche, of morality, and of the spirit of the place, they have, and are intended to have, no intrinsic supernaturalness.

Many twentieth-century fantasists also have been both myth seekers and myth makers. That is, they have used the inherited mythologies; they have made their own, sometimes anew and sometimes by reworking the traditional materials. Often too they have blended the received and the new-made. But always they have kept the supernatural content of whatever kind not only prominent but essential.

If space permitted, it would be possible to discuss many mythological fantasies, the best of which are Robert Graves's *Seven Days in New Crete*; Max Beerbohm's *Zuleika Dobson*, a complete myth of Aphrodite in Oxford, despite its being comic; and two fantasies by Lord Dunsany, *The King of Elfland's Daughter* and *The Charwoman's Shadow*. This last work is based on a persistent theme, that the loss of a shadow signifies the loss of human substance and communication, which is central in *Peter Schlemihls wundersame Geschichte* by Adelbert von Chamisso, in several romances by George Macdonald, and in the story by Hugo von Hofmannsthal that he made into the libretto for Richard Strauss's *Die Frau ohne Schatten*.

Like Kenneth Grahame's *The Wind in the Willows* and the Alice books of Lewis Carroll, J. R. R. Tolkien's trilogy, *The Lord of the Rings,* had its inception as a children's book, *The Hobbit.* Like these earlier works also, it kept its attractiveness for children, but as it developed, extended its fascination to adults and proved to be the most impressive mythological fantasy of the twentieth century. Soon after publication, *The Lord of the Rings* became the center of a popular cult. Even so, it is a work of great learning, which invests the whole narrative and the elaborate documentation that accompanies it. Even in the midst of violent action, the reader is not allowed to forget the comprehensive lore that surrounds actors and events. All this mobilization of scholarship is not just an exercise in Tolkien's ingenuity. The learning continually stresses the long continuity of tradition behind the immediate happenings and thus contributes to two tactically advantageous aspects of the total illusion: an impression that Middle Earth, over its long span from an antiquity for which there is no chronology, is the whole world; and a sense that the narrative presents the final conflict, with a foredoomed result, of forces in movement since the beginning of time. A tremendous span of history, as well as ultimate forces, reaches a culmination in *The Lord of the Rings.* Even though this trilogy lacks the cosmic range of C. S. Lewis's, the sense of a finality long awaited and historically decisive is inescapable. Edmund Fuller compares Tolkien's work with Wagner's *Der Ring des Nibelungen* and places his earlier brief narrative *The Hobbit* in the position of *Das Rheingold.*[6] This is a suggestive comparison, although *The Lord of the Rings* lacks that fiery destruction of *Die Götterdämmerung,* which is necessary to bring forth the final purity and the redemption of love. Herein lies the difference between catastrophe and what, in his essay on fairy stories, Tolkien calls *eucatastrophe.*

For his generous providing of information Tolkien offers several reasons. The entire fabric of created legend and history is both a construct of his own interest, antedating the composition of the work, and an attempt to satisfy the curiosity of

6. "The Lord of the Hobbits: J. R. R. Tolkien," in *Tolkien and the Critics,* ed. Neil D. Isaacs and Rose A. Zumbardo (Notre Dame, Ind.: University of Notre Dame Press, 1968), p. 18. Fuller's essay first appeared in a volume entitled *Books with Men behind Them* (1962).

readers. Also, he says, "the story was drawn irresistibly towards the older world, and became an account, as it were, of its end and passing away before its beginning and middle had been told." [7] Even in *The Hobbit* there had been "glimpses that had arisen unbidden of things higher or deeper or darker than the surface." It is possible, I believe, to infer some additional effects, which may or may not have been part of Tolkien's intent. The trilogy presents a massive created mythology, seemingly unique and self-contained. He denies that it is either allegorical or topical. But one of Tolkien's triumphs is that his creation reminds one on almost every page of the inherited mythologies of many times and cultures, particularly Teutonic, Scandinavian, Anglo-Saxon, and Celtic. Of course, certain beings of the work are traditional; there is nothing essentially original in his dwarves, elves, wizards, magicians, wolves, and trolls. But these interact with his own Ringwraiths, orcs, ents, and (most of all) hobbits so fully and naturally that any discrimination between derivative and original material becomes impossible. Thus Tolkien gained for his work the dignity of epic.

There is, however, in *The Lord of the Rings*, one decisive departure from the norms of the conventional epic that is formed from myth. The central actors are not superbeings, not even men. They are hobbits, sometimes called halflings. Small, sturdy, comfort-loving, earthy, shy, and tough, they ordinarily live in holes and have no wish to be concerned with worldwide upheavals. Their involvement in the War of the Rings is half accidental. By nature they are not heroic, but pressed by circumstances and by knowledge that their participation in fearsome events is necessary, they become heroic and achieve their proper *arete*. Acting with and against them are epic figures of the traditional kind—Gandalf the white wizard; Aragorn the Strider, finally crowned as King Ellessar; Sauron; and many more. But virtue is concentrated in the few hobbits who undertake the perilous quest of destroying the last ring of power.

The hobbits, then, are accessible, familiar beings. The reader learns a great deal about them. With his passion for imparting

7. Foreword to *The Lord of the Rings* (New York: Ballantine Books, [1965]), part I, p. viii.

information, Tolkien provides a long prologue describing hobbits; sketching their history, customs, habits, and institutions; characterizing prominent families among them; and relating the way in which they became entangled in a conflict that convulsed the whole world beyond the Shire. But even without this prologue, the whole narrative abounds in hobbit lore, and even in their moments of desperation and of glory, his halflings remain simple, amiable beings, easy to understand. Whatever the moral implications of this presentation, the accessibility of the hobbits is part of a shrewd and sustained tactical maneuver. Most epic figures are far separated from readers by distance and awe. Since they are superior beings, suitable to be admired, this is proper enough. But no one thinks of admiring the hobbits; they are far too agreeable, close, and well known for this. We would like to see ourselves in them, but no man can, without hubris, see himself in Aeneas or Odysseus. The familiarity of his central actors contributes to Tolkien's total effort, which is to make the entire remote, lofty, mysterious, cataclysmic action familiar.

In his foreword, Tolkien professes a dislike and mistrust of allegory. "I must prefer history, true or feigned, with its varied applicability to the thought and experience of readers" (p. xi). Here is the key to Tolkien's method and the principle that makes *The Lord of the Rings* a fantasy. With unbroken sobriety, Tolkien pretends to be relating a history of events that have been moving toward culmination since their half-known origins in the dim past. The elements are many and complex; yet all are arranged in a system that has the clarity Gibbon imposed on the innumerable details of the waning of the Roman Empire. Magic, marvelous events, and mysteries are discussed as matters of fact. A perspective is maintained whereby the relationship of small events to large patterns is never obscured, and the bearing of occurrences in antiquity on current happenings is always as evident as knowledge will allow. Because the power of the enemy, Sauron, works as much as possible in secret, there are facts, particularly in the early stages of the conflict, that cannot be known at once. In these instances there is no attempt to satisfy or bemuse the reader with unreliable information. The ignorance is acknowledged. But in time it is dispelled, for one of the

major movements of the story is to expose Sauron's conceal-
ments; this is part of the sustained effort to force him out of
conspiracy, his favored method, into confrontation, for in open
contest he cannot win. Because it always appears as history,
known and revealing itself as the action progresses, the massive
myth is plausible and persuasive. Tolkien is as careful as Dreiser
to give his readers the fullest and most accurate information
available. The entire narrative and all the accompanying apparatus are determined by this game of persuasive historicity. In a
word, Tolkien's total method is rhetorical.

This pretense of factual recounting offers no interference to
the rapid movement of action or to the sense of emerging destiny,
which pervades *The Lord of the Rings*. Indeed, both are reinforced by the clarity, particularly the latter, for this can be regarded as the operation of historical process. In connection with
the awesome forces that work toward the fulfillment of destiny,
a curious characteristic of the work reveals itself. The trilogy
abounds in the supernatural, but there is no hint in it of a deity
or divine powers and no experience that may be understood as
religious. This has puzzled some readers, for Tolkien as man and
writer was for years closely associated with that literary-religious
coterie at Oxford that included C. S. Lewis and Charles Williams. In the essay on fairy tales, Tolkien claims that the chief
value of such literature is the access it gives to Christian truths.
But he avoids such revelation in *The Lord of the Rings*, and
specifically denies that he intended any allegorical understanding.
To be sure, the ethical principles that may be inferred are consistent with traditional Christian ethics, but if the reader is to
take comfort from this, he must make the inferences without
Tolkien's assistance.

I cannot account for this omission, which departs from standard epic practice. And I do not wish to speculate about its
significance. But whatever else may be said, the absence of the
sacred strengthens the conflict of good and evil as forces in a
created world and serves his pretense that the action represents
secular history.[8] In Tolkien's world the supernatural exists as

8. See Patricia Meyer Spacks, "Power and Meaning in *The Lord of the
Rings*," in *Tolkien and the Critics*, pp. 81–99.

fact and is manifested in phenomena; he writes mythic history and feigns that it is real. In doing so he does not lose the impressive effect of the marvelous, which is maintained by the awesomeness of the slowly revealed forces that are in conflict. But these are the more awesome for being credible and for impinging not only on the lives of the familiarized hobbits but also on an entire created and documented civilization that is in jeopardy, even though the reader remains confident throughout that evil cannot prevail.

The workings of good and evil through the trilogy also contribute to the pretended veracity. I have said that the morality of the story is consistent with traditional Christian ethics, though without evident divine sanction. But it does not follow that the ideas of good and evil are abstract or prescriptive, as they often are in epic and romance. Tolkien is far from being a psychological novelist and far from a finder of virtues and vices in unlikely people. But he does go so far as to execute much of his characterization on the principles that good and evil often conflict in motives to action, and that a commitment to good may result from willful purgation and a commitment to evil from a deterioration that is opposed even as it is succeeding. Frodo Baggins must struggle with himself to resist the lust for power that the ring he is to destroy fosters in him. At the culminating moment he does not throw the ring into the fiery Crack of Doom; it is snatched from him by Gollum, a miserable agent of the mighty Sauron's evil power, who then tumbles into the pit. Gollum was at first a decent enough hobbit, but he cannot resist the ring, murders his brother for it, and then painfully deteriorates into sliminess without completely losing faint impulses to do good. We understand that even Saruman was once the mightiest of the white wizards. Thus Tolkien throughout takes account of the ambiguities that attention to experience always reveals in moral reality before this has been transformed into abstraction or figuration. This, as much as anything else, elevates *The Lord of the Rings* above the level of learned melodrama and contributes to the pretended historical veracity that is the central rhetorical strategy of the work.

Before I conclude this discussion of *The Lord of the Rings*, I wish to bring before the reader several observations by Douglass Parker in an essay that is, in my view, the most perceptive and cogent piece of Tolkien criticism yet published.[9] Parker posits three interrelated criteria of fantasy: "the solidity and variety of the developed structure, its relation to reality, and its viability" (p. 598). By the first, he means that a fantasy must show a creation of thought that departs from the "real" and yet is logically complete and on its own terms acceptable. By the second, he requires "a connection between the real world and the fantasy world," a way for the reader to contemplate one against the other. By viability, Parker means a quality that causes the reader to accept the creation and participate in its results. *The Lord of the Rings* meets not only these requisites but also another that is even more important, in that it is "a means toward a perception, or perceptions, of reality that can better be attained and expressed in that genre than in any other" (p. 601). The effectiveness of the work, Parker proposes, results from Tolkien's ability to direct his learning into the creation of a credible situation and to keep a balance, chiefly by the nature of the hobbits, between genuine heroics and common sense. Thus Tolkien can show an archetypal and not at all simplistic conflict of good versus evil and the nature of the end of an era, in which are revealed truths of importance about the human condition. As in *Beowulf*, which Tolkien "has rewritten, or rather recreated," there emerges "a sense of man's *Vergänglichkeit*, his impermanence, his perishability" (p. 608). Parker's reading of *The Lord of the Rings* demonstrates that it is a work to take seriously, not the juvenile trash with pretensions to learning that detractors, such as Edmund Wilson, have proclaimed it to be.

"Theological romance" is a strange term, seemingly not quite cohesive, and it requires explanation. The concept of romance itself offers little difficulty despite the variety of its manifestations. Theology, however, is an intellectual discipline, the science of the being and attributes of a divinity, or divinities, of sufficient importance to be central in a system of beliefs and observances that are embodied in a visible church. "Natural theology," such as Browning set forth in "Caliban upon Setebos,"

9. "Hwaet We Holbytla . . . ," *Hudson Review*, 9 (1956–57), 598–609.

may have its function in the prehistory of the discipline, but until there are a rational formulation and a coherent tradition, theology, as it is conceived in the major religions of the world, does not exist.

Part of the rationale whereby "theological romance" becomes a usable term is suggested by C. S. Lewis, one of the principal practitioners of such fiction. He characterizes his friend and colleague Charles Williams as a "romantic theologian." Continuing, Lewis offers a definition: "A romantic theologian does not mean one who is romantic about theology but one who is theological about romance, one who considers the theological implications of those experiences which are called romantic. The belief that the most serious and ecstatic experiences either of human love or of imaginative literature have such theological implications, and that they can be healthy and fruitful only if the implications are diligently thought out and severely lived, is the root principle of all his work." [10] "Untheologized romanticism" is, by sad contrast, "sterile and mythological." Elsewhere in his critical writings Lewis is approving, rather than harsh, about the mythological.

It seems plausible that if a romantic theologian as here described were to write fiction, the result might properly be called theological romance. This is not mere play on words. It is quite consistent with Lewis's definition that the material, the purposes, and the methods of Williams, Lewis himself, and the other producers of this specialized kind of fiction be within the range of heroic romance. They seek to impart a sense of high adventure, wonder, and moral loftiness triumphant over evil. The aim of those writers whose theological romances are fantasies is not enlightenment alone, but enlargement and support of the reader's religious beliefs, perhaps even proselytization. They are self-appointed agents for the propagation of the Christian faith, and theological romance is a subdivision of the novel of purpose.

The principal modern writers of theological romance—C. S. Lewis and Charles Williams—belonged to a cohesive group who called themselves the Inklings. During an extended period of

10. *Essays Presented to Charles Williams* (London: Oxford University Press, 1947), p. vi.

their productivity they formed a coterie at Magdalen College, Oxford, and gathered irregularly to discuss their work in progress. Lord David Cecil says of them: "They combined voluminous learning . . . with a strong liking for fantasy. But this fantasy was not indulged independently of their ideas; it was fantasy *about* their ideas." [11]

The ideas here adverted to were many and wide-ranging, but they all concerned the spiritual problems of modern life, the rich mythology of Catholic Christianity, and the persuasive representation, through fiction, of orthodoxy. Of the writers themselves, Williams and Lewis were Anglo-Catholic, and Tolkien Roman Catholic. It is impossible, however, to infer doctrinal differences from their imaginative works, and dissensions seem never to have disturbed their personal friendship. As apologists and teachers they concentrate on that large area which is common to Roman and Anglican Catholicism.

Behind and filigreed into the romances of Williams and Lewis is most of the humanistic learning of the Western world and not a little from the East. Literature and criticism, linguistics and philology, philosophy, history—the catalog of their knowledge would read like the headings of a humanistic curriculum. Mythologies are for them not sources of decoration but systems of feeling, reference, and imaginative order pervasive through both the form and content of their works. They exploit Christian mythology most, Graeco-Roman least, and others are invoked or echoed with the effortlessness that bespeaks possession. Lewis and Williams are, moreover, as near as men can be to born syncretists; they make mythologies blend almost into uniformity, and all serve their most Christian purposes.

I do not propose any extended discussion of the influences upon Lewis and Williams. Several scholars have already performed parts of this formidable task, and much is yet to be done. One predecessor, however, should be briefly treated: the little-known Scottish romancer George Macdonald. C. S. Lewis several times acknowledges Macdonald as a teacher. Of his first

11. "Is There an Oxford School of Writing?" *Twentieth Century*, 157 (1955), 562. This essay is in the form of a dialogue between Rachel Trickett and Lord David Cecil.

reading of Macdonald's *Phantastes: A Faery Romance* (1858) he says: "That night my imagination was, in a certain sense, baptised. . . ." It is evident, moreover, that in two of his books, *Phantastes* and *Lilith* (1895), Macdonald was an early practitioner of theological romance.

From 1851 to 1897 Macdonald wrote some fifty books, mainly novels and fairy tales. Of these only the two mentioned in the preceding paragraph were clearly intended for adult readers, though it may be that like C. S. Lewis he made less than the usual differentiation between adult and juvenile readers. Macdonald, too, was a man of capacious, though somewhat disorderly, learning. Through his narratives are intimations of a Neoplatonic lore, of Böhme, Swedenborg, Blake. He was devoted to the German writers of tales of wonder and *Kunstmärchen*; *Phantastes* was intended as an essay in the latter form. The strongest single influence on him was that of Novalis, whose *Geistliche Lieder* he translated and whose apothegms he often quoted. Like his successors', Macdonald's learning and his narrative effort were directed to a Christian end, particularly to exemplification of the nature and power of love, which is the essence of life itself. Greville Macdonald stated that the "allegorical revelation" of *Lilith* might be summarized in a passage from one of his father's earlier romances, *Weighed and Wanting* (1882): "Love, and love alone, as from the first it is the source of life, love alone, wise at once and simple as a child, can redeem life. It is life drawing nigh to life, person to person, the human to the human, that conquers death."

George Macdonald proceeded from the premise frequently expressed in mystical thought though best known to most readers in the apothegm of Blake, "For everything that lives is holy, life delights in life." For Macdonald the necessary corollary is that living consists in assent to the divine. All retrograde allegiances are participations in death, and the worst of these is self-will, the end product of which is the seeking of damnation. "For very love of self himself he slew" may be applied not only to the egoist Sir Willoughby Patterne but also, more grimly than Meredith intended, to those who will their own ruin. In C. S. Lewis's *The Great Divorce*, George Macdonald is made a character, a saintly joyous expositor of the new life. In this embodiment the Scottish romancer is made to say: "All that are in Hell, choose it. Without that self-choice, there could be no Hell." The cheerful converse is that redemption may come, as it did to Lilith, even to those whose assent to the divine is almost lost in self-will, though their purgation will be painful almost beyond endurance.

I have found no external proof that Charles Williams was acquainted with the theological romances of George Macdonald, but it is hard to believe that Williams, widely read and for years closely associated with C. S. Lewis, would have missed so like-minded an author. The conformity of their principles and sensibilities is evident at once. Both were somewhat God-intoxicated, though with no loss of control over their imaginings. Both found a more compelling reality in the unseen than in the seen. Both envisioned the world as a battleground of virtue and vice, with virtue—that is, goodness made moral strength by trial—the destined victor in God's time and way. There is thus a joyousness prevalent in their works, even in parts where the conflicts are both grave and desperate.

All of Williams's seven fantasies, from *War in Heaven* (1930) to *All Hallows' Eve* (1944), are founded on essentially the same mythic plan. He posits the embodiment of primordial good and evil in forms, persons, or physical substances of great intrinsic energy. In other words, in place of the dead metaphors and abstractions in which archetypal principles are usually expressed, Williams establishes vivid and disruptive incarnations. These forces are then let loose in ordinary modern society—and here his method differs from that of Macdonald, who is fond of faërie and other remote settings—and their conflicts produce either widespread or concentrated convulsion until evil is suppressed and order secured.

A context for possession and power is the thematic center of five of Williams's romances: *War in Heaven, Many Dimensions, The Greater Trumps, Shadows of Ecstasy,* and *All Hallows' Eve.* Those who wish to deprecate his fiction sometimes call them "spiritual thrillers." I doubt that Williams would have resented this label, for it expresses a major part of his purpose, to show by narrative action the potency of spiritual forces in the world as we know it and the urgency of contests between good and evil.

The evil forces of *War in Heaven* are purposeful destroyers, who wish to command the Holy Grail because of their hope that a corrupt use of the power that inheres in it will enable them to magnify their mischief. This mischief, like that of Milton's Satan and of the evildoers in most romances, has no object beyond expressing their vengeful hatred of the good. The protectors of the Grail have motives that range from piety to decency. They understand, dimly at first and then with progressive enlightenment, what the impious never understand, that the Grail itself is less significant than the intentions of its would-be possessors. The power of the ungodly is limited. They can achieve hell for themselves and carry out a ritual murder on a consenting victim, who is demented by his belief that he cannot escape the devil. But against resistance they cannot triumph; on the stubbornly unconsenting they can inflict confusion, pain, even death, but not defeat. Within their own ranks the loyalty of the diabolists to their own effort is insecure, for they are committed to no more than a destructive principle. As one of them says, "I have no tears and no desire. I am weary beyond all mortal weariness and my heart is sick and my eyes blind with the sight of the nothing through which we fall." [12] It is no surprise, then, when one of their number confesses his crime and saves himself, though he will be hanged for murder.

Throughout *War in Heaven* Williams maintains an interpenetrating relationship between doctrine and the devices of fantasy. Once the reader has accepted as fiat the presence of the Grail in the church of a small parish in Hertfordshire, the way is prepared for a narrative of benign magic and *maleficium*, angelic visitation, and translation. Williams makes no attempt to give these events a mundane rationalization. Indeed, given his commitment to the immanence of the spiritual, any such attempt would be a worse tactical error than the post facto explanations of Anne Radcliffe.

In *The Place of the Lion* a contest for possession and power is less prominent. Williams requires that the reader believe in the physical presence of the ideal animals of Neoplatonic lore. Lion, serpent, butterflies, lamb, eagle, horse, and unicorn are loosed upon the Hertfordshire countryside in all their strength

12. *War in Heaven* (New York: Pellegrini and Cudahy, 1949), p. 163.

and glory. Human normality is reduced to chaos, for these creatures not only disrupt the mundane tenor but exert their influence upon human beings.[13] One person is rapt in a vision of
the Holy Spirit as he beholds the swarming, dancing butterflies;
two others realize their snaky natures by becoming snakes themselves. Another, a bluestocking student of philosophy, is terrified
into understanding that Pythagoras, Plato, and Abelard, whom
she has exploited only to advance her intellectual ambitions, were
indeed concerned with mighty realities. It remains for Anthony
Durrant to learn in his humility that these beings, though divine
in origin, must be controlled by man. And so, a new Adam, he
names and tames the beasts and restores the proper order of
nature.

Anthony Durrant is at once himself and Adam. This fact,
presented in action without explanation, points to a puzzle in
Williams's methods of characterization. Given to showing conflicts of mighty opposites, he might be expected to have made
protagonists and antagonists of the mighty figures from myth
and history and thus to have erred by including within fantasy
embodiments too potent for the mode to contain. Rather than
this, he portrayed ordinary people who, usually with a delayed
self-awareness, are invested as agents of superhuman powers.
When he did import a mythic figure, Williams gave the personage ordinary human form and manners. Thus Chloe Burnett of
Many Dimensions is a secretary of no notable personality, but
because of her obedience to divine will she can wield the power
of Solomon's magical stone, incised with the characters of the
tetragrammaton. Ordinary and humble, she is an agent of salva-
tion, at the cost of her life, a willing sacrifice.

Thus, too, when Prester John, the legendary priest-king of
Asia and Africa, joins the action of *War in Heaven*,[14] he comes
as a modestly dressed, mild, sociable young man and remains

13. Somewhat the same representation is central in *The Terror*, by Arthur
Machen, except that in this the creatures are acting in vengeful rebellion against
man because he has forfeited his rightful supremacy.

14. I will note in passing that a Kaffir inheritor of the mission of this lengen-
dary figure is the honored antagonist in John Buchan's *Prester John* (1910).
Buchan's character is heroic and tragic and lacks the amiability of Charles
Williams's.

such, even when he announces his oneness with Saint John the Baptist, Galahad, and the Virgin Mary, and at a crucial point remarks to a companion, "Tonight thou shalt be with me in Paradise." I surmise that in such characterization, risky as it was of itself, Williams was not just exercising a technique or indulging in extravagance. He was actually putting into narrative practice one aspect of a cherished belief, the complex doctrine of co-inherence. This is a unitary principle which proposes, among other things, that individual uniqueness is illusory, that one person may contain many and the many are ultimately parts of one. This doctrine goes beyond the power of sympathy, that favored belief of benevolists, which is only a means of vicarious sharing and communication. The doctrine of co-inherence posits a universal community, in which the accidents of time, space, language, endowment, station, personal identity, all that makes for seeming finitude and isolation, are subsumed in the essence of the one. I mean no disrespect when I suggest that this is an apposite doctrine for a practitioner of theological romance. Certainly Williams used it to great advantage.

It is very easy to generalize about the romances of Charles Williams, for his work in this genre is remarkably uniform. He puts the supernatural into being and action in a commonplace setting. Part of its distinctiveness, however, lies in the ease with which prodigies seem to occur; the reader is little afflicted with the strain and parade that often attend representations of the otherworldly. The accommodation derives somewhat from Williams's own beliefs about the comprehensive and unitive nature of reality, but irrespective of its source, it is one mark of the successful practitioner of fantasy. Not only do the marvels seem plausible within the ordinary, but the ordinary is in turn invested with wonder. A susceptible reader of *War in Heaven*, for example, may thereafter see the Holy Grail in any communion chalice.

Consistent with this intense objectification of the abstract is the rapidity of action that characterizes his work. Williams presents spiritual crises which so engage his persons that their thoughts are invested with strong feeling. The fundamental conflicts promote partisanship and anxious movement toward resolution. Regularly too, Williams builds his romances to climactic scenes of enlightenment, in which the great truths revealed seem both new and familiar.

In an account of his progress from atheism to Christian faith, C. S. Lewis makes clear that he had a lifelong commitment to fantasy. As soon as he could follow his own taste, his "allegiance" went to romance, to all books in which he could hear "the horns of elf-land." [15] He records also that he early created, in drawing and writing, a region called Animal-Land and that from this entertainment grew chivalric tales, history, and elaborate geographical description. He wove a "web of childhood," less lurid than what the Brontë children fabricated but no less expressive of a lively and consuming fancy. As Lewis continued toward maturity, various kinds of reading engaged his interest, either transiently or permanently. Some prepared him for a life of literary scholarship, some for his years of prominence as a lay propagator of the Christian faith. Beyond these he mentions specifically the children's stories of Edith Nesbit Bland and Beatrix Potter, *Gulliver's Travels*, the exotic productions of H. Rider Haggard, the pioneering science fiction of H. G. Wells, fairy tales of all kinds, Norse and Germanic mythology, William Morris, and George Macdonald. Macdonald was, as I have earlier suggested, decisive as much to Lewis's spiritual development as to his literary. It seems, in short, that Lewis's contribution to prose fiction fantasy came from a lifelong preparation undertaken in response to personal interest rather than professional demands.

His simplest fantasy is *The Great Divorce* (1946). It is a narrative demonstration of the irreconcilable difference between good and evil. Attempts to deny or mitigate this opposition Lewis considers to be among the gravest errors of modern thought. The narrative takes the form of a dream-vision, in which the major contrasts between good and evil, as Heaven and Hell, are schematically objectified. Heaven is intensely real and vivid. Its light is blinding, its music penetrating, its matter preternaturally substantial. Visitors in Heaven cannot lift its golden apples; they cut their unaccustomed feet on its brilliant

15. *Surprised by Joy: The Shape of My Early Life* (London: Geoffrey Bles, 1955), p. 12.

grass. The principle is simple: "Heaven is not a state of mind. Heaven is reality itself. All that is fully real is Heavenly." [16]

Hell, embodied chiefly in the windy, desolate, murky town from which the visitors depart for Heaven, is by contrast all shadow and no substance. As with matter, so with inhabitants. The heavenly beings are ageless, joyous, gloriously naked, loving, and giving. Their characteristic expression is laughter and song. Those who are visiting are wraithlike, timid, quarrelsome; they find Heaven painful alike to their hell-bound senses and constricted opinions. All the visitors, the "ghosts," may stay among and become of the saved if they will undergo rebirth, which means sharp separation from their old lives and selves. Many are so devoted to their sins and blindness that they beg to return to their familiar earthly hell. The few who make the change enter, after the pains of purification, upon an eternity of joy and certainty. There is no place for doubt and speculation in Heaven; the saved not only rejoice in certainty, but are delivered from any compulsion to discuss it.

All fantasy is contrived, but in *The Great Divorce* Lewis made little attempt to absorb the contrivance into a fully developed and autonomously persuasive illusion. Presumably he considered the narrative, characterization, and imagery self-contained and intrinsically meaningful. Perhaps they are, though one wonders what the book might signify to a reader ignorant of Christian eschatology. It is evidently for people with such knowledge that Lewis wrote *The Great Divorce*, just as Charles Williams assumed a knowledge of one or several standard mythologies.

On first reading, *The Great Divorce* prompts comparison with E. M. Forster's "The Celestial Omnibus." They have the same basic narrative device, and both favor the pure in heart. Forster is concerned with the contrast between innocent wonder as a response to literary beauty and spurious worship of culture. There is some resemblance between Forster's Mr. Bons, who cannot endure the reality of the immortals, and the "ghosts" who find Heaven intolerable. But the heavenly beings in *The Great Divorce* are not so through initial innocence; there are murderers

16. *The Great Divorce* (New York: Macmillan, 1946), p. vi.

and adulterers among them. They have reached their beatitude by the touch of grace upon their repentance, faith, and will. Forster attempted no such illustration of Christian doctrine.

C. S. Lewis's principal contribution to fantasy is the trilogy of what he called "planetary romances"—*Out of the Silent Planet* (1938), *Perelandra* (1943), *That Hideous Strength* (1945). A single idea and source of narrative energy control all three: that the universe is still, as it always has been, the object of a tremendous struggle provoked by the conquering, destructive ambition of the Bent One (Satan). The evil agents are principally human beings who in their demonic possession employ extraordinary powers and intelligence, great technical and scientistic ability, in the service of interplanetary subjugation. They work—whether on Malacandra (Mars), Perelandra (Venus), or Thulcandra (Earth, the silent plant long enthralled to the Bent One)—by force, fraud, temptation, intimidation, perversion of thought and language, and a limited kind of magic. They are subtle and compelling, but like the evildoers in most romances, incapable of victory in the final conflict. The human agents of Maleldil, the universal deity of good, are in varying degrees conscious of the gravity of the contest in which they participate. The most active and successful is the numinously named Elwin Ransom, hero of the trilogy. Through his progressively awakened understanding, the cosmic dimensions of the struggle emerge. Ransom draws several staggering assignments, none more awesome than combatting the temptation to disobedience offered to Tinidril, the Eve of Perelandra, a young planet where the efforts of the Bent One are for the first time being exerted.

This singleness of a cosmic conflict throughout the three romances does much to bind them together. Unity of effect, as well as of result, is a primary object of the sustained narrative illusion that Lewis creates. The planetary system is one. The *eldila*, spirit emanations both benign and malignant, have from the beginning ranged at will through outer space. Now men have also learned such travel and have found not only that they can live on other planets but also that they can communicate with nonearthly and nonhuman beings, most of whom, unlike the planetary bogeymen of H. G. Wells, are agreeable creatures. It becomes evident that one language, Old Solar, once was common throughout creation. This can yet be learned and used abroad. Moreover, there is one spiritual government, with Maleldil its supreme deity. Time is a single continuum, not of Earth alone but of the entire system. Its span is astronomical rather than geological, and the planets are of differing ages within it. Malacandra is ancient beyond imagining, cold, moving toward its twilight.[17] Venus, on the other hand, is young, yet a seaworld, green, vital, paradisiac, a plausible setting for an attempt to implant a new—and graver—original sin. Unity is promoted finally by making a power struggle on Earth, in *That Hideous Strength*, simply a further development in the contests that have taken place on Mars and Venus. The same powers of Deep Heaven are behind the alliance of Elwin Ransom (now Mr. Fisher-King) and Logres as embodied in the awakened Merlin Ambrosius, and the same powers behind the busy diabolists of the National Institute of Co-ordinated Experiments (N.I.C.E.) at Belbury. This focusing of one phase of the cosmic conflict on a familiar setting and a familiar aspect of modern culture, the research institute, was Lewis's shrewdest device toward unity and verisimilitude.

The need for a sense of action throughout the universe, however, impelled Lewis to seek further means toward verisimilitude and immediacy. The tactics of a novelist, strictly defined, would not enable him to deal with the heart of his matter, which is beyond society, human psychology, and experience. Like others before him who proposed to assert eternal Providence, Lewis needed a cosmic narrative and imaginative structure, and he achieved it by combining traditional myth with that of his own creation. In doing so he reflects his conviction that in essence myth is preverbal and thus preliterary. Two statements somewhat clarify his belief. In discussing George Macdonald, he remarks: "The critical problem with which we are confronted is whether

17. In *The War of the Worlds* (1898) Wells cited that age, increasing cold, and exhaustion of the planet as the primary motive for Martian invasion of the earth: "Their world is far gone in its cooling and this world is still crowded with life, but crowded only with what they regard as inferior animals. To carry warfare sunward is, indeed, their only escape from the destruction that generation after generation creeps upon them." *Seven Famous Novels by H. G. Wells* (New York: Knopf, 1934), p. 266.

this art—the art of myth-making—is a species of the literary art. The objection to so classifying it is that the Myth does not essentially exist in words at all." [18] Similarly in *Miracles* (1947) he sketches a theory that, though not directly applied to literary creation, is yet pertinent: "The truth first appears in *mythical* form and then by a long process of condensing or focussing finally becomes incarnate as History. This involves the belief that Myth in general is not merely misunderstood history . . . nor diabolical illusion . . . nor priestly lying . . . but, at its best, a real though unfocussed gleam of divine truth falling on human imagination." [19]

The "history" Lewis here cites is not, of course, the same as the history to which writers of fiction, even romance, have often claimed kinship for their works. But neither is it totally different. Chronicling historian and romancer alike, when they deal with matters grand and remote, are faced with problems of objectification and ordering, and both are likely to feel the inadequacy of language and sequential narrative—which call attention to their own finitude—for expressing the truths with which they are concerned. The difficulties are severe, and the writer of prose fiction cannot directly avail himself of the devices of an epic poet. Particularly he can do but little to achieve that sublimity of imagery, syntax, and sound that Milton trusted, though uneasily, in presenting his cosmic vision. But the writer of fiction can use myth, that known through inheritance and that created by himself, as a means of displaying an orderly progression of events and meanings that, understood analogically, will provide the reader with access to a conceptual system otherwise statable only in abstractions and dogmas. Lewis's presentation of this kind of "fictive analogue" has prompted some to call him a popularizer, and Lewis would not at all have resented this label. He was attempting to reach a variety of readers. Regularly in his fiction his syncretized myth directs attention to the essentials of complex doctrine, represented imaginatively rather than speculatively. No reader can miss his adaptation of the fundamental Christian

18. *George Macdonald: An Anthology* (New York: Macmillan, 1947), pp. 14–15.
19. *Miracles: A Preliminary Study* (New York: Macmillan, 1947), p. 161n.

story. Readers who wish to follow the range of Lewis's allusiveness will find his fundamental, easily understood meanings enriched by learning that is rarely extraneous. Those who wish to read for the story alone can scarcely miss his major contentions. For either kind of reader, his clear narration and brisk, plausible dialogue will be a pleasure.

In part for the skillful narration and in part for more, Marjorie Nicolson has high praise for *Out of the Silent Planet:* "Just when I most despaired, believing that the kind of imagination I have been discussing was entirely lost in our generation, a novel appeared that gave the lie to my pessimism, a modern interplanetary voyage whose author need not bow before any of the masters of the past. . . . *Out of the Silent Planet* . . . is to me the most beautiful of all cosmic voyages and in some ways the most moving." [20]

As is consistent with the general practice of romances, Lewis's characterization is little given to nuances and deep penetrations, even when he is representing in *That Hideous Strength* two human beings whose values are confused and divided. Their difficulties in making a choice between the powers that impinge upon them are regularly externalized in speech, action, and directly reported thought. About their dark psychic and emotional stirrings the reader, seeing little, may guess if he wishes. Most of the characters are committed to good or evil before they ever appear in narrative action, and though their natures may develop along determined lines, they do not significantly change. The clearest example of this is Weston. In *Out of the Silent Planet* he shows himself a perverter of science, an activist, and a "life worshiper." It is no surprise in *Perelandra* when he turns megalomaniac and, possessed by a demon, raves and froths, rips up birds and frogs with his fingernails, goes through "a whole repertory of obscenities" upon his own body, though all the while he remains a dangerous tempter, with the devil's eloquence in the Old Solar language, to the Venusian Eve. From the beginning Weston has been destined to embody the Unman. This is scarcely subtle characterization, but Lewis's purpose did not call for subtlety in this respect, any more than did Milton's. How-

20. *Voyages to the Moon* (New York: Macmillan, 1968), pp. 251–52.

ever devious his ways, the devil of standard Christian mythology is a simplistic destroyer.

C. S. Lewis brought theological romance to a higher artistry, and a higher persuasiveness, than did Charles Williams. Lewis's greater technical skill I have already suggested. Moreover, he manages more adroitly the interfusion of doctrine and action. Except perhaps in *Perelandra*, moral theology and cosmogony are totally objectified and made operative in the story. It is always the mark of a successful romancer of purpose that his doctrine seems transformed into narrative action. And this impression remains with readers, even after the immediate engagement is past. The presented doctrine may be discussed of itself, but it has been liberated from its abstract condition and made living. This is the artistic analogue of the word made flesh.

As a purveyor of myth Lewis is likewise most accomplished. He does not offer his readers the rich mélange of the familiar and the esoteric tradition, and Lewis is much less noticeably than Williams a syncretist. He stays pretty much with Christian mythology and with those aspects of the Arthurian that center on Merlin and Logres; Professor Nicolson notes his familiarity with "the long tradition stemming from Kepler and the *Somnium*" (p. 253). Lewis himself many times acknowledged his debt to previous writers about planets and interplanetary travel. But he is also among the myth makers. In his hands the familiar becomes new and the new familiar. Though one can in analysis separate what he inherited (and relied upon his readers to know) from what he created, the two remain bound together and interactive. Not only do the inherited and the created form a technical unity; they combine also in their evocation of the reader's feeling. Professor Nicolson credits Lewis, "the scholar-poet," with achieving "something unachieved by previous imaginary voyagers in space." Earlier writers had created new worlds from legend, from mythology, from fairy tale. "Mr. Lewis has created *myth* itself, myth woven of desires and aspiration deep-seated in some, at least, of the human race" (p. 254). As she points out, Elwin Ransom himself discovers progressively the mythical dimension of what he is experiencing, and the reader shares these discoveries with him. Thus in another way the familiar and the new become one. The trilogy of C. S. Lewis is a triumph in theological romance.[21]

21. Kathryn Hume describes in detail the "architectonic accomplishment" of Lewis's three romances and concludes: "Together, they can truly be said to form a cosmic romance, a work which expands the bounds and interests of the genre to higher spiritual levels than any romancer since Spenser at least has attempted or achieved in English." "C. S. Lewis' Trilogy: A Cosmic Romance," *Modern Fiction Studies*, 20 (Winter, 1974–75), 517.

eleven   *The Value of Fantasy*

After the examination of the principles of fantasy and the illustration of these in exemplary works, one task remains. This is to suggest an answer to the question, What is the value of fantasy as a mode of prose fiction? There are signs that consideration of this question is appropriate. As I have noted earlier, though fantasies have been written in many periods, fantasy has no history, that is, no continuous developmental movement. Rather, it tends to be prominent through a span of years, emerging for no clearly ascertainable reasons, then receding. Its time of longest prominence is the one I have chosen to review.

Between 1880 and the mid-1950s numerous authors, many of them eminent, played with fantasy, wrote one or two, then abandoned it. Only Ronald Firbank, Elinor Wylie, Charles Williams, and Tolkien made it a major part of their literary careers. The members of the majority have left no stated reasons for their desertion. I think it safe to guess that they undertook their fantasies as experiments, perhaps learned from writing them, then found the form insufficiently rewarding for further expense of time and effort. There are hints, for example, that long before he prepared the lectures that became *Aspects of the Novel*, E. M. Forster committed himself to fantasy in *A Room with a View*, only to become impatient with his choice before he had finished writing it. Like others—among them Walter de la Mare, Algernon Blackwood, and "Saki"—his chief contributions to the mode are in short fiction.

What are the attractions of fantasy, especially to a writer who is in an experimental phase of development? First, it relies on ingenuity of a kind that other narrating does not demand. That is to say, it invites the play of wit within a controlled situation. One mark of a lively mind is its desire to depart from the familiar and the conventional. This provides not only release but also a chance for novel speculative formations. Often these are sheer whimsy, appropriate to such conversation as makes an evening's entertainment, forgotten the next morning. Only when affectation or self-gratification dominates does such sport lapse into preciosity. But sometimes these formations of the fancy constitute a critique of the established truths that they playfully reject. Thus, for example, *Zuleika Dobson* sets a factitious standard against which the hoary dignities of Oxford and the pretensions of its members may be measured.

Two facts must be noted again. The ambience of fantasy, in which the "false" displaces the "true," is intellectual. Its maneuvers do not compromise any further serious affective or tendentious purpose that the author may have. Though I cannot think of a fantasy that could be called sentimental in any gross way, there are many in which the fanciful establishment of the impossible makes possible an engagement of the reader's emotions. In *The Lord of the Flies* a demonstration against the standard concept of innocence permits a horrifying vision of human depravity where the reader least expects to find such. This work is as much a fantasy as Abbott's *Flatland*, which has no affective content at all.

Just as fantasy does not exclude emotion, so it does not fundamentally attack the norms it denies. It may leave the reader enriched with an intellectual modification that prevents his ever again holding to his original naïve understanding of the norm, but it will cause no revolution. This was what Forster wished to suggest when he observed that fantasy is dominated by "small gods," that its power "penetrates into every corner of the universe, but not into the forces that govern it. . . ." Nothing is immune from fantasy, but nothing of any conceptual validity is destroyed or overturned by it. I have repeatedly stressed that wit turned to making fanciful narrative operates according to the principles of play. Whatever else they may be, revolutionists are not playful. A whimsical Lenin or a Blake who wished his prophetic books to be regarded as so much sporting is unthinkable. Yet to say that fantasy strikes against convention with no zeal to alter or subvert is not to suggest that fantasy is quite frivolous. A fantasist may really hope that his story will have some lasting effect of modifying the way in which his readers accept the norm that he has playfully violated.

The impingement of fantasy on understanding suggests another reason for its appeal, especially to the writer who is testing his capabilities to find his strength. It gives him an opportunity for a direct and simple control of the reader's intellectual response. We are all accustomed to a novelist's management of his reader's thoughts and feelings, even when there is an appearance of abstention. Consideration of the methods whereby control may be unobtrusively exercised forms a great part of Wayne Booth's *The Rhetoric of Fiction;* these are both complex and subtle. In a fantasy, however, there is one strategy of control, from which all tactical development follows. This is the subversive intellectual construct. It is not at all, or very little, concealed, and the very candor of positing the impossible invites a peculiar participation by the reader. He knows, as well as does the author, that this is a game, and he joins it without illusions. Thus fantasy promotes a community that is likely not so profound as that generated by other fiction, but certainly simpler and closer.

With these attractions, we may wonder why fantasy is inconstantly prevalent through literary history, why it from time to time recedes. From 1880 to about 1957 fantasies appeared frequently; since then there have been very few, despite an increased use of the fantastic as material by many writers of what is called postrealistic fiction. Why should this be?

One answer, I believe, is that fantasy suffers from the defects of its virtues. Because it is rationalistic, manipulative, and playful, it rarely contains the visions and outrages of writers—and readers—whose sense of urgency and imminent disaster has overcome their capability of consideration. In 1947 W. H. Auden chose to call his long poem *The Age of Anxiety.* For the time the phrase was apt, but it will no longer serve. Since the mid-1950s it has been borne in upon us that we live in an age of panic—or perhaps panic and emptiness. That this view is both hysterical and ahistorical, that the alarms of one time become the amusements of a later time, offers no immediate assurance. However right it may be, the poise of perspective can be but precariously maintained. Even though our comfortable homes, offices, and communities seem yet inviolate, the menaces that stalk through our newspapers and across our television screens are out there, not far away, moving toward us. This and a hundred other well-known predicaments of the recent years give no encouragement to satisfaction with the play of wit.

Of the novelists who represent and interpret the modern temper, many deal in the fantastic. This seem inevitable, for as computers, automation, surgical transplants, various "mysticisms," pollution, drug culture, poverty and revolution, potentials for mass destruction, and foreign policies that gamble with disaster have become part of daily experience, the present has become a time in which the fantastic is familiar as it never was before. It permeates our present culture. There are countless readers of science fiction, and usage has established the identity of science fiction and fantasy. Elsewhere I have argued that conceptually and formally they are distinct. Even so, the prevalence of such writing is a symptom of engagement with the fantastic. Likewise the current spate of romances that convey adult readers—not children and adolescents—into experiences with the remote, the exotic, and the magical.[1]

Evidence of this heightened taste does not come from literature alone. Popular interest can unfailingly be aroused by stories of UFOs or ESP, by indications that dolphins have a language, by intimations that plants may be sentient and responsive to love or hostility, by forecasts that medication and surgery may alter the facts of human biology as we know them. And so it goes. The fantastic abounds in current films, in music, psychology, sociology, anthropology, theology. Manifestations prompt the whole range of emotions from horror to rapture; the only thing they do not generate is indifference. Harvey Cox, in a rich and exciting theological essay, sees an unlimited range for "fantasy," if only people will regain for themselves the freedom it requires. And he sees in it also a forecast perhaps of renewed life: "We have spent the last few hundred years with our cultural attention focused fixedly on the 'outside' factual world—exploring, investigating, mastering it. Those with a penchant for fantasy never really felt at home. But now there are signs that a new age of fantasy is about to begin, that there are new worlds

1. See Patrick Merla, " 'What Is Real?' Asked the Rabbit One Day," *Saturday Review of the Arts*, 45 (November, 1972), 43–50.

to explore. We may be on the threshold of an exciting period of symbol formation and myth creation. It could be an age in which the fantasy side of our civilization once again flowers." [2]

What does all this stir and confusion mean? That the Lord of Misrule has broken loose? That we are dead to any but gross and violent stimulants? That the psyche finds disruptive ways of exercising itself? That we are responding vitally to the world we live in? At present we cannot know, and years may pass before we do. Meanwhile, the symptoms are all about us; few people can avoid observing—or displaying—them.

Thus it is no accident that in their different ways such novelists as John Barth, Iris Murdoch, Muriel Spark, William Burroughs, Kurt Vonnegut, Philip Roth, John Updike, Samuel Beckett, John Hawkes, and James Purdy make it central in their work. This list of names could easily be extended, but in the fiction of whatever writers might be named would be found very few authentic fantasies.[3]

Though this is no place for a comprehensive review of recent fiction, the generalizations suggested above may be tested by some further consideration. During the past ten years there has been seemingly no end to the bizarrerie, extremity, and idiosyncrasy intrinsic in the material of English and American novels. Representation of extravagance in an extravagant manner has ceased to be a mark of the avant-garde; it is now to be expected. Readers accommodate themselves, willingly if not easily, to the religious aberrations that Flannery O'Connor details, to the experiences of drug taking and the sexual grotesqueries of Burroughs's *Naked Lunch*, to the elaborate Alexandrian world of Lawrence Durrell and the postcatastrophic world, just emerging from the dark ages, of Miller's *A Canticle for Leibowitz*, to black humor of many varieties. Sometimes one can readily spec-

2. *The Feast of Fools: A Theological Essay on Festivity and Fantasy* (Cambridge, Mass.: Harvard University Press, 1969), pp. 66–67. This book provides a comprehensive view of the range and variety of the fantastic.

3. In the early pages Philip Roth's *The Breast* seems to be developing as a fantasy of metamorphosis made persuasive by carefully reported clinical detail. But as the work proceeds, objective narration is more and more replaced by the self-revelations of a psyche sick with the impotence of the modern male. Roth abandoned the method of play for that of organized introspection. For an opinion that judges *The Breast* to be unified throughout, see a review by Webster Schott, in *Life*, 73 (September 22, 1972), 12.

ify what a novel is "about." There are novels about alienation, autism, computers gone mad, the exotic effects of mass media, minority experience, counterculture, riot, revolution, all forms of sexual normality and abnormality. Muriel Spark's *Memento Mori* is about those intimations of mortality that come, sooner or later, to all; Golding's *Free Fall* is about a search for self-understanding; Terry Southern's *The Magic Christian* is about a campaign to discomfit "automata, governed by stock responses to various stimuli—mainly economic." [4] But it is impossible to state in a phrase the central matter of *Giles Goat-Boy, Pincher Martin,* or any novel (except perhaps *The Italian Girl*) of Iris Murdoch.

These and many other assertions of freedom in the concerns of recent fiction are only aspects of a more general dissociation from the realistic heritage of the nineteenth century. Such a revolt, with its accompanying antinomies, has appeared recurrently in the history of prose fiction. When it does, some critics worry about "the death of the novel" or its atomization; others welcome the changes as movements toward rebirth. That there is a need for rebirth, if not yet vital signs, is a central contention of John Aldridge:

> For there is abundant evidence that the imagination of the contemporary novel has remained locked in certain stereotyped modes of perceiving and recording reality that it has inherited from the modern classic literary past, but that, as stereotypes, have now ceased to relate meaningfully to the reality of which we are, or ought to be, most intensely aware. . . . All [theater and film, both American and European] have, like the novel, been subsisting for years on visions and fantasies of experience that have nothing to do with the way we actually think or live, but that represent merely increments of style, struck attitudes, ceremonial poses of anguish, passion, perversion, hysteria, and boredom that belong to a tradition of pioneering realism that is now dead and to a convention of feeling and action derived not from life but from other plays, films, and novels. [5]

4. Robert Scholes, *The Fabulators* (New York: Oxford University Press, 1967), p. 64. The whole discussion of *The Magic Christian* (pp. 62–66) reveals that the book is not so simple as my reference suggests.

5. *Time to Murder and Create: The Contemporary Novel in Crisis* (New York: McKay, 1966), pp. xi–xii.

In dissatisfaction with stereotypes Ihab Hassan finds the "common impulse" of what seems "a scattering of trends and forms"; they unite in "an attack on the accepted view of reality." He continues: "The decline in realistic techniques, the dearth of public themes, the aversion to ideology suggests a redefinition of the function of the novel which in the past has always tried to keep its vision centered on the highroads of life." [6] Redefinition, rebirth, and murdering to create are all metaphors for the same essential operation.

To such violent reformation, if that be what it is, fantasy can contribute nothing, for fantasy is bound to realistic traditions and methods. Let us examine the contrast between fantasy and recent fiction that embodies the fantastic via some of the language of the two passages quoted above. Much recent fiction deals with the "stereotypes" that Aldridge cites by destroying, denying, denouncing them, or otherwise making a radical departure from them or a fundamental replacement of them. The typical attitudes and procedures of the fantasist are not so drastic. He offers a speculative alternative, which is developed in a narration not intended to break up the idol; sometimes it does not disturb it at all. The fantasist's approach to a stereotype is intellectual; the reforming novelist, though he may use the weapons of intellect in his attack, is scarcely content with these alone.

There is also more often than not a difference in the targets. Aldridge refers to the "increments of style, struck attitudes, ceremonial poses of anguish, passion, perversion, hysteria, and boredom" that he believes present novelists should reject and that indeed many current practitioners do reject. These are the reliquary instruments of an obsolete heritage "from the modern classic literary past." Many recent revolutionary efforts are accordingly time-bound, part of a process of dynamic historical development, in which the revolutionary novelist asserts against the outworn traditions a representation of "the way we actually think or live" now. Thus he usually stays with contemporary concerns, even though these, as in *The Sot-Weed Factor*, may be enriched by strong historical and mythical associations. The

6. *Radical Innocence: Studies in the Contemporary American Novel* (Princeton: Princeton University Press, 1961), p. 103.

fantasist is not so closely held to immediate "relevance." Certainly the writer who posits an impossible society wishes his readers to compare this construct with the society of their current experience. But the society of *Looking Backward* or 1984 is impossible not only in relation to the contemporary formation but also in relation to any historically known society and even to the very idea of a society. And in those fantasies that are conceptually simpler, such as those originating in metamorphosis, there is no concern with a time setting at all. A lady changed into a fox is an impossibility whenever it occurs. The propositions against which a fantasist makes counterdemonstration are not stereotypes of limited duration such as Aldridge scorns, but rather general truths and conventions of understanding reality so widely accepted as to be suprahistorical. Perhaps this detachment from developmental phenomena accounts in part for the fact that fantasy has no history.

I have said that fantasy is bound to realistic traditions and methods, though the relationship is not one of subservience. A scrutiny of this proposition will reveal another aspect of difference between fantasy and recent reforming fiction. In many works of fiction, presentational realism, that is, a sustained verisimilitude, demonstrates and supports the realism of content. The assumption is that in such works "realism" and "reality" are either directly synonymous or so closely related that the former is only the agent of the latter, whose validity is self-evident. This equivalence can be seen in *Emma, Dombey and Son, Middlemarch, The Old Wives Tale,* and many another, which likely still form the main tradition of the English novel. In fantasy there is the playful pretense that the content is real, but the only "realism" is in presentation, which because it exists alone must be persuasive. But the revolutionary novelist, of whatever period, is playing no game. Such a one says, as did Virginia Woolf in her essay "Mr. Bennett and Mrs. Brown," that the "reality" revealed by "realism" is either invalid or fraudulent or both. Things are not what they have been made to seem. The "highroads of life" are not necessarily the ways to clear knowing; the customary representations are routes that mislead. Reality is there, but it must be reached by seizure, depth exploration, metaphoric or symbolic systems, refraction, total mythic recasting, or other means that, however devious in execution, gets to the heart of the matter. If this forces readers to move without the supports of usual story-telling and the usual assumptions about what is real—and indeed makes some readers refuse the effort—so much the better for them. They have been deprived of a familiar comfort and re-warded with a way to the truth, however disquieting this may be when confronted as it is.

I would not like to see the scheme of the preceding paragraph made into a paradigm. Realistic fiction, fantasy, and antirealistic fiction are alike in offering the possibility of complex, rather than monistic, execution. But the posture of fantasy, vis-à-vis realism and antirealism, reveals its nature. It imitates the validating process of the former, plausible and coherent presentation, with a completeness not always found in realistic novels themselves, but it does so in support of a fictive "reality" that violates conventions as to reality. On the other hand, fantasy and antirealistic fiction deal with materials that are or seem to be, according to some convention, "untrue." But whereas antirealistic fiction insists that its materials are experientially valid, fantasy never makes this claim. Writers who set forth the fantastic may play games, but ultimately these games are tactical maneuvers instrumenting some serious strategy. In fantasy itself play is essential. Thus fantasy exists in an intellectually closed system; antirealistic fiction, however bizarre, expresses a vision or a version of life itself. The one calls for contemplative, the other for direct, participation.

Two exhibits of the fantastic not confined in fantasy will illuminate the recent practices more than any further abstract analysis. For the purpose I choose Kurt Vonnegut's *God Bless You, Mr. Rosewater* (1965) and *A Clockwork Orange* (1962), by Anthony Burgess.

God Bless You, Mr. Rosewater; or, Pearls before Swine (1965), by Vonnegut, was immediately labeled in reviews with such terms as "fantasy" and "fantastic," along with "satire," "black humor," "scathing," "wacky," and others. That it is fantasy, within the understanding I have attempted to establish, does not appear from examination. Neither in premise, major action, nor significant details does any impossibility show itself. The action represents no more than what is conventionally improbable. Even the astonishing final gesture, in which Eliot Rosewater instructs the counsel of his foundation "to draw up . . . papers that will legally acknowledge that every child in Rosewater County said to be mine *is* mine, regardless of blood type," seems in context both legally and psychologically feasible. We are not given the enlightenment of an attorney's advice about what might happen when such an expression of will is subjected to probate proceedings. The wildly improbable is Vonnegut's métier, and that absurdity which can usually be reached when essentially ordinary phenomena, such as the organization and functioning of a benevolent foundation, are carried to an unlikely but logically permissible conclusion.

Why, then, call *God Bless You, Mr. Rosewater* fantastic? For several reasons both substantial and stylistic. One is a sustained polarization of values, whereby a familiar combination of business enterprise and philanthropy is rendered depraved and compassion resides only in a fatuous wreck of a man who loves everybody, but particularly the insulted and injured. Quite possibly Eliot Rosewater is "the sanest man in America" and the affluent society itself, as Vonnegut opines, a fabric of knavery and folly. Such an ideological contention is familiar enough, and has been for years. Vonnegut reverses the contrast of values normally implied in the image of pearls before swine. The pearls, far from embodying wisdom or being of great price, are the growths of rottenness, and the swine deserve much better. Indeed, if they had ever received better, they might be other than swine.

But lest anyone believe that *God Bless You, Mr. Rosewater* is a sentimental fable, it must quickly be added that the whole tone of the book is mocking and mimicking. This major aspect of style and expression of attitude set up not a distortion of truth but an extreme formulation that exposes what Vonnegut takes to be the clichés, illusions, self-deceptions, and pious frauds of our time. Disrespectfulness permeates the work, in small details and overall development. This appears most clearly in some of the proper names—Eliot Rosewater, Senator Lister Ames Rosewater, Leonard Leech, Geraldine Ames Rockefeller, Sylvia Du Vrais Zetterling (affiliated with Rothschilds and DuPonts), Diana Moon Glampers. Here is one of the standard tricks of formal satire, and readers need only see these names to make for themselves the desired associations. Beyond this Vonnegut's mockery extends to all aspects of American affluence, privilege, self-serving, and self-delusion.

Much more might be written to describe Vonnegut's principles and method, but all would only illustrate the central fact that he has created the fantastic by improbable characterological and narrative extensions from the familiar. Thus he has produced absurdity, a frequent emanation from recent fiction, of persons, actions, relationships. Absurdity is different from impossibility in being a situation experientially present or potential, for which reason it bothers people even when it amuses them. And in recent thinking the absurd and the fantastic are more often than not synonymous. Perception of both has become a daily occurrence; thus *God Bless You, Mr. Rosewater* answers the call for the replacement of stereotypes by vital responses implied in Aldridge's statement. And so, in their different ways, have many other recent novelists who are grouped within the unsatisfactory term "postrealistic." Many of these deal with the fantastic because it is with us, perhaps too much with us. The writer of fantasy, however, has a radically different concern; he deals with what is not, pretending that it is.

The man known to most readers by the pseudonym Anthony Burgess has since 1956 followed a career of astonishing versatility. He has published a score of novels, several studies of Shakespeare and Joyce, translations, essays in linguistics and literary criticism, studies in the history and culture of travel, and a guide to contemporary fiction. He is also a composer of music. Though he modestly professes to regard his novels as "works of craftsmanship for sale, objects as well-made as I can make them," his contributions to fiction are varied and exciting. His Malayan trilogy, based on experience as an education officer in the Colonial Civil Service, reminds one of the novels with which Joyce Cary began his career; both men made a vocation of an avocation, after being invalided out of the service. Anthony Burgess's works include two that come close to being fantasies, *Devil of a*

State and *The Wanting Seed*, and one realized mythological fantasy, *The Eve of St. Venus*. He could have made *A Clockwork Orange* such also, had he so chosen, but one may infer from the book itself that a rationalistic method was not adequate for what he wished to represent.

It is a story of a future that is both drab and depraved, when the violence of teen-age gangs is the routine occurrence of a city at night and few dare to venture out. The central figure may justly be called a hoodlum, a punk, a rocker, or any other disapproving name one might wish to use of the juvenile delinquent. For Alex, women exist to be raped, old men to be beaten, parents and authorities to be despised, and property to be smashed. He is fond of listening to Bach, Mozart, Beethoven, Schoenberg, Orff, and others on his stereo hi-fi, but as he does, sadistic and orgasmic daydreams run through his mind and pace themselves to the music. He is arrested for murder in the act of burglary, and sentenced. In prison he is treated and "cured" by a method more horrible to him than any brutality could be, being forced to watch seemingly endless movies of unrelieved torture, dismemberment, and mayhem. They make him sick. At the end of the treatment all violence of action has left him; he refuses to participate in an antigovernment campaign that holds him up as the "boy victim of criminal reform." He is only grateful to the state, which will give him a job, protect him from his enemies, and give him back his music. As the book ends, he listens again to the Ninth Symphony of Beethoven: "Oh, it was gorgeosity and yumyumyum. When it came to the Scherzo I could viddy myself very clean running and running on like very light and mysterious nogas, carving the whole litso of the creeching world with my cutthroat britva. And there was the slow movement and the lovely last singing movement still to come. I was cured all right."

For readers inexperienced in this novel and not yet familiar with the film version, the foregoing often quoted passage provides a sample of the language in which it is written. The whole work is cast in an argot composed of neologisms, slang, puns, mockeries ("baddiwad" for bad), elemental images ("panhandle" for erection), and words derived, and probably degraded, from Russian. The glossary compiled by Stanley Edgar Hyman, from which I have taken my illustrations, is indispensable, though as he says, the reader who persists beyond the first shock of non-recognition will find context an aid to understanding. The language of *A Clockwork Orange* is as ingenious as Joyce's and like his expresses pathos, comedy, exaltation, contempt, bewilderment—indeed, the whole range of human response. Like Joyce's further, this language is no nonfunctional tour de force or display of idiosyncrasy. The whole book is a monologue narrative, and young Alex is his language.

The uniqueness of language in *A Clockwork Orange* is a symptom of its being other than a fantasy. In an earlier chapter I demonstrated that in diction, syntax, and style, fantasists ordinarily stay within standard English, for the writing itself is meant to contribute to that realism of presentation which is requisite. But in *A Clockwork Orange* Anthony Burgess wishes to convey the reader into the nightmare that is Alex's being and his world. As nonliterary occurrences, nightmares and dreams generally are fantastic, but they lack evident order and significance. These must be ascertained by a process of rationalization. Anthony Burgess's effort—and it is the effort of many writers of current fiction—is to make the reader confront experience as it is, in all its apparent chaos and distortion. This method of achieving immediacy has a long history; some critics say that it had an early manifestation in *Tristram Shandy*. This is the occasion not for tracing that history, but rather for asserting that such directness is radically inconsistent with the intellectual play and the formation of an apparently plausible construct that are essential in fantasy.

It would, however, be foolish to pretend that fantasy becomes inadequate only when times are so distressing that most writers and readers abandon their faith in reason. Were this so, fantasy never could be written. Historians repeatedly caution us against the error of assuming that simply because the oncoming disasters of the past do not upset us now, they never seemed real threats and never warranted the anxiety they provoked. George Saintsbury entitled a book on early eighteenth-century English literature *The Peace of the Augustans*; on the title page this work is described as "a survey of eighteenth century literature as a place of rest and refreshment." What a caper of irony! One needs little acquaintance with contemporaneous events to know that an Augustan temper was the insecure possession of a few and that the literary scene and the public events of the time were anything but peaceful. An ignorant or willfully blind nostalgia allows many people to see in the years just before World War I the last sweet dream of peace. It is not difficult to shatter this illusion. In the last chapters of *The Education of Henry Adams* that perceptive commentator, extraordinarily privileged in the range of his experience, expressed the uneasiness with which he learned between 1900 and 1905 that the forces of acceleration and multiplicity were altering the world so drastically that man's traditional ways of regarding himself and his history had become childish. *The 42nd Parallel*, the first novel of Dos Passos's trilogy, *U.S.A.*, offers overwhelming evidence of a violent tenor of life, especially in the conflict of labor organizers and the established interests that opposed them. Two later historians, Barbara Tuchman in *The Proud Tower* and Samuel Hynes in *The Edwardian Turn of Mind*, have detailed the menaces and portents of disaster that between 1890 and 1914 were there to be seen by anyone who could or would look about him. A generalization in Miss Tuchman's foreword is pertinent:

> The period was not a Golden Age or *Belle Epoque* except to the thin crust of the privileged class. It was not a time exclusively of confidence, innocence, comfort, stability, security and peace. All these qualities were certainly present. People *were* more confident of values and standards, more innocent in the sense of retaining more hope of mankind, than they are today, although they were not more peaceful nor, except for the upper few, more comfortable. Our misconception lies in assuming that doubt and fear, ferment, protest, violence and hate were not equally present. We have been misled by the people of the time themselves who, in looking back across the gulf of the War, see that earlier half of their lives misted over by a lovely sunset haze of peace and security. It did not seem so golden when they were in the midst of it. . . . A phenomenon of such extended malignance as the Great War does not come out of a Golden Age. . . .[7]

7. *The Proud Tower: A Portrait of the World before the War, 1890–1914* (New York: Macmillan, 1962), pp. xiii–xiv. The temporal range of Professor Hynes's book is more restricted, and he investigates some aspects of cultural and

All this is not introduced to astonish the reader with what he has never known or suspected. Rather, I wish to note that fantasy flourished in this time of dismay and that among the fantasists were authors like Wells, Forster, Arthur Machen, Virginia Woolf, and George Orwell, who were aware that darkness lay about and ahead of them. From this one may conclude that though the stresses that provoke irrationalism may discourage the writing of fantasy, its prevalence or absence is not determined by circumstances.

Thus I am forced back to the question of value, that is, of the preferences that writers and readers feel as to ultimate literary worth. And there is no doubt. For better or worse, those forms are more prestigious that open the way to elevated imagination and profound insight. In competition with these, the play of wit and the formations of fancy, however ingenious, provide no more than diversions. Forster names four novelists who in his judgment achieved that highest excellence which he called prophecy: Melville, Emily Brontë, Dostoevsky, and D. H. Lawrence. All had some command of reason, but no one would think of valuing their novels principally for the enlightenment they provide. They give us visions, not just clarification. And so it is through literary history. For better or worse again, the purveyors of wit may provide amusement, liberate the mind, expand judgment, and preserve sanity. For these, readers are grateful, but they give their veneration to the authors and works in which rationality is either transcended or transformed.

What I have been describing is an aspect of established taste, which in turn is a symptom of human waywardness in regard to reason. Repeatedly one of two mistakes manifests itself: either reason is elevated into a law and a godhead justifying blind worship and tyranny, or it is degraded to an enemy that prompts any excess of anti-intellectualism. That poise which uses reason as an instrument of the good life, an ally of feeling and imagination, seems attainable by a few only, and even for them it is sometimes a precarious balance. Perhaps man is an *animal rationis capax*, but the optimism latent in this phrase is more often than

intellectual history that Miss Tuchman does not consider. But his conclusions are much the same.

not disappointed. One of many consequences of this condition is that works of literature which make a strong appeal to, or demand on, the reasonable faculty rarely enjoy the wide acclaim of those which exploit the feelings. All this might be made the theme of a diatribe, but no combination of cogency and eloquence would change a condition that has resisted the best efforts of Erasmus, More, Rabelais, Swift, and many other defeated proponent of sanity.

Earlier in this study I attempted to demonstrate that fantasy is a result of intellectual play. The capacity for play is an amiable human characteristic, certainly a promoter of culture, perhaps even, as Romano Guardini and Hugo Rahner hold, the way in which man best imitates God and assumes what he can of divine nature. But human play is a diversion, and after the game is over, the "serious business of living" must be resumed. A subversive person might suggest that "must" in the preceding sentence is a symptom of widespread illusion, for the discipline of play is demanding, and after it a return to the familiar brings its own relief, along with that self-congratulation fostered by a conviction of being engaged in the work that makes the world go forward. That this work includes the manufacture of holocaustal weapons; the exhaustion, defacement, and poisoning of the physical environment; and campaigns to stultify independent thought seems little to disturb the perpetual possession of being well deceived.

But likely it is as well that the diversions of play are occasional and limited, not because the departure from a norm deserves less praise than does adherence, but because uninterrupted play would lose its identity as play and with this the restorative power that is its value. Thus I think it is with fantasy also. It is a diversion; it rarely has been and rarely will be the main occupation of writers for the main taste of readers. This very intermittency is a function of its utility. Fantasy provides not only entertainment but one means to keeping a clear perspective on our required concerns of thought and feeling.

Suggested Reading

There follows a list, far from exhaustive, of fantasies and related fictions that may be agreeable for those who wish to read further. I do not include here books discussed extensively in the body of this study. Some of those noted below have been named in the text, though so briskly as to give little idea of their content; others have not even been mentioned. All works listed were originally published in English.

Those interested in even further exploration of the subject will find several thousand titles specified in *The Checklist of Fantastic Literature: A Bibliography of Fantasy, Weird and Science Fiction Books Published in the United States,* edited by Everett F. Bleiler ([Naperville, Ill.?]: FAX Collector's Editions, 1972). This bibliographer does not cite works that were published after 1947, the date of the first issue of his compilation. So inclusive is Bleiler's understanding of "fantastic literature" that he includes a wide miscellany from several genres. There is also a bare author and title listing under the heading "fantasies" in *Fiction Catalog*, 8th ed., edited by Estelle A. Fidell (New York: Wilson, 1971).

Barrie, Sir James. *Farewell, Miss Julie Logan: A Wintry Tale.* New York: Scribner's, 1932. A revenant, who aided the escape of Prince Charles Edward in 1745, bemuses a Scottish clergyman.

Beagle, Peter. *A Fine and Private Place.* New York: Viking, 1960. (Paperback edition: Ballantine.) Interaction of the "dead" and the "living" in a Bronx cemetery.

Beerbohm, Sir Max. *The Dreadful Dragon of Hay Hill.* London: Heinemann, 1928. A comic myth. In 39000 B.C. a dragon is killed and revived.

———. *The Happy Hypocrite.* London: Heinemann, 1897. Lord George Hell adopts a mask of purity and becomes the mask. A parody of *The Picture of Dorian Gray.*

———. *Zuleika Dobson: An Oxford Love Story.* London: Heinemann, 1911. A mock myth of undergraduates driven to suicide by the bewitchment of a beauty.

Benson, Stella. *Living Alone*. London: Macmillan, 1919. The story of a witch who keeps a refuge for strays and outcasts.

———. *Tobit Transplanted*. London: Macmillan, 1931. (American title: *The Far-away Bride*; in print: Greenwood.) An adaptation of the apocryphal Book of Tobit.

Blackwood, Algernon. *Dudley and Gilderoy: A Nonsense*. New York: Dutton, 1929. (Paperback edition: Curtis.) A cat and a parrot, longtime friends, escape from home and pursue their adventures through London.

Burdekin, Kay. *The Burning Ring*. London: Butterworth; New York: Morrow, 1927. A magic ring enables a man to live through several historical periods.

Burgess, Anthony. *The Eve of St. Venus*. London: Sidgwick & Jackson, 1964. A young man slips a wedding ring on the correct finger of a statue of Venus and finds himself, for a short time, with a goddess-bride. Adapted from a story told in Burton's *Anatomy of Melancholy*.

Chesterton, G. K. *The Man Who Was Thursday: A Nightmare*. New York: Dodd, Mead, 1908. (Paperback edition: Putnam.) Seven formidable men, each named for a day of the week, ally themselves to chase evil from the world. Thursday perhaps represents divine love.

Collier, John. *Full Circle*. New York: Appleton, 1933. Continued wars produce a primitive and savage society in 1995.

de la Mare, Walter. *Henry Brocken: His Travels and Adventures in Strange, Scarce-Imaginable Regions of Romance*. New York: Knopf, 1924. In his travels a boy meets famous figures from literary history.

———. *The Return*. New York and London: Putnam, 1911. A man is possessed and transformed by the spirit of a seventeenth-century Huguenot who committed suicide.

———. *The Three Mulla-Mulgars*. London: Duckworth, 1910. (In print: Knopf.) Three pure and sentient animals return to the region where they are kings.

Douglas, Norman. *In the Beginning*. New York: John Day, 1928. (In print: Scholarly Books.) A story of premoral pagan harmony.

———. *Nerinda*. New York: John Day, 1929. A young man's disastrous quest for union with Nerinda, the other part of the whole self they once formed. Since the destruction of Pompeii, she has been only ashes.

———. *They Went*. London: Chapman & Hall, 1920. The history of a city of mythical beauty and pleasure before it and its inhabitants were destroyed.

Dunsany, Edward John Moreton Drax Plunkett, 18th Baron. *The Charwoman's Shadow.* New York and London: Putnam, 1926. (In print: Folcroft; paperback edition: Ballantine.) The charwoman's shadow, stolen from her years before, is restored by a young magician, and she becomes again a marriageable maiden.

————. *The Curse of the Wise Woman.* New York and Toronto: Longmans, Green, 1933 (In print: Folcroft.) An old woman's curse brings down supernatural forces that rout the efforts of the Peat Development (Ireland) Syndicate, which has tried to reclaim some Irish bog land.

————. *The King of Elfland's Daughter.* New York and London: Putnam, 1924. A king's son wins the daughter, who brings with her a magical tide that transforms the world into a place of harmony.

————. *The Story of Mona Sheehy.* London and Toronto: Heinemann, 1939. Because she is thought the daughter of the Queen of the Fairies, Mona Sheehy is exiled from her village, lives among tinkers, and presently returns to her home and acceptance.

Eddison, E. R. *The Worm Ouroboros.* New York: Boni, 1926. (Paperback edition: Ballantine.) A epic of the warfare between Witchland and Demonland, ending in the defeat of the King of Witchland, the Satan of this created myth.

Firbank, Ronald. *The Artificial Princess.* London: Duckworth, 1934 [published posthumously]. (In print: New Directions.) Firbank's version of the Salome theme, with borrowings from Aubrey Beardsley, Oscar Wilde, and Richard Strauss.

————. *Vainglory.* London: Richards, 1915. (In print: New Directions.) This has no real plot. It gives a series of scenes involving people whose culture has ended in pretense and preciosity.

————. *Valmouth.* London: Duckworth, 1919. (In print: New Directions.) Aged residents of a health resort amuse themselves with a variety of perversions.

Garnett, David. *A Man in the Zoo.* London: Chatto & Windus, 1924. A reversible metamorphosis in which a man temporarily becomes an exhibit (*Homo sapiens*) in a London zoo.

————. *Two by Two: A Story of Survival.* New York: Atheneum, 1964. Two girls are stowaways on Noah's ark. Once landed, they become mothers of the new race.

Golding, William, *The Inheritors.* London: Faber & Faber, 1955.

(Paperback edition: Pocket Books.) The innocence of a Neanderthal family cannot match the predatoriness and corruption of civilized man.

――――. *The Lord of the Flies.* London: Faber & Faber, 1954. (In print: Coward; paperback edition: Putnam.) The defeat of innocence in an island society of well-bred boys, who become devotees of Beelzebub.

Grahame, Kenneth, *The Wind in the Willows.* New York: Scribner's, 1908. (Paperback editions: Airmont, Avon, Dell.) The central actors of this beast fable—a mole, a water rat, and a badger—are embodiments of organized innocence.

Graves, Robert. *Seven Days in New Crete.* London: Cassell, 1949. (American title: *Watch the North Wind Rise.*) A future society dominated by the ninefold goddess, who rules by benign witchcraft.

Hudson, William Henry. *A Crystal Age.* London: Unwin, 1887. Human society in its forest period. A dream of the future.

――――. *A Little Boy Lost.* London: Duckworth, 1905. (In print: Folcroft.) The boy, an innocent like Rima in *Green Mansions,* loves everything that lives, but the nature he encounters is sometimes fair, sometimes menacing.

Hughes, Richard. *A High Wind in Jamaica.* London: Chatto & Windus, 1929. (American title: *The Innocent Voyage;* paperback edition: Harper and Row.) A group of children who, captured by pirates, dominate and destroy their captors.

Lindsay, David. *A Voyage to Arcturus.* London: Methuen, 1920. (Paperback edition: Ballantine.) A theological romance, with science fiction machinery, stressing trial and redemption.

Macdonald, George, *Lilith.* London: Chatto & Windus, 1895. (Paperback edition: Eerdmans.) An allegory of the conquest of evil by love.

Machen, Arthur. *The Great God Pan.* Boston: Roberts, 1894. (In print: Books for Libraries.) The spirit of Pan possesses a young woman who thereafter prompts a series of suicides.

――――. *The Terror.* New York: McBride, 1917. Angered because man has forfeited his rightful dominance, the animals revolt and begin a campaign of killing.

Matson, Norman. *Flecker's Magic.* New York: Boni and Liveright, 1926. A girl who claims to be a witch gives a "magic" ring to an art student in Paris, so that he may have his wish. But she is a fake witch and the ring has no special powers.

Meynell, Esther. *Time's Door.* London: Chapman & Hall, 1935. A young violinist, a pupil of Paganini, has a love affair with the musical past and especially with J. S. Bach's long-dead daughter Catherina Dorothea.

Miller, Walter M. *A Canticle for Leibowitz.* New York: Lippincott, 1959. (Paperback editions: Lippincott, Bantam.) An impossible society in a monastery founded after the destruction by hydrogen bomb of the present civilization.

Morley, Christopher. *Where the Blue Begins.* Garden City: Doubleday, Page, 1922. A fable about dogs. One of them undertakes a quest for freedom and content. Failing to find these in worldly occupations, he discovers them at home.

Munro, H. H. [Saki]. *The Unbearable Bassington.* London: Lane, 1912. (In print: Scholarly Books.) The misadventures of a pleasure seeker named Comus as he revels through an exotic society.

Nathan, Robert. *Portrait of Jennie.* New York: Knopf, 1940. (In print: Knopf; paperback edition: Popular Library.) Jennie is a revenant who both haunts and inspires an artist.

Peattie, Louise Redfield. *Pan's Parish.* New York and London: Century, 1931. An area of Provence enjoys the benign, disorderly rule of Pan.

Priestley, J. B. *Adam in Moonshine.* London: Heinemann, 1927. Adam Stewart finds his life changed from the routine to that of the Young Pretender.

Russell, George William [AE]. *The Avatars: A Futurist Fantasy.* New York: Macmillan, 1933. The dreams of a group of mystics are realized in two otherworldly visitors.

Sackville-West, Victoria. *Grand Canyon.* New York: Doubleday, 1942. In a remote part of the Grand Canyon where a power restores the dead to life, the survivors of a total war preserve themselves.

————. *Seducers in Ecuador.* London: Woolf, 1924. A man who wears magical spectacles gains extraordinary and destructive vision.

Sinclair, Andrew. *Gog.* New York: Macmillan, 1967. (Paperback edition: Avon.) A story of innocence. A giant encounters characters from several periods of history.

Spark, Muriel. *The Ballad of Peckham Rye.* New York: Lippincott, 1960. A Scottish demon convulses the life of Peckham.

Stephens, James. *The Crock of Gold.* New York: Macmillan, 1929. (Paperback edition: Macmillan.) A mythical conflict of Pan and Angus Óg for the devotion of Caitilin ni Murrachu.

————. *The Demi-Gods.* New York: Macmillan, 1925. Three picaresque "angels" find an agreeable life on earth.

Stewart, George R. *Earth Abides*. New York: Random House, 1949. (Paperback edition: Fawcett World.) The remaking of a patriarchal civilization after "the Great Disaster" kills all but a few Americans.

Thurber, James. *The White Deer*. New York: Harcourt, Brace, 1945. (In print: Harcourt, Brace, Jovanovich.) A myth of the soul seeking redemption.

Warner, Rex. *The Aerodrome*. London: Lane, 1941. A military elite and a purified state are established by the Air Vice-Marshal, but cannot be maintained against ordinary human feeling.

————. *Men of Stones*. Philadelphia: Lippincott, 1950. A warning story about the exercise of power and the opposition to it.

————. *The Wild Goose Chase*. London: Boriswood, 1937. A successful quest to find the life principle.

Warner, Sylvia Townsend. *Lolly Willowes; or the Loving Huntsman*. New York: Viking, 1926. (Paperback edition: Popular Library.) A woman transformed into a witch finds that demonic control is gentle.

West, Rebecca. *Harriet Hume: A London Fantasy*. (Garden City: Doubleday, Doran, 1929. (Paperback edition: Popular Library.) Harriet Hume is a psychic whose insight penetrates any pretense in human conduct and discovers the reality.

White, Terence Hanbury. *The Master*. London: Cape, 1957. Twelve-year-old twins and a dog frustrate the Master's plan for domination of the world.

————. *Mistress Masham's Repose*. New York: Putnam, 1946. (Paperback edition: Putnam.) The alliance of a girl and the descendants of the Lilliputians frustrates attempts to steal her inheritance.

Williams, Charles. *All Hallows' Eve*. London: Faber & Faber, 1945. (Paperback edition: Avon.) Simon the Clerk (Simon Magus) tries and fails to control both matter and spirit by magic.

————. *Descent into Hell*. London: Faber & Faber, 1937. A demonstration of the power of love over fear, self-seeking, and hatred.

————. *The Greater Trumps*. London: Gollancz, 1932. (Paperback edition: Avon.) Manipulation of a Tarot pack can control physical and human nature.

————. *Many Dimensions*. London: Gollancz, 1931. A struggle for the power inherent in a magical stone from the crown of Solomon.

————. *Shadows of Ecstasy*. London: Gollancz, 1933. A Scottish clergyman defeats the megalomania of Nigel Considine, who plans to conquer Europe by mobilizing the dark powers of Africa.

Wilson, Angus. *The Old Men at the Zoo.* London: Secker and Warburg, 1961. A bizarre zoo is a microcosm of an impossible society.

Wylie, Elinor. *Jennifer Lorn: A Sedate Extravaganza.* New York: Doran, 1923. An impossible couple in an exotic society of late eighteenth-century India.

———. *Mr. Hodge and Mr. Hazard.* New York: Knopf, 1928. Mr. Hazard is a distillation of nineteenth-century English romantic sensibility whose brief period of joy is spoiled by Mr. Hodge, an embodiment of crassness.

———. *The Venetian Glass Nephew.* New York: Doran, 1925. The nephew of a cardinal is a young man made of glass. Because he is fragile, his mistress is transformed into Sèvres china. Perhaps an adaptation from *The Licentiate of Glass,* by Cervantes.

Index